RSPB Nature Watch

Published 2011 by A&C Black Publishers Ltd,
36 Soho Square, London W1D 3QY

ISBN (print) 978-1-4081-3974-5

A CIP catalogue record for this book is available
from the British Library

This book is produced using paper that is made
from wood grown in managed sustainable forests.
It is natural, renewable and recyclable. The logging
and manufacturing processes conform to the
environmental regulations of the country of origin.

Commissioning Editor: Nigel Redman
Project Editor: Lisa Thomas
Design by Austin Taylor

Printed in China
10 9 8 7 6 5 4 3 2 1

Visit www.acblack.com/naturalhistory to find out
more about our authors and their books. You will
find extracts, author interviews and our blog, and
you can sign up for newsletters to be the first to
hear about our latest releases and special offers.

RSPB

RSPB Nature Watch

How to discover, explore and enjoy wildlife

Marianne Taylor

A & C BLACK · LONDON

CONTENTS

INTRODUCTION

We live in one of the most crowded nations in the world, but British people still love little more than exploring the great outdoors. We tend and cherish our gardens, while away sunny afternoons in our local park, and when we get the chance to go walking in the woods or fields, along the river or by the sea, most of us jump at it.

Along with this enthusiasm for time spent outdoors comes an interest shared by most of us for the wild animals and plants that share our countryside. Who has not marvelled at the sight and scent of a woodland glade carpeted with Bluebells, or watched with fascination a flying gull at play in a strong sea breeze? Take a closer look around whenever you're outside and you'll see more and more interesting things – perhaps a Robin discreetly visiting its nest in your garden, an exquisitely patterned moth resting inconspicuously on a brick wall, a deer grazing on the edge of a woodland.

Something for everyone

Wildlife-watching is a hobby that anyone can enjoy, regardless of age, mobility and where you live. There's no need to blow your savings on expensive equipment, or travel vast distances – there is wonderful wildlife to enjoy on everyone's doorstep. Nature has a way of seeking you out even when you're not looking for it – the sudden drama of a bird of prey attack in your back garden, that weird insect that flew into your living room when you left the window open after dark... it can be the smallest thing that entices you in and gets you hooked.

Our wildlife and wild places

At first glance the wildlife we have in the UK is unimpressive compared to elsewhere in the world. We have few large and imposing animals, and little in the way of real wilderness for them to roam even if they were here. However, when you start to look at what we do have, you might be surprised. In terms of wildlife, we have a list of nearly 600 species of bird, enigmatic mammals such as Red Deer, Grey Seals, Arctic Hares and Red Squirrels, more than 2,000 species of moth and another 60 or so of butterflies, and several thousand different kinds of plants.

Our wild places range from precious ancient forests to rolling heathlands, plains and mountains. With nearly 12,500km of coastline, we have internationally important populations of shoreline and marine wildlife, with great seabird 'cities' on the remote and rugged cliff-faces of the north, and swarms of marshland birds that gather each autumn on wide estuaries up and down the country.

The secret life of your garden

The animals and plants that live in your garden are a subset of the species that you'll find in the wider countryside – the deciduous woodlands or meadows that have been replaced by our homes. A study of 'ordinary gardens' in Sheffield found more than 1,100 plant species and 700 species of insects and other invertebrates in the average garden, along with an assortment of mammals and birds and a handful of reptiles and amphibians.

Go a little further afield and you'll find an even greater range of plants and animals. Any countryside walk offers the chance to see something new, and if you are willing to make longer trips you can see some of the best-known and most iconic species found anywhere, from dazzling and rare orchids to stunning bird species like Golden Eagles, Bitterns and Puffins. Every corner of the country has its own local specialities.

← Many of us first became interested in wildlife after watching beautiful birds like Chaffinches in our gardens.

↑ Colourful butterflies are harbingers of summer, but the Comma and some other species may be seen as early as February and as late as November.

↑ It may not be our most popular wild animal, but the Grey Squirrel's intelligence and cheeky charm makes it great fun to watch.

WATCHING AND LEARNING

There is a lot more to wildlife-watching than simply ticking off the species that you've seen. If you take the time to watch and study plants and animals, the rewards will be far greater.

You'll experience the incredible satisfaction of mastering fieldcraft to the point that animals will actually approach you as you sit quietly, and you can enjoy watching them as they go about their daily lives. Their behaviour is always engaging and sometimes extraordinary – a Stoat or a spider stalking its prey holds all the drama of any natural history documentary, and the sight of any animal from an earwig to an egret caring for its young is enchanting.

Studying plants and fungi

If your interest lies in plants or fungi, you can enjoy detailed study of them without any worries about causing disturbance. You can get to know the flowering seasons of the different plants, and the variety of ingenious methods they use to achieve pollination and to disperse their seed. Fungi have an ephemeral, magical quality, springing up overnight when the weather has been just right, and sometimes persisting for just a couple of hours in dewy perfection before they start to decay or are devoured by hungry animals.

↑ Discovering an array of exotic-looking fungi, freshly sprouted after a rainy night is one of the highlights of an autumn woodland walk.

→ Britain is home to many species of orchids, some beautiful, some peculiar and several extremely rare. Seeing as many species as you can is an exciting challenge.

Encouraging young naturalists

Wildlife-watching is something that captures the imaginations of children, and it's easy to encourage them to get more out of their hobby by carrying out simple 'nature studies'. From seeing how many different birds they can spot on a country walk, to using a pitfall trap to study the insects in the back garden, there are numerous activities to help them enjoy nature. Children lead far more sedentary lives than was the case just a couple of decades ago, to the detriment of their health and general wellbeing. Wildlife-watching is a fantastic way to encourage them to get outside, take some exercise and gain more awareness of the real and wonderful world of wildlife that surrounds them.

ALL ABILITIES

Not everyone is up to long walks through the countryside, but having limited mobility need not stop you from enjoying a hobby of wildlife-watching. Your garden or outside space can easily be turned into a haven for wildlife. When you want to go further afield, many of the nature reserves managed by the RSPB have excellent facilities for the mobility-impaired. Hides can be built with access ramps and low-set viewing windows for wheelchair-users. You can hire a buggy at some reserves, while others permit disabled visitors to use special parking places close to the best viewpoints. Also, interpretive displays are provided at some reserves to help those with sight or hearing problems.

↑ Cultivating a family interest in nature is the perfect way to get your children off the sofa and out enjoying fresh air and exercise, as well as the beauty of the natural world.

HOW TO USE THIS BOOK

This book has been written for anyone who's ever stopped for a second look at nature, and decided that they want to discover more.

The first chapter covers places to go, with a look at the main different habitat types you'll find in the UK, from town to farmland, river to sea shore, woodland to mountain and moor. You'll discover the wildlife you can expect to find in each, and some tips for how best to explore each habitat.

The next chapter covers fieldcraft – how to get close to wild animals without causing any alarm or disturbance. **Then we look** at equipment for wildlife-watching, including how to choose binoculars and other optical equipment, what kind of clothing to wear, and advice about using technical gadgets to help with your wildlife-watching. **Chapter 4** introduces the why and how of species identification – why it matters, and how to do it for animals, plants and fungi.

Chapter 5 is an introduction to drawing and painting wildlife, from making useful sketches to help you identify particular species, to using various media to create wildlife artworks. **Chapter 6** is devoted to wildlife photography for everyone, whether you're using a simple camera phone or a DSLR. The jargon is explained, different camera types are described and there's advice on using (and bending) the rules of composition to take better photos.

The following chapter helps you organise your observations and make more use of them, including ways to show off your photos and artwork, and publishing your words and pictures online. **Chapter 8** invites you to take a more active role in your wildlife-watching, from transforming your garden into a miniature nature reserve, to introducing more formalised study – including its value and how to undertake it.

The last chapter is about how to make your own contributions to wildlife conservation, through submitting your records of unusual sightings to giving your time and growing expertise as a volunteer at your local nature reserve and further afield. The book concludes with lists of useful addresses and recommended further reading.

ABOUT THE RSPB

The Royal Society for the Protection of Birds exists not just to protect birds but is a million-strong voice for all wildlife. The society is open to members of all ages, and your support helps with its vital work in conserving wildlife habitats, researching how best to proceed with future conservation projects, and educating everyone, from politicians to school-children, about how to live in better harmony with the natural world. The RSPB is also committed to helping everyone, whatever their age and background, to enjoy our nation's glorious wildlife and its wealth of natural beauty.

← A boat trip is a great way to see our marine wildlife, and could bring you eye to eye with fantastic seabirds like the Gannet.

WOODY WONDERLAND

A single mature tree can be a temporary or permanent home for an amazing variety and quantity of other living things. Insects feed on its leaves and sap, while squirrels and birds feast on its fruit. Fungi and lichen grow on its bark and birds nest high in its branches. Now, just imagine what happens if you multiply that one tree's wildlife by many thousands. Welcome to the woodland, one of our richest and most rewarding wildlife habitats.

TYPES OF WOODLAND

Woods in the UK can be divided into two basic types – deciduous (composed primarily of trees which drop their leaves in autumn) and coniferous (evergreen conifer trees). While the kinds of trees you'll find there, other things that influence the wildlife mix include whether you're in the lowlands or uplands, whether the soil is wet or dry, and how the woodland is (or isn't) managed.

Typical wildlife of a deciduous wood

Let's consider a fairly large woodland composed mainly of oak, Beech and Sweet Chestnut trees. Who lives there? Mammalwise, there will be Badgers, Foxes, Roe

THE WILDWOOD

Over the last 5,000 years, people have eroded away the wildwood – at first slowly, but more recently at a startling rate. The trees provided construction material, and the cleared land was used to grow food.

THE WILDWOOD

Over the last 5,000 years, pe the wildwood – at first slow at a startling rate. The trees material, and the cleared la The great predators were ex they posed to livestock – eve

Generic text box

↖ Throughout the book a series of general boxes provide definitions or additional information.

Mixing your media

As if that weren't enough, ma artists have fun combining two or more different paintin or drawing media in the same artwork. Some classic

Techniques box

↖ Whether you want to improve your photography or drawing technique or learn how to get close to wildlife, these boxes tell you how.

ZOOM OR PRIME?

A lens which has just one fo lens. Such lenses are often b which give you a range of fo zoom lens gives you flexibili of different subjects at diffe are often easier to use than

Equipment box

↖ Once you're hooked on nature watching it's possible to buy a whole range of equipment. These features give you the lowdown on a range of items.

PAINTING MATERIALS

CHOOSING DSLR LENSES

FEEDING GARDEN BIRDS

WILDLIFE IS EVERYWHERE!

You don't have to hike miles into the countryside to see wonderful wildlife. You don't need to live in the back of beyond or have a nature reserve on your doorstep to enjoy sights to match anything David Attenborough might show you on the tv. It's easy to suppose that we humans with our buildings, roads, noise and pollution have pushed the wild world out of reach to all but a few, but it's not true – wildlife finds ways to thrive all around us, and you don't have to go very far at all to immerse yourself in a world of nature.

NO BOUNDARIES

It's true that some animals and plants will only survive in very specific conditions. There's no two ways about it – to see a Puffin or Pasqueflower you will have to head for the right stretch of coastline or chalk/limestone meadow respectively. However, many others are adaptable pioneers – adventurers, travellers and tough survivors which can live right alongside us in the most unpromising settings. Give them just a little encouragement and they will not only survive but thrive. Once you tune your senses in to the wild world, you'll be amazed at what you can find and where.

PATCHWORK

Most people who develop a real interest in wildlife will have at least one 'local patch', whether they set out to have one or not. This is the place which is close enough to where you live or work that you can visit it frequently. You go there often and it becomes your special area of study. Through visit after visit, you build an intimate knowledge of its wildlife.

Your local patch doesn't have to be a wonderful wildlife wilderness. It can be your local town park, the beach, a walk along a canal. If you have a garden,

↓ Seeing shy animals like Fallow Deer is always a thrill. With care and planning you can watch them going about their business without knowing you are there.

↑ RSPB reserves offer you the chance to encounter scarce and exciting wildlife, such as these Bearded Tits at Titchwell Marsh in Norfolk.

→ This Holly Blue butterfly was photographed in a tiny city back yard. Many other adaptable species have found ways to thrive right on our doorsteps.

you already have the makings of a local patch of your own, and it's one which you can manipulate to make it more attractive to wildlife. While travelling around to great places in search of exciting wildlife is always a joy, getting to know your local area offers a different kind of pleasure – that of real in-depth understanding and 'tuning in' to the rhythms of nature around you.

EVERYONE'S INVITED

Wildlife-watching is a hobby that has no limits on age or ability. Of course, wildlife-watching encompasses a great variety of activities and not all of them are suitable for everyone. There will come a time in all our lives when hiking up Ben Nevis to see a Snow Bunting is no longer an option, and for small children the excitement of waiting silently in a forest hideout for a deer to come by is likely to wear thin rather quickly. However, with imagination and enthusiasm everyone in the family can enjoy spending time exploring nature.

For children, plan tips that include some fun activities – pond-dipping, minibeast hunting and so on, and make sure you're not out too long so that overtiredness spoils the day. For the infirm and disabled, many country parks and nature reserves have facilities that make a visit easy – wheelchair-friendly trails and birdwatching hides, and frequent benches for a sit-down.

PREPARE TO BE HOOKED

Once you become seriously interested in wildlife, your life will never be the same again... It will, however, be better, because the more you look, the more you'll see. Even a simple walk to the shops can turn into an adventure – a silhouette flying over catches your eye and you realise it's a hunting Sparrowhawk. You find yourself checking walls and fences for moths, after finding that gorgeous Garden Tiger on the neighbour's wall last week. You become obsessed with attracting more wildlife to your garden, and when you book your seaside holiday you'll try to convince the family that the best place to go is the one that offers the biggest choice of whale-watching boat trips. Don't worry, all this is perfectly normal – and the more people in your life that you can persuade to share your new and exciting view of the world, the better.

WILD ABOUT TOWN

Many parts of the UK are built up and, at first glance, not very promising for wildlife. In the centre of a big and flat city, such as London, it's hard to see any sign of non-human life among the high buildings and the busy roads that separate them. But even here there is wildlife to see – migrating birds fly overhead, windblown plant seeds take root in road cracks and gutterings, and their flowers attract wandering insects. City parks are oases of life – and it's often much easier to see a shy animal like a Jay or a Fox in a city setting than it is in the 'proper countryside'. Out into the suburbs, the network of gardens form a substitute open woodland that attracts a wide variety of species, and even houses themselves have animal residents alongside the human ones.

THE WOODS REBORN

Back in medieval times, most of the UK was covered in ancient woodland. We went on to develop sophisticated tree-chopping tools and methods, and cleared away the woods to create farmland and towns. However, with town houses come gardens, and they offer at least some of the benefits of the original woodland.

Most of the birds that you know as 'garden' birds were originally woodland birds, and where the woodland remains so do the birds. But Blue Tits, Blackbirds, Chaffinches and many of our other favourite bird-table visitors thrive just as well in our gardens as they do in proper woodland. Our gardens don't have the same rich natural food supplies as woodland does, but we can make up for that to some extent by supplying artificial food in the form of nuts, seeds, fat and even mealworms.

↑ Many animals have found suburban gardens an adequate substitute for deciduous woodland, including the Speckled Wood butterfly.

Gardens at their best
Your garden is a small piece of a much larger network of gardens. The barriers between gardens count for little to flying animals but become significant for smaller and less mobile animals, and when animal populations get broken up into smaller fragments which can't find each other, they are more likely to disappear. So the more 'good' gardens around, the more likely you'll have a variety of wildlife in your garden as it will draw in wildlife from surrounding gardens.

NO GARDEN?

If you live in a flat, that doesn't mean no at-home wildlife-watching for you. Watching the skies can be a rewarding way to pass the time, especially during

GOOD OR BAD?

Here are some of the attributes of a 'good' (from a wildlife point of view) garden and its 'bad' counterpart.

GOOD **Trees** Especially if they are native species which support more insects – but even non-natives offer shelter and nest sites for birds.

BAD **Concrete** If your garden is mostly patio, the lack of plants will equate to a lack of insects, birds and everything else.

GOOD **Wild patches** Parts of the garden left to 'run wild' a little will become full of native plants, which will attract more insects.

BAD **Tidiness** If every inch is manicured, your garden will lack attractive sheltered hiding places for assorted minibeasts.

GOOD **Water features** Naturally landscaped ponds, stocked with native water plants, offer drinking places for animals and boost wildlife variety.

↑ Leave a patch of your lawn to grow wild and you could find it produces beautiful meadowland wild flowers like Ox-eye Daisies.

BAD **Foreigners** If your garden is stocked with non-native plants, they will appeal less to insects which means fewer birds, bats and other small mammals.

GOOD **Natural clutter** Woodpiles, stone slabs, tangly bramble patches all provide shelter for animals.

BAD **Poison**. Don't use slug pellets or other toxic agents to kill 'pests'. They don't just harm the target animals but everything else too.

GOOD **Housing options**. Nestboxes may attract tits, sparrows and Starlings. You can also provide homes for Hedgehogs, toads and many insects.

BAD **Too much lawn**. Lawn-mowing is a chore, and more importantly short grass is bad for wildlife and is also very thirsty as it's never allowed to stop growing. Let some of it grow long and flower.

spring and autumn when birds are migrating. Many towns and cities have resident Peregrine Falcons and Sparrowhawks, and these birds perform their courtship flights in early spring. Nestboxes for Swifts and House Martins are made to be fixed to buildings – boxes for other birds can be attached to walls too. For smaller beasts, try putting out window boxes stocked with nectar-bearing flowers and see which insects come to visit. You can do the same at your workplace if you're able to sweet-talk whoever's in charge into taking up the idea.

↙ The House Sparrow is closely associated with humans and our buildings, and its recent severe decline underlines the importance of gardens as a habitat.

PARKLIFE

No town of a certain size is complete without a town park. This is usually a general-purpose open space, offering sports fields, play areas for the kids, pleasant walks through the trees for grown-ups, and a duck pond for everyone to enjoy. It can also be a happy hunting ground for a wildlife watcher, offering a good range of habitats within easy reach of home. Town parks can be great places to get familiar with more common wildlife, as the animals are often well accustomed to people and so are more laid-back and approachable than their country cousins. Parks also provide good environments for you to hone your skills with your camera or to try out drawing and painting some of the more obliging residents.

↑ Traditionally a bird of upland rivers, the Grey Wagtail is equally attracted to urban parks with landscaped, fast-flowing streams.

HALFWAY HOUSE

The semi-natural environment of the typical town park attracts a range of wildlife including some species which you'd find in the average garden and some which would usually occur in more rural woodland and open countryside. For example, you might find Treecreepers on the trees, Mistle Thrushes bounding across the football fields or Pied Wagtails strutting along the paths – birds that rarely show up in the average garden.

The park is likely to have a greater variety of mammals than most gardens, too, with shrews and Wood mice rummaging in the leaf-litter, and various bats flycatching over the pond on summer nights. A 'nature garden' in a park is likely to have plenty of interesting insects, invertebrates and plants – if your park doesn't have one, you could try speaking nicely to the local authority about considering adding a dedicated space for wildlife.

THE PARK POND

Most parks have a duck pond or two, complete with a crowd of Mallards. Sometimes the Mallards will have some domestic duck ancestry which shows

← The ubiquitous parkland mammal of most of England and Wales, the Grey Squirrel is often delightfully approachable and photogenic.

→ Where there is water there will be damselflies, even in the heart of town. The Common Blue Damselfly is one of our most abundant species.

up in the form of confusing plumage patterns that you won't find in your field guide. Alongside the ducks may be a pair of Mute Swans and the odd Moorhen shyly working its way along the margins. Bigger ponds means more birdlife. You might find Great Crested Grebes, Tufted Ducks and visiting gulls. Ponds with some natural landscaping and water plants will host populations of insects, such as damselflies, mayflies and caddisflies, which spend their early months living under water – such ponds should also have fish, and frogs, newts and toads.

TIME IT RIGHT

It can be hard to find wildlife (except for hungry ducks) when there are too many people visiting the park. To see the most birds overall and to improve your chances of encountering a mammal, your best bet is to visit early in the day, close to dawn if you can manage it. If you can get up before all the joggers and dog walkers you'd be doing very well, but in general earlier means quieter, and most birds are more active and more vocal in the early mornings.

Dawn is also the best time to look for migrating birds in spring and autumn. Migrants will stop off in unpromising places overnight, especially in bad weather, but they are likely to move on pretty soon. If you are hoping to see insects, try waiting until a little later, when the air has warmed up a bit.

PARKWATCH
The RSPB runs 'Date with Nature' events in some city parks to introduce you to interesting park wildlife. For example, in London you can meet Tawny Owls in Kensington Gardens and Grey Herons in Regent's Park.

FERAL FAKERS

One pitfall for the amateur birdwatcher checking out a park lake is the presence of exciting unusual birds which look wild but aren't. Many parks keep a collection of exotic ducks which have their wing feathers clipped so they can't fly beyond the confines of the park, but are otherwise unconstrained. Sometimes the keepers don't clip their birds' wings in time after the moult, so the wings reach full size and the ducks escape, often colonising new parks nearby and starting to breed in the wild.

It's easy enough to tell a captive duck – when it stretches up and flaps its wings one of them is half the size of the other. With escapee full-winged 'ferals', it's much harder to be sure. Some exotic species have done so well in the wild that they can now be seen in many town parks. They include Red-crested Pochard and Mandarin Duck, as well as Canada and Greylag Geese.

→ Among the standard-issue ducks and swans, your park lake may attract more exotic fare. This is a male Pochard, a handsome diving duck.

WOODY WONDERLAND

A single mature tree can be a temporary or permanent home for an amazing variety and quantity of other living things. Insects feed on its leaves and sap, while squirrels and birds feast on its fruit. Fungi and lichen grow on its bark and birds nest high in its branches. Now, just imagine what happens if you multiply that one tree's wildlife by many thousands. Welcome to the woodland, one of our richest and most rewarding wildlife habitats.

TYPES OF WOODLAND

→ The Marsh Tit is a bird of mature deciduous woodland, using holes drilled in trees by woodpeckers in which to nest.

↓ This view across the North Downs shows recently planted woodlands flourishing in between patches of more mature tree cover.

Woods in the UK can be divided into two basic types – deciduous (composed primarily of trees which drop their leaves in autumn) and coniferous (evergreen conifer trees). While the kinds of trees in your wood are the most important factor determining what wildlife you'll find there, other things that influence the wildlife mix include whether you're in the lowlands or uplands, whether the soil is wet or dry, and how the woodland is (or isn't) managed.

Typical wildlife of a deciduous wood
Let's consider a fairly large woodland composed mainly of oak, Beech and Sweet Chestnut trees. Who lives there? Mammalwise, there will be Badgers, Foxes, Roe and Fallow Deer, Grey Squirrels and a range of other rodents and bats. The birds could include Nuthatch, Treecreeper, possibly all three of Britain's woodpecker species, various warblers, Spotted and perhaps Pied Flycatchers, Redstart, Woodcock, Tawny Owl, plus many familiar garden birds.

THE WILDWOOD

Over the last 5,000 years, people have eroded away the wildwood – at first slowly, but more recently at a startling rate. The trees provided construction material, and the cleared land was used to grow food. The great predators were exterminated for the risk they posed to livestock – even the superbly elusive Lynx was extinct here by the 17th century. By 1900, the UK's forest cover was down to just 5 per cent.

Today, only fragments of original forest remain – an estimated 15 per cent of woodland in the UK is considered 'ancient'. Examples include the Forest of Dean on the England/Wales border and Abernethy Forest in the Spey Valley of Scotland. Even these have been modified to some extent, but they remain among the best places to see a great variety of wildlife. Meanwhile, a reduction in deforestation and increased tree planting have seen forest cover in the UK increase from just over 200,000 hectares in 1980 to nearly 300,000 in 2005. More considered and sensitive woodland management is helping to make our 'new' woodlands gain the rich wildlife diversity of the ancient forest they have replaced.

There will be numerous moths, and some butterflies, such as Speckled Wood and perhaps Purple Hairstreak and White Admiral. If the woodland has some open, sunny paths or clearings, they will encourage a great variety of flowers which will in turn attract additional butterflies, moths, bees and hoverflies. In early spring, before the trees' leaves appear, the wood floor may be carpeted with flowers like Bluebell and Wood Anemone.

Typical wildlife of a coniferous wood
Pine woods tend to have less varied wildlife. Their year-round leaf cover shades out smaller plants, and fewer different kinds of plants means fewer animals. Also, many pine woods are commercial forestry plantations – regimented rows of fast-growing, densely planted trees with little room for anything else. Species that do really like pine woods include Coal Tits and Goldcrests, while the often heathy margins of plantations may attract reptiles, and birds, such as Nightjar and Tree Pipit. In Scotland there are a few patches of 'original' Scots Pine forest with a more open structure than the plantations, and these hold some special wildlife such as Red Squirrel, Capercaillie, Crested Tit and Scottish Crossbill.

↓ The Scots Pine, our only native conifer, forms the basis of wildlife-rich evergreen woodlands in the Scottish Highlands.

YOUR LOCAL WOODLAND
You will probably have most luck exploring mature deciduous woodland with a mix of native tree species. If there are clearings and wide 'rides' (pathways) to bring sunshine into the wood, so much the better; the presence of streams and ponds will add another new dimension to your woodland wildlife-watching.

DOWN ON THE FARM

A huge proportion of our countryside is used for growing crops or rearing animals for food. There's not much arguing with that – we all need to eat, and home-grown produce is better for the planet as a whole than foods flown in from overseas. Farmland can be great for wildlife, but it can also be as sterile as any desert – it all depends on what's being grown or kept, and what methods are used. Major declines in many of our farmland birds towards the end of the 20th century have led to lots of new incentives for farmers to adopt more wildlife-friendly farming methods, and today many nature reserves include farmland fields that are managed to boost plant, insect and bird numbers.

Play it safe

When walking in farmland, always keep to the footpaths – remember you're on a public right of way through the farmer's private workspace. Keep your dog under control and take care when crossing a field containing livestock.

ARABLE VERSUS PASTURE

There are few habitats less promising than a huge field planted from edge to edge with a single plant crop. Chemicals used to wipe out insects and wild plants mean there's no food for the birds or mammals, and grubbing up hedgerows to enlarge fields removes even more wildlife habitat. However, if you divide the field up with generous hedgerows, cut down or eliminate pesticide use, and leave the margins of the field as unsown 'headlands', the same patch of land instantly becomes much more wildlife-friendly.

Fields grazed by sheep or cattle can be rich in wildlife, with interesting communities of grassland plants, and insects attracted by the animals themselves as well as the plants. Organic farming is much better for wildlife, and mixed farms with a diversity of crops in smaller fields are preferable to large-scale monocultures.

WILD FARMS

Some nature reserves include open land that's managed by grazing – so the livestock is working to benefit the wildlife. The grazing ensures that wet grazing marsh stays that way, rather than slowly drying out and turning into wet and then dry woodland. RSPB reserves like Pulborough Brooks in West Sussex and West Sedgemoor in Somerset have acres of wet grassland which offer perfect nesting habitat for wading birds in summer, and when winter comes the fields flood which attracts great flocks of ducks and many other kinds of wildfowl.

← Several species of wading birds feed and nest on damp grazing pasture. The most striking of them is the handsome Lapwing.

FIND YOUR FARM

The kind of farming that goes on in your local area will probably be determined by the soil type and other geographic factors. High and hilly fields lend themselves to sheep grazing, while the heavy soils of fenland are often used to grow vegetables. To find a good farmland walk, get hold of a local Ordnance Survey map and check out where the public footpaths go – try to find a landscape of smaller 'patchwork' fields for the best chance of a good mix of wildlife. The most rewarding walk will mix a bit of farmland with other habitats, such as patches of woodland or stretches that follow a river bank. Farmers rotate the use of their fields, though, so what's a fantastic butterfly-filled meadow one year could be a dull block of wheat the next.

WHAT TO LOOK FOR AND WHEN

Because most farmland is not managed with wildlife in mind, looking for interesting plants and animals in this habitat can be a bit hit-and-miss. In spring, breeding birds, such as Skylarks and Lapwings, may be displaying over the fields. Summer can be good for mammals, with Stoats hunting Rabbits in pastures and Roe Deer venturing out of the woods to feed on field edges. In autumn and winter, large flocks of birds may gather on cut arable fields to hoover up the grains that the combine harvester missed.

Hedge your bets
Good thick hedgerows provide a very important wildlife habitat. The hedge itself may contain a great variety of native plant species. An ancient hedge (one which has been *in situ* since the early 19th century at least) is often composed of five or more 'woody' species, backed up by dozens of herbaceous plants (those which die back in winter). These plants produce insect-attracting blossom and nourishing seed for birds and mammals. Small birds, such as buntings and whitethroats, nest in the hedge's thorny depths and rodents live in tunnels among their root systems – these in turn attract hunters like Weasels and Barn Owls.

↑ Where field margins are kept free of pesticides, a mixed community of wild plants grows, supporting insects like the Small Copper butterfly.

↓ The rolling hills across much of southern England, enjoyed by many walkers, offer a patchwork landscape with plenty to interest open-country wildlife.

HEATHLAND TO MOUNTAIN

We Brits cleared a great deal of our tree-covered countryside for farming, but not all areas proved to be up to the job. On some less fertile, sandy soils, crops refused to grow well and instead tough plants like heathers and gorses took over. Heather-dominated, open landscapes are known as heathland in low-lying areas and moorland in the uplands. In a few places the uplands ascend into true mountain habitat, where vegetation is sparse and little wildlife can survive. Heath, moor and mountain can seem rather bleak compared to woods or meadowland, but they have their own special range of wildlife and are exciting places to explore.

↓ In the mountains of the Scottish Highlands, you could see Golden Eagles, Mountain Hares and other exciting wildlife.

ROUGH AND READY

Heathlands and moorlands have few trees, though conifers grow more readily on this sort of soil than deciduous trees, so some heathy areas have been turned into conifer plantations. The classic lowland heath is a very open landscape of mainly heather, up to a couple of feet high, cut through with sandy pathways. The lack of shade means heathlands get very hot in summer, which makes them popular with reptiles and insects. However, this also makes them chilly in winter, and at this time of year they can be very bleak and seemingly empty of wildlife.

Upland moorlands tend to be wetter and cooler all year round, and they become even quieter in winter than their lowland equivalents. In the mountains, where any exploration requires great care and planning to ensure you'll be safe, wildlife is thin on the ground throughout the year but includes wonderful species, such as Mountain Hare, Ptarmigan and Golden Eagle.

SAY NO TO PEAT

Peat, the decomposing remains of heathland and moorland plants, has long been used as a growing medium by gardeners. However, its removal damages and destroys wet moorland and heathland habitats, and to regain the peat deposits would take thousands of years. Use a compost bin to make an eco-friendly garden fertiliser instead.

Fire hazard

Lowland heaths can be devastated by fire, especially in hot summers. While fires can prompt regeneration of the heather, there is so little lowland heath left in Britain that accidental fires can destroy fragile animal populations, so take extreme care.

BOGGED DOWN

Soggy, boggy areas of trapped water over or around peat deposits are characteristic of both heath and moor. Several species of insects that spend their early life stages under water thrive in the acidic waters of bogs. The National Nature Reserve of Thursley Common in Surrey has lowland raised bog, a rare habitat in South-east England, and an impressive tally of more than 25 species of dragonflies and damselflies. Bog plants are also interesting, including the beautiful Cotton-grass and the tiny insect-trapping sundews. Most boggy nature reserves have boardwalks over the wet areas so you can traverse them safely.

↑ Acidic heathland and moorland pools are breeding grounds for some of our most striking dragonflies. This is a male Black Darter.

↙ The Stonechat is an archetypal bird of heathland and gorse-rich moorland, though like many others it tends to move to lower, warmer ground in winter.

DAWN TILL DUSK – SUMMER ON THE HEATH

The open skies over heathland are ideal for watching birds on the move. Make an early start to see some 'visible migration' and to watch the resident birds of the heath at their most active. Some Lowland heaths, like the RSPB's Arne reserve in Dorset, offer the chance to see all six of Britain's native reptiles – look out for them basking in sunny spots. Insects like dragonflies are active in the warmest parts of the day, too, hunting for prey over the pools and being hunted themselves by hungry Hobbies. As dusk falls, listen for the soft rippling churr of male Nightjars proclaiming their territories, and watch for their silent long-winged shapes as they vie with bats to catch moths.

BIRDS OF HEATH AND MOOR

Heathland birds include some particularly enchanting species. At heathy RSPB reserves, such as Aylesbeare Common in Devon, you can see Dartford Warblers, Nightjars and Hobbies. Up on the moors, a different set of birds make their living, with Hen Harriers, Merlins, Red Grouse and Short-eared Owls among the more exciting. Most of these birds move to the lowlands in autumn – the hardy Red Grouse has the winter moorlands almost to itself.

GO WITH THE FLOW

Our countryside is cut through by many rivers and streams, delivering fresh water to, and draining it from, the surrounding countryside. These waterways hold as much importance for wildlife as they do for humans. They also offer some of the most enjoyable wildlife-watching around, with riverside pathways providing a constantly changing view and an exciting variety of wildlife. Whether you're walking alongside a noisy, rocky stream tumbling downhill through an upland forest or a wide and lazy river wending its way slowly seawards through flowery meadowland, you're bound to see interesting wildlife at every turn.

PATHS OF PLENTY

↑ A river slows and widens as it nears the sea. A wildlife-watching walk along a riverside footpath is a blissful way to spend an afternoon.

→ So often seen just as a bolt of blue zooming down a river, the Kingfisher is one of our most dazzling birds.

Many major rivers have well-established footpaths running along considerable stretches of their length, making them ideal for long countryside walks that often take in a good mix of habitat types. You can walk the entire length of the Thames from its source in the Cotswolds to the Thames Barrier on the outskirts of East London – the 174-mile trail will take you several days to complete, but you'll enjoy some very picturesque surroundings, and there's tremendous wildlife-watching potential along the way. Even as it runs through the city of London itself, the Thames is an important conduit for birds moving across the country. Check your local map to find your own nearest riverside walk.

RIVERSIDE CHARACTERS

Fast upland streams and rivers are home to birds like Dippers, Grey Wagtails and Common Sandpipers, all of them hunting the insects which live in or around the water. The clear, cold waters suit strong-swimming fish like trout and Salmon, which snap up mayflies and other insects as they emerge on spring days, and these fish attract Goosanders, handsome diving ducks which enjoy fast-moving water.

As the river slows down, plant life proliferates on its banks and under water, and the wildlife variety tends to increase. Almost every lowland river will have resident Kingfishers most of the year, dashing like blue bullets just over the surface. Waterfowl, including ducks and grebes, will find nesting places when the river is slow enough for lush vegetation to grow at its margins. A different set of insects will appear over the slower water, and a greater variety of fish will live in these more hospitable rivers, while you might spot Water Voles, Water Shrews and Grass Snakes swimming in the water. When rivers get close to the sea, seabirds may visit and the occasional seal may venture a short distance upriver.

↑ A Common Mayfly rests on riverside vegetation.

↓ A fast-flowing river, best enjoyed from the shore.

UNDERWATER INSECTS

Some kinds of insects undergo two distinct phases of life after hatching from their eggs – each one starts out as a wingless nymph which lives under water, and then some weeks or months later the nymph climbs out of the water, its skin splits and the winged adult insect emerges. This life cycle is called incomplete metamorphosis, as it misses the pupa stage that occurs in some other groups such as butterflies, beetles and bees. Insects that live this amphibious lifestyle include dragonflies, damselflies, mayflies and stoneflies. In complete metamorphosis, the hatchling insect is called a larva rather than a nymph, as with the various 'true flies' that start their lives under water.

Large emergences of insects attract excitement from insect-eating birds, which may flock over the river to feast on the bounty. Fish also rise to the surface to catch the newly formed adult insects as they try to take off. If you search the reed stems along the riverside, you may find the old casing of the nymph from which an adult insect broke free, still clinging to the plant with its empty legs. This perfect, paper-thin shell is called an exuvium.

RIVER RESPECT

We're all aware of the dangers of sea currents but tend to be a bit more blasé about rivers. However, large rivers can have powerful currents and dangerous undertows, and they are rarely clear enough to see whether you can wade across. For safety's sake, stay on the bank. Another less serious riverside hazard comes in the form of swarming mosquitoes or other biting insects. Insect repellent is a must if you decide to explore the riverside towards the end of the day.

LAKELAND

From puddle to inland sea, still fresh water is a wildlife magnet. If you have added a pond to your garden, you'll have seen what a difference it makes to the variety of animals that visit. Scale up that pond a bit to lake size and you'll find an ever-increasing array of creatures making their homes in and around the water. A walk around the shores of a lake is a pleasant way to pass an afternoon, or just pick a shady spot at the at the water's edge that gives you a good view across the lake, unfold your chair and just wait and see who comes to join you.

A QUESTION OF NUTRIENTS

You may have learned in geography classes that there are two main kinds of lakes – oligotrophic and eutrophic. These alarming-sounding words simply describe how rich the lake's waters are in the kinds of chemicals that encourage plant growth. Oligotrophic lakes are low in nutrients, so have little in the way of aquatic plant life. They tend to be clear, cold and not very rich in wildlife. Eutrophic lakes have lots of plant-friendly nutrients. You'll recognise them by the rich variety of plants growing in, on and out of the water, and these plants in turn support plenty of wildlife of all kinds. Lakes in steep upland valleys, such as the Lake District lakes, tend to have a more oligotrophic character, while lowland lakes in flatter surroundings are likely to be eutrophic.

DEEP OR SHALLOW?

↓ The Great Crested Grebe is a consummate fisher which thrives on our lowland lakes. This one has caught a Perch.

Waterbirds feed in a variety of different ways. Some pick their food from the surface, others upend to immerse their heads and necks, some make short, shallow dives and others dive deep and long. A lake that is too shallow won't attract the deep divers, but a lake that's too deep will exclude the non-divers.

Often when you look out at the birds sitting on a lake you'll notice the surface-feeders like Moorhens stay close to the shore, while divers such as Tufted Ducks are out closer to the middle. If your lake slopes away very gradually from the shores, a few rainless days will shrink the lake and leave some exposed mud on the shore which may attract wading birds.

FISH AND FISHERS

There are many different species of freshwater fish living in our lakes. As a wildlife-watcher you'll have trouble seeing them, though if you pick a sunny day and walk quietly close to the shore you could spot shoals sunbathing in the shallows or coming up to

try to catch insects at the surface. Rather easier to see are the fishers – birds and mammals that hunt fish.

Most lakes will provide you with views of Great Crested Grebes and Grey Herons – the former diving for their prey, the latter waiting motionless for a fish to swim close enough to grab. Kingfishers plunge-dive for fish from a perch – if you find a favourite Kingfisher spot and a place from where you can watch it without being seen, you could be rewarded with some fantastic views of this jewel of a bird. Otters, on the increase in Britain, can also be seen at some lakes, though you'll need lots of patience or luck.

BED TIME

Many inland lakes have tall reedbeds at their margins, which offer homes for some special wildlife. Even small reedbeds may attract a pair of two of Reed Warblers, while larger ones could have Marsh Harriers, Bitterns and Bearded Tits. Some unusual moth species live in reedbeds, while in the Norfolk Broads the rare and spectacular Swallowtail butterfly is found in extensive marshy, reedy areas like the RSPB's Strumpshaw Fen reserve.

↑ Lowland lakes have lots of nutrients in their waters, so plants grow luxuriantly around their fringes and a wide variety of wildlife lives in, on and around them.

↓ Purple Loosestrife is a beautiful wild flower associated with lakes and other areas of fresh water, producing its vibrant flowerheads in midsummer.

MARSH AND ESTUARY

The excitement of birdwatching close to the sea, in a wide landscape of marshland, reedbed and muddy river mouth, is hard to match. It's no wonder that many of the RSPB's best known and most visited nature reserves encompass this kind of habitat. Seeing wildlife other than birds here is more difficult – most of those massed crowds of waders and ducks are feeding on plants or tiny invertebrates hidden in the water or mud – but you could see specialised saltmarsh plants, spot uncommon moths among the reeds or perhaps see a water-loving mammal like a Water Vole or Water Shrew swimming in the shallows.

BIRDS FOR ALL SEASONS

There's never a bad time of year for a birdwatcher to visit a coastal marshland. Spring brings the migrants – waders in colourful breeding plumage stopping off on their way further north, and warblers which will be here for the whole summer. Marsh Harriers perform their dazzling courtship dance high in the skies, and Bitterns boom from deep in the thick of the reeds. In summertime, the reedbeds are alive with the incessant songs of Reed and Sedge Warblers while Lapwings and Redshanks rear their adorable chicks on the wet grassland. In autumn the migrant waders are back, this time joined by that year's crop of youngsters, and unusual visitors may turn up. In winter the sheltered marsh waters attract masses of wildfowl and waders, and a number of different birds of prey visit to take advantage of this amazing abundance.

↓ RSPB Lodmoor in Dorset is a reserve of open, shallow water, marshy fields and reedbeds, and is alive with wildlife all year round.

RESERVE A SEAT

The soggy character of marshland as well as the height of the reedbeds mean that many marshland reserves need to be amply equipped with birdwatching hides to allow visitors to see the open water in comfort and safety. RSPB Minsmere on the Suffolk coast has seven hides, most of them looking out onto open water. From the hides you can enjoy wonderful close views of the birds on and around the water.

Marshland provides rich feeding grounds for birds like geese and waders, which may gather in massive numbers through the winter months.

SEA DEFENCES

The RSPB manages several reserves that hold coastal marshland. Much of our marshes have been drained for farming, so this is a scarce and precious habitat. It is also difficult to look after, as the natural processes of erosion constantly work to reshape our coastline and change its character. The famous RSPB reserve of Titchwell Marsh in Norfolk, with its extensive reedbed and rare breeding birds, has both saltwater and freshwater areas, and the RSPB uses drainage systems, flood defences and vegetation management to ensure all of the habitats are protected.

In an imaginary Britain without people, the coastline would constantly shift around, and the sea would create and destroy habitat all of the time, with the birds moving from area to area as it became suitable for them. But in real life, so much of our marshlands have been lost that we can no longer afford to let the sea damage those that remain.

RARE AND ICONIC

Our coastal wetlands have some of the most exciting breeding birds anywhere in Britain. A walk around an RSPB reserve such as Titchwell, Minsmere or Leighton Moss in spring should reveal several of them. The Avocet, unmistakable emblem of the RSPB, nests on islands in the open water, and vigorously defends its sweet fluffy chicks from any other bird that looks even vaguely threatening. Over the reeds skim Marsh Harriers, large and powerful birds of prey which were virtually extinct in Britain as recently as 1971 but are now thriving at places like this. The secretive Bittern gives its foghorn call from deep in the reeds – with luck you could spot one flapping ponderously to a new feeding spot. And Bearded Tits, exquisite little long-tailed birds, dance through the reeds in noisy gangs.

↑ Many wading birds gather to feed on the rich mud around estuaries at low tide. The Curlew uses its long bill to extract worms from the mud.

RIVER MOUTH

Marshland naturally develops around places where rivers reach the sea. The river mouth itself is typically surrounded by an expanse of thick and squishy mud, too dangerous for humans to walk across, which is packed with worms, shellfish and other invertebrates, and wading birds are equipped to exploit this cornucopia of delights. The long-billed species, like Curlew and Bar-tailed Godwit, can probe deep and catch tunnelling worms, while agile little Sanderlings rush after scuttling sandhoppers. When the advancing tide covers up most or all of the mud, the waders will often decamp en masse to a favourite roosting spot. At RSPB Snettisham in Norfolk, waders pushed off the muddy expanse of The Wash roost on lake islands, right in front of cunningly sited birdwatching hides.

BY THE SEA

Wherever you live in Britain, the sea is no more than 70 miles away. Our island nation has a strong attachment to the seaside – most seaside towns are holiday resorts of some kind or another – and any sunny day flicks the 'go to the beach' switch in the average British brain. The seaside is a wonderful Mecca for wildlife-watchers as well as sunseekers, and our remarkably varied coastline is home to an equally varied selection of plants and animals for us to see and enjoy.

WALKING ON THE BEACHES

↓ A classic West Highlands beach. The sandy bay is edged by seaweed-covered rocks, a perfect spot for picnics, ball games and searching for rock-pool wildlife.

An expanse of golden sand might be the only kind of seashore you'll find depicted in a holiday brochure, but it's just one of the seaside options available out there. Shingle beaches are composed of small pebbles rather than fine sand, and where they are not heavily used by people, both beach types develop their own unique plant communities as you move away from where the sea breaks on the shore. Marram Grass binds sand dunes together, while on shingle grow oddities like Sea Kale and the dramatic Yellow-horned Poppy. Dune systems can be great for insects, while the few undisturbed shingle beaches around our coasts provide breeding grounds for terns and Ringed Plovers. Wading birds forage on exposed beach sand in winter.

SEASIDE SAFETY

Always treat the sea with respect. There are plenty of trouble spots around our coast where swimming is seriously inadvisable, and it's frighteningly easy to be trapped by a fast-flowing incoming tide. Do your research, and always stay within easy reach of the high-tide mark. When you're rock-pooling, be very careful moving over the rocks as they can be extremely slippery, and seaweed can disguise perilous chasms.

CLIFF RICHES

Where tall cliffs flank the sea, you'll often find seabird colonies. The limestone cliffs of northern England and Scotland are probably best, but chalk and even sandstone cliffs can attract nesting seabirds too. The colonies are often densely packed and constantly buzzing with activity, and visiting one is an unforgettable assault on the senses. Among the commoner birds such as Guillemots and Kittiwakes, some colonies hold sought-after species like Puffins and Black Guillemots. They arrive from early spring, and by midsummer the adults are constantly commuting out to sea and returning with fish for their growing chicks.

By late summer, parents and babies all depart and the cliffs are suddenly almost birdless, except for residents like Jackdaws and Peregrine Falcons. Areas where cliffs have crumbled to leave a beach and an 'undercliff' can be great hunting grounds for fossils – Lyme Regis in Dorset is a famous example of a fossil-rich undercliff.

↑ Inaccessible rocky shores may attract nesting seabirds. Shags are glossy blackish-green with curly top-knots in their summer plumage.

ROCKING OUT

The mini-worlds of life that live in rock pools offer endless fascination for the wildlife enthusiast. Made of sea water trapped in a rocky hollow when the tide retreats, the average rock pool is home to an array of sealife from tiny fishes to sea anemones. Delicate crabs and shrimps hide in the shadows, while molluscs, such as limpets, periwinkles and mussels, cling to the rocky walls. Sandy coves are often flanked by rocky clusters with plenty of pool potential. Treat your rock pool with consideration – if you move a rock to see what's underneath, carefully replace it afterwards.

WATCHING THE WAVES

Seawatching is a bit of a minority interest among birdwatchers. Keen seawatchers may spend dawn till dusk (or dawn till lunchtime at least) in a single spot, watching for birds moving out over the sea. Often the best times and places for seawatching are also the most uncomfortable –

sitting on an exposed headland while a strong autumnal onshore wind is blowing offers the best chances of seeing lots of seabirds, including more unusual species.

If that doesn't sound like your cup of tea, you can still enjoy seawatching in greater comfort. A sunny picnic on an elevated seaside position can be delightful. You might not see as many birds, but you'll probably have a nicer time. You may see whales or Basking Sharks from headlands, or try a whale-watching boat trip.

↑ Boat trips out of the north-west of Scotland provide wonderful views landward, and are great for seeing sealife such as Common Dolphins.

NATURAL HAVENS

Although wildlife does truly live everywhere, nature reserves offer some of the best opportunities for seeing it. Chosen because they already have good wildlife communities and managed to help those communities thrive, nature reserves will almost invariably have a richer range of species than the countryside in general. They are also visitor-friendly – the trails around the area are designed to show you the best spots without allowing you to disturb more vulnerable habitats. Some reserves are packed with facilities to ensure an exciting family day out, while others are more minimalist, enabling you to really get away from it all so it's just you and the wildlife.

↑ Broadwater Warren RSPB in Sussex is an area of conifer plantation which the RSPB is gradually restoring to lowland heath.

MAKING RESERVATIONS

Nature reserves offer safe havens for wildlife, protected from the threat of land redevelopment or too much human disturbance. They are managed in a way that will encourage more wildlife and maintain conditions that are suitable for any particularly uncommon species that live there. The best thing about nature reserves, though, is that they are everywhere, and each one practically guarantees you the opportunity for exciting and enthralling wildlife encounters. Some reserves are not open to the public but can be viewed from nearby footpaths, but most are set up to receive visitors.

Who looks after the reserves? In theory, anyone who owns a piece of land could manage it as a nature reserve and let visitors come to see it. There are a few privately owned and managed nature reserves around Britain, but the majority are run, if not owned, by a charity or government organisation.

- **The RSPB** owns more than 200 nature reserves around the UK. They include remote cliffsides holding deafening seabird cities, wide shimmering marshlands and wild ancient forests, but also meadows, parkland and riversides in or on the edge of towns and cities.
- **The Wildlife Trusts** is divided up by county into 47 branches, and each branch looks after several reserves of all shapes and sizes.
- **The Wildfowl and Wetlands Trust** has nine large wetland reserves around the UK, managed to attract wildfowl and other watery wildlife.
- **Butterfly Conservation** runs 33 nature reserves, all chosen because they hold populations of uncommon butterfly species.

▓ **The National Trust** isn't just about stately homes. The Trust also looks after some of our most delectable outdoor scenery, much of which is also important wildlife habitat.

▓ **National Nature Reserves** hold the most interesting and important of the UK's Sites of Special Scientific Interest. Some NNRs are designated and cared for by government bodies such as Natural England, Scottish Natural Heritage and the Countryside Council for Wales.

▓ **Local nature reserves** are often declared and managed by local authorities.

Whoever manages them, reserves are for all nature, and whether you're a general nature-lover, a budding botanist, a dragonfly-chaser or a beginner birdwatcher, you'll find something to interest you on virtually every nature reserve.

↑ Birdwatchers gather on the bridge at RSPB Radipole Lake in Dorset, watching the waters for waders and gulls and the skies for migrating birds of prey.

↓ Not all nature reserves are open to the public. The Grey and Common Seals at Blakeney Point in Norfolk can generally be seen only from special boat trips.

WHAT TO EXPECT

Most nature reserves have a car park, and many have a visitor centre. This may be a basic shed with information pinned to its walls or a lavish building with shop, café, art gallery and lecture room, with outside play and exploration areas for children. There will usually be a map of the reserve, a list of recent sightings and information on the local wildlife. There will often be a network of nature trails of varying lengths, and along the way there could be birdwatching hides. When you are out on the reserve, keep to the footpaths. Some reserves don't allow dogs – if they do, it's your responsibility to keep your dog under control so it doesn't disturb wildlife. Keep to the Countryside Code at all times, just as you should wherever you go in the countryside. The full details of the code can be found here: **www.naturalengland.org.uk/ourwork/enjoying/countrysidecode**. Its main premises are simple courtesy and common sense – keep yourself safe, don't disturb people or wildlife, and leave places as you find them.

FURTHER AFIELD

Depending on your budget, how you feel about your carbon footprint and your time commitments, you can take yourself off almost anywhere on Earth these days. Watching wildlife overseas doesn't require a dedicated wildlife holiday – you can find interesting wildlife to see whether you're on a shopping trip to New York or soaking up the sun on a Thai beach. Of course, a more wildlife-oriented holiday is an option too – you might take a couple of days on safari in between beach-basking in The Gambia, or you could go for a full-on birdwatching trek tour of somewhere as remote as Bhutan or Tierra del Fuego. There's no need to leave British shores for a wonderful wildlife holiday either – for a lifelong southerner a trip to the Scottish Highlands offers a whole new world of wildlife, and the Highlander will find just as much excitement on their first visit to the wide open marshlands of East Anglia.

IT'S ALL ABOUT COMPROMISE

↓ Voluntary conservation work abroad is exciting and rewarding. This volunteer is observing bird migration in Malta.

When you're planning a family holiday, everyone's needs have to be considered. Some people, exhausted from their daily routine, want to spend their week away doing as little as possible. Others will want to go on adventures, see sights and squeeze as much fun out of each day as possible. Luckily, wildlife-watching is a flexible hobby, and any holiday will have some opportunities.

As soon as you venture beyond our corner of Europe you'll start to encounter new and exciting wildlife in all habitats. Try to choose accommodation away from town centres and pick somewhere that has some outside space so you can sit with a drink and watch the wild world go by. Look out for places that offer bike or moped hire so you can take yourself off into the countryside when you get the urge.

GUIDED TOURS

There are numerous travel companies out there offering dedicated wildlife-watching holidays in some of the most exciting parts of the world. The companies vary widely in their approach. Birdquest, for example, is popular with keen birdwatchers with a 'hit list' of species they want to see. The itinerary is tough, with long days out birdwatching. Gentler-paced tours abound, too, and some companies offer holidays that combine wildlife-watching with other specialist interests. Avian Leisure, for example, offers South African tours combining birdwatching with wine-tasting.

↑ Camber Sands in East Sussex is a popular summer holiday destination, but is an exciting, wildlife-rich place to explore in winter too, both on foot or horseback.

→ When you go overseas, you'll find new wildlife to enjoy almost anywhere you look. This Japanese White-eye was photographed in a Kyoto park.

WORKING HOLIDAYS

Voluntary work is a great way to have an affordable and rewarding holiday somewhere you might not otherwise get the chance to go. The RSPB runs a busy volunteering programme on its reserves in the UK – accommodation is provided and during your stay you could do anything from practical land management, wildlife surveys, helping with school visits or keeping watch over rare breeding birds. Overseas, there are opportunities to work on wild animal orphanages in Africa, to carry out sealife surveying on research ships and to help fight illegal bird hunting in the Mediterranean. The website **www.environmentjob.co.uk** has a database of voluntary work from around the world.

↓ Take nothing for granted when wildlife-watching abroad. Cities in parts of southern Europe are full of Spanish Sparrows rather than House Sparrows.

LOCAL KNOWLEDGE

Hooking up with a local expert can really boost your chances of seeing the special wildlife that lives around your holiday destination. In some areas you can book a freelance guide for the day. The owners of your accommodation can also be a valuable source of local info. The RSPB's magazine *Birds* (supplied quarterly to RSPB members) has listings of wildlife-friendly accommodation in its classified section, covering the UK and further afield. Here you could choose a Scottish guest house which has Pine Martens visiting the garden, or find a Spanish *casa* whose owners will be able to tell you exactly where you need to go to see Lesser Kestrels or Great Bustards.

THE ART OF FIELDCRAFT

Fieldcraft isn't about making daisy chains. It's a blanket term for all of the little tricks you can employ to make it easier to find and get closer to wild animals when you're out. Fieldcraft comes into its own when you're watching shy or fast-moving animals which would rather avoid a close encounter with a human being. Wild animals are highly motivated and well equipped to keep out of sight, but if you work on developing great fieldcraft you should be able to get close to a shy animal, watch it going about its business and leave again without it ever knowing you were there.

SENSE AND SENSITIVITY

Animals, like people, use their senses to interpret their world. The sight of an approaching human is interpreted as bad news by most animals and they will disappear when you get too close for comfort. Vision is an important sense for many animals, especially birds and flying insects, but for others hearing and smell are equally, or more, important.

Mammals can only smell you at a distance if there's a breeze going from you to them, but most have acute hearing and will take a worst-case-scenario approach to any unfamiliar sound, whether it be the snap of a twig or the beep-beep of an arriving text message. Reptiles are extremely sensitive to ground vibrations and will slip away if they feel a heavy footfall nearby. A photogenically posing butterfly will almost certainly take flight if you let your shadow fall across it.

SHY AND RETIRING

As well as using their senses to detect and avoid you, many animals are also doing their utmost to evade detection by your senses. Some birds have such confidence in their camouflage that they will stay put, motionless, while you amble past a couple of feet away, oblivious to the Snipe, Woodcock or Nightjar

← With those huge eyes, this Common Darter dragonfly is ultra-sensitive to movement. To get close to it, you'll need to move slowly.

→ Common Lizards often bask on sunlit boardwalks. To stand a chance of seeing them, slow down and step as softly as you can.

sitting quietly there among the leaf-litter. Mammals tend to move quietly, and while some species of birds are show-offs, others skulk deep in vegetation and refuse to show themselves (though they may taunt you by loudly singing from their hiding places). So fieldcraft is not just about being quiet and discreet, it's also about being observant and, above all, patient.

CONSIDER THE LILIES

You don't need special skills to creep up on a plant. However, you still need to consider plants when you're out and about, even if they're not what you're looking for that day. In general, stick to footpaths. If you do go 'off path', watch where you step to make sure you avoid crushing plants. As well as sparing the plants themselves, this will help minimise the chances of animals detecting you – squashing plant stems makes noise and also releases smells that can inform mammals that something big, heavy and clumsy is wandering about nearby. When you are photographing a particular flower, resist the temptation to pull up or cut down other plants that might be getting in the way of your shot. Carefully fold grass stems out of the way and replace everything when you've finished.

The same goes for searching for small ground animals. By all means take a look under that stone, but move it slowly and gently, and carefully replace it exactly where it was afterwards so you don't make dozens of woodlice, earwigs and other 'minibeasts' homeless.

↙ No-one likes being woken up, and that includes a Fox dozing in the sun. Don't try to get too close, and enjoy the satisfaction of watching without being watched.

DO NOT DISTURB

Getting better and closer views of animals is just one reason why it's good to improve your fieldcraft. More importantly, it helps prevent you disturbing the animals and interrupting their normal and natural behaviour. Animals have enough to cope with already in the day-to-day struggle to survive and breed, so being careful not to alarm them unnecessarily is more than just a courtesy – it could make the difference between life and death. If you're close to a bird nest and the adult birds know you're there, they may not go near the nest until you've gone, which places the chicks at risk. Wading birds resting at high tide are conserving precious energy while they wait for the tide to expose their feeding grounds again. Forcing them to take flight depletes those energy stores and puts them in danger of starvation.

KEEPING A LOW PROFILE

So now that we've established you have to make yourself as invisible, inaudible and unsmellable as possible to get close to wildlife, how do you go about achieving this personal transformation? The answer is a mixture of preparation before you set off and careful behaviour once you're out there in the field. The degree to which all of this matters depends a great deal on where you're going and what you're looking for. If you're visiting a nature reserve with lots of hides on a busy day, you're as likely as anyone to see the best of the wildlife however you prepare and conduct yourself. But if it's a solo expedition to a quiet forest, good fieldcraft could make all the difference.

WHAT NOT TO WEAR

↓ Two rules of fieldcraft in one – get low so your outline doesn't break the horizon, and wear something that's dull-coloured so you blend in.

You may not want to invest in a full wardrobe of camouflage gear, but it's always a good idea to wear dull, neutral colours when you go out wildlife-watching. A flash of fluorescent yellow among the trees is a bit of a giveaway, and while many mammals have poor colour vision their eyes are well adapted to pick out strongly contrasting tones.

'Loud' clothing doesn't just cover dazzling colours, either. Many a fine-looking khaki-green jacket is completely unsuitable for wildlife-watching because it makes a veritable cacophony of swishing and crinkling sounds as you move. So walk about in your prospective new outdoors jacket to make sure it's soundless.

Blowing in the wind

Minimising your smelliness to wild creatures is a difficult problem. It's not about spending longer in the shower – the scent of soap and deodorant is just as noticeable to sensitive-nosed mammals as more natural human smells. You can make sure you're clean and avoid applying strongly perfumed products to your hair or skin and you'll still probably be sniffed out if the wind is blowing the wrong way. So work with the wind instead, and if you're approaching a mammal you've spotted, or heading somewhere you know mammals might be, make sure the wind or breeze is blowing towards you. If it's coming from behind you, it will carry your smell right to the animal.

THE COMFORT COMPROMISE

If you're too hot, too cold, feel constricted or even ridiculous while you're out, you won't enjoy yourself and you'll probably be too preoccupied with how bad you feel to notice much wildlife. Wearing head-to-toe camo gear might help you get closer to wildlife, but won't always 'feel' right. So always make sure you'll be comfortable in your chosen attire. Wear layers so you can take some off if you get too hot. A hat will protect your head from sun and cold – choose one that doesn't interfere with your hearing too much. Use suncream on any exposed bits, even if it's not sunny when you set out. Sturdy walking boots are the best footwear choice in most circumstances, while wellies are a necessity in others.

SOFT-STEPPING

Effective wildlife-watching requires a particular kind of walk. Every step you take could be the one that disturbs the as-yet-unseen animal ahead of you, so make sure your feet land gently. Proceed slowly, scanning all around you as you go and pausing now and then to listen. You can also lower your profile by positioning yourself carefully in relation to the surrounding terrain. If you're crossing a field, you're less likely to draw attention to yourself if you stick to the edges rather than striding across the middle. The outline of a human against the sky is very recognisable and alarms many animals, so try to disguise yours by keeping close to taller things – a hedge, a line of trees or even a wall.

↖ Take advantage of opportunities for a sit-down while you're out. You'll be amazed how closely some animals will approach when you're sitting quietly.

↓ Fish such as Common Carp are sensitive to movement, and when basking in sunny shallows will often dart away if you allow your shadow to fall onto them.

STOP!

It's tempting to get into the 'out for a walk' mindset when you're wildlife-watching, and keep striding on to see what's up ahead. Change this habit and take some breaks where you just stand (or sit) and wait. Ideally, pick somewhere where you have a reasonable view around but can make yourself quite inconspicuous. Standing with your back to a broad tree will hide your outline, and if you don't move there's a good chance animals won't realise you're there. Birds in particular may become quite blasé about your presence. If you are a confident tree-climber (be very careful though!) ascending a few feet into the branches can give you an excellent vantage point.

THE EYES HAVE IT

Being outdoors in search of wildlife involves all our senses (though admittedly taste and touch play a minor role!). However, rewarding though it is to hear a Nightingale or smell a glade of Bluebells, most of us will not be completely satisfied with a wildlife encounter where the subject remains unseen. The trouble is that many animals do all they can to avoid our gaze... But with practice we can learn how to use our eyes more effectively and see a wider world than we ever imagined.

[a]

DIRECTING YOUR GAZE

When you're out wildlife-watching, some things will catch your eye much more readily than others. A bird flying against the sky is much more noticeable than one flying below the horizon. An insect feeding on a bright flower will draw your attention more than one lurking among the leaves below. So the golden rule is to look *everywhere*, but look particularly carefully at spots which offer good hiding places. The bird in the top of a bare tree will catch your eye straight away,

↓ Crab Spiders are not only small, but also beautifully camouflaged to hide from their insect prey. You'll need to look hard and closely at the flowers to spot one.

but further down among the tangled lower branches there may be more. Move slowly and stop often to thoroughly scan promising-looking spots.

When searching for unobtrusive insects and other small animals, you will need a different approach. This means slowing down and engaging your close-focus vision. It may also mean getting low – from your eye-level when standing, you will miss a great deal of what's going on closer to your feet. When you're in a meadow, try crouching or kneeling down and looking through the grass stems – it's a window into another world in miniature.

LOOK AHEAD

The reason why binoculars are such an essential part of your wildlife-watching kit concerns the 'flight distance' of animals. Often when you are watching an animal, it is watching you too, and if you get too close for its comfort, it will retreat. Some animals will tolerate a much closer approach than others, but

← For every bird which sits obligingly out in full view like this Goldfinch (a), there will be ten more which lurk among the leaf cover like this Chiffchaff (b).

with many species you will never get close enough for a decent view unless you use binoculars. So as you walk, pause often to scan the path ahead of you with your binoculars. If you see something interesting in the distance, you can then plan a stealthy approach to get a better look.

DO YOUR HOMEWORK

If you are looking for a specific species, some knowledge of its habits will help guide your search. Birds of prey, for example, tend to be most active on warm still days, so scan the skies if you're blessed with fine weather on your raptor search. On gloomier days, you're more likely to find your raptor doing 'sit and wait' hunting from a perch, so scan along lines of fence posts and along walls. Roe Deer will often stay close to field edges adjoining woodland when grazing, ready to dash into cover, while woodland butterflies will be drawn to any sunny clearings.

Following directions

When you're out wildlife-watching with others, you'll soon need to point something out to a companion or have them point something out to you. This isn't always straightforward – 'just look where I'm pointing' or 'it's right there, you idiot!' are not terribly helpful, but there are tricks you can use to make the process easier.

1 Clock-face Let's say you want to point out a bird in a tree. Pick an obvious striking feature of the tree, for example, where the first branch comes off the trunk or a contrastingly coloured clump of leaves. Treat this as the centre of the clock-face and give the bird's position in relation to that centre point: 'It's nine o'clock from the big patch of moss on the trunk.' This works in many other contexts, too, including high-flying birds when there are some clearly describable clouds in the sky.

2 Landmarks. If you need to point out a flying bird or running mammal, note the direction in which it's moving, pick a feature on the horizon that it will shortly reach, and say 'it's going left, above/below the horizon, about to go over/under the red house, going over/under the red house now.'

3 Tracking along boundaries. Let's say you've found a Fox sleeping in long grass in a field. It's quite obscured and there's nothing obvious to use as the centre of a clock-face. Look for linear features that the eye can track along – a fence, a ditch, a ridge of taller grass. Then you can say something like 'follow the darker strip of grass from left to right, about two-thirds of the way along from the left edge, come forwards in a straight line and it's halfway between that and the line of greener grass.'

BEYOND VISION

An experienced birdwatcher can go into the woods on a spring dawn and come back with an impressively long list of species they've noted without actually having seen more than a handful of birds. When you're a beginner, this ability to identify birds by their voices can seem almost magical, but it's something anyone can master and it adds a huge new dimension to your wildlife-watching. Using your ears can also help you find shy mammals and other animals. One of the great things about wildlife-watching is that the rustling you hear in the undergrowth could be almost anything – a foraging Blackbird, a hunting Adder, a Hedgehog searching for slugs... So wherever you go, keep your ears open.

BIRDSONG

⬂ Some birds sing from perches, while others deliver their song in flight. Then there are those like the Swallow which may do either.

It's probably our favourite of all natural sounds, and listening to birdsong is soothing and uplifting. However, if you're keen to find out the identity of the singers, those pleasant feelings can quickly turn to frustration.

Some birds habitually sing from a prominent spot, and it's easy to match the voice to the bird. This group includes most of our resident songsters, such as Blackbird, Mistle Thrush, Dunnock and Chaffinch. Early spring is the best time to get familiar with these common birds' songs, as the trees are leafless and the birds easy to see. By mid-spring, things become complicated as the buds open and a new set of singers arrives. When you have to deal with the songs of warblers,

SONG OR CALL?

Birdsong describes the 'advertising' sound made by an adult male bird to declare his territory and attract a mate. Songs are best developed in the group of mostly small birds known as passerines or, appropriately, songbirds. Songs vary a great deal but in general involve quite elaborate combinations of sounds and are delivered regularly over long periods.

Not all birds sing, but almost all give calls. Bird calls are simpler sounds than songs and are given by adults of both sexes as well as youngsters. They have varied purposes: 'contact calls' help members of a flock stay together when on the move, alarm calls warn when danger is around, and 'begging calls' are are given by baby birds to encourage their parents to feed them.

Learning calls is more difficult than learning songs. In some cases it's practically impossible. For example, when small songbirds spot a very dangerous predator, such as a Sparrowhawk, they give a very similar short high-pitched whistle as an alarm call. Using recordings will help you get a handle on the more distinctive calls, as well as the non-vocal bird noises – the drumming of woodpeckers, for example, or the wing-clapping of Nightjars.

flycatchers, Nightingales, Whinchats, Redstarts and assorted other migrants, you'll be glad you put in the hours learning the resident birdsongs first.

In its simplest form, learning birdsong goes like this: hear the song, find the bird that's singing it, match the two in your mind and you'll recognise the song next time you hear it. However, you can learn and revise birdsong at home using recordings. There are many CDs of British bird songs and calls on the market, plus numerous recordings online. The RSPB's online bird guide (**www.rspb.org.uk/wildlife/birdguide**) includes recordings of songs and calls for almost all species. While some songs are very distinctive, others are easily muddled (Garden Warbler and Blackcap, for example, have bewilderingly similar songs), and recordings are a really helpful resource in cases like this.

↑ Plaintive squeaky calls building in pitch and excitement indicate a bird begging for food – in this case it is a female Robin soliciting a 'courtship feed' from her mate.

↓ The pungent aroma of the invasive Himalayan Balsam characterises riverbanks in midsummer.

OTHER NOISES

Many mammals make distinctive sounds, though hearing them is rarely easy. You may know the harsh shrieks and barks of amorous Foxes or have heard the noisy snuffling of foraging Hedgehogs. Bats are extremely vocal but most of their insect-locating squeaks are pitched too high for human hearing – an electronic bat detector will pick them up and help you identify them. Grasshoppers and crickets advertise for mates with distinctive mechanical sounds called 'stridulating', made by rubbing the wings or legs.

SMELL YOU LATER

Humans aren't blessed with a great sense of smell. However, we can pick up aromas at close range and they can help us identify wildlife as well as enhance our experience of the natural world. Scent is a useful aid to identifying certain kinds of fungi. Some male butterflies produce scents from modified scales on their wings, intended to delight female butterflies but detectable to human noses. The keen and practised nose can detect mammal scent-markings, while everyone enjoys sniffing wild flowers.

KEEP ON TRACK

No matter how hard you try, you won't always see the animals you want to see. However, if you can find some sign that they are living in the area, you'll know you're in the right place to see them one day. Not all animals leave obvious signs of their presence lying around but many do. Turn wildlife detective, and keep your eyes open for feathers, fur, footprints, droppings, nibbled food remains, nests, animal pathways through the undergrowth and other evidence.

KINDS OF SIGNS

↑ When a raptor like this Peregrine Falcon eats a bird it has caught, it must first pluck out the feathers, which may get scattered over a wide area.

It would be easy to fill a whole book with the various signs animals leave behind. To tackle the topic more concisely, let's consider the main categories of signs.

■ **Discarded body parts** Birds moult their feathers, mammals moult fur and reptiles moult their skin. You could find feathers anywhere, though larger ones are easiest to spot. Individual mammal hairs are hard to find, but you may find tufts of fur caught on barbed wire or on thorns. Lizards shed their skin in small patches, but snakes lose it all at once and leave a complete empty skin behind.

■ **Movement signs** Mud, snow and sand are all good for capturing animal tracks. Field guides to tracks and signs will help you identify whose feet left the prints. You can make a cast of a print by surrounding it with a card frame and pouring plaster of Paris inside, though a photograph is quicker and more reliable. Mammals create their own narrow pathways through undergrowth – following one may lead you to the animal, or to its home or favourite feeding ground.

■ **Animal homes** Bird nests are easiest to spot in winter, when revealed by fallen leaves. Don't search for nests in spring and summer when they may be in use. Holes in trees, made by woodpeckers or by natural causes, make homes for all sorts of birds. Some mammals build nests in trees or bushes, while others dig burrows. A cluster of large tunnels close together in woodland is probably a Badger sett; freshly disturbed earth suggests it's in use.

■ **Feeding signs** The appearance of the indigestible parts of a meal can give clues as to who ate it. Pine cones with the scales chewed through to the central stem indicate squirrels, while a hazelnut accessed via a neatly gnawed round hole is the work of a Dormouse. Herbivorous insects and their larvae often leave a clear pattern of damage on their food plant. Large quantities of bird feathers indicate that a predator killed the bird: feathers pulled out whole suggest the killer was a bird of prey; feather shafts bitten through indicate the predator was a mammal. An empty bird's egg with a hole in the side and traces of yellow within was probably opened by a predator. Piles of broken snail shells around a stone are the work of a Song Thrush.

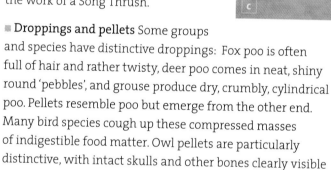

■ **Droppings and pellets** Some groups and species have distinctive droppings: Fox poo is often full of hair and rather twisty, deer poo comes in neat, shiny round 'pebbles', and grouse produce dry, crumbly, cylindrical poo. Pellets resemble poo but emerge from the other end. Many bird species cough up these compressed masses of indigestible food matter. Owl pellets are particularly distinctive, with intact skulls and other bones clearly visible on the pellet's surface.

↑ (a) An intriguing-looking opening in long grass may be a 'run' used by medium-sized mammals.
(b) A neat hole in a tree trunk is the work of a woodpecker, but may in subsequent years become home to another hole-nesting species.
(c) This distinctive 'two short, two long' print was left by a Rabbit.
(d) A clump of feathers discovered on the lawn is a good indication that your local Sparrowhawk has recently made a kill.

One for the collection?

The idea of keeping a collection of wildlife-related bits and pieces (well, maybe not the poo) may appeal to you. However, there are certain things that you're not allowed to own, so be careful when considering whether to pick it up or leave it where it is.

Taking wild birds' eggs from their nests has been an offence for many years and no right-minded naturalist would consider doing it. But what about broken eggshells that you've found on the ground? Still best to leave them where they are. The same goes for dead birds or parts of them, though you shouldn't have any problem owning the odd moulted feather.

→ This small collection of natural objects includes shells, stones, a blue wing feather from a Jay and a curly tail feather from a drake Mallard.

IN HIDING

What wildlife-watcher wouldn't jump at the chance to wear an invisibility cloak? Until some bright spark invents them, the next best thing we can do is hide behind things – or, in the case of purpose-built hides, inside things. Some nature reserves have very comfortable and well-equipped hides. While getting outdoors is part of the fun of wildlife-watching, it's hard to rival the kinds of views you can get from inside a hide.

↗ Finding a well-concealed hiding place and keeping still is a good way to get close views of very shy birds such as Cetti's Warbler.

↓ A simple viewing screen in front of a bird feeding station means people can walk past without disturbing the birds, or watch through viewing slots.

AU NATUREL

As we've already seen, using natural cover to disguise your outline is one of the basics of fieldcraft. When out and about, keep an eye open for suitable hidey-holes which will enable you to tuck yourself into the vegetation but still have a good view ahead of you. A folding chair will make things much more comfortable if you settle in for a long wait.

If there's no handy cover, getting low can help you get closer views of wildlife, as it hides your human outline that can be so alarming to wild animals. Mastering the 'commando crawl' on one's belly while holding a camera is a crucial skill for wildlife photographers – if you notice a wader, for example, working its way along a shoreline, try going round it in a wide circle so you're ahead of it and then lying down flat close to the shore – it may well keep going right past you.

BUILD YOUR OWN

You can make a basic hide from natural materials without damaging wildlife habitats. Try tying branches together to make a screen in a wood, or on a beach build up a low bank of pebbles to hide behind. If you're willing to introduce some man-made elements, there's a material called scrim which is designed specifically for creating inconspicuous screening. It is patterned with camouflage designs and you can hang it up to make a screen or just throw it over yourself for an instant hide. It is available from outlets like Wildlife-watching Supplies – **www.wildlifewatchingsupplies.co.uk.**

PORTABLE HIDES

The place where you bought your scrim probably also sells a range of small, portable hides. These may be very simple, perhaps just a big bag of camouflaged material with a viewing slot. There are also more sophisticated designs that give you space to sit in reasonable comfort – ideal for those long waits to get a much-coveted photo of a special animal. Portable hides often resemble dome tents, and indeed you could use a tent or a fisherman's bivouac as a hide, though you'll need to devise a way to see out of it in comfort. When siting your hide, you'll find wildlife accepts it more readily if you blend it into the vegetation a bit. Bear in mind that you should seek the landowner's permission before setting up a hide on property that's not your own.

Hide on wheels

Animals are often a good deal less frightened by cars than they are by people (a pity, given how much more dangerous cars are, on average, to wildlife). You can use this tendency to your advantage and stay in your car to get views of animals that would not hang around long if you got out. Quiet country roads offer the most wildlife-watching potential – just make sure you pull safely off the road. Access tracks to nature reserves, such as the long track through grazing marsh to RSPB Elmley Marshes in Kent, are ideal for car-based wildlife-watching.

HIDES ON NATURE RESERVE

Permanent hides on nature reserves are purpose-built to give you great views of the best areas. Their approach is screened off, so often when you go into a hide, what you see from the viewing slots is quite different to the views while out on the reserve trails. The most productive hides tend to overlook wetland areas, where waterbirds come to breed or feed.

Hide etiquette is simple. First of all, keep quiet. Turn your mobile phone to silent, and ask your children to talk in soft voices as the birds will be able to hear them. The viewing slots may have fold-up wooden covers – if so, replace them before you leave. Don't poke your arms or long camera lenses out of the viewing slots, and if the hide is busy don't put your belongings on the bench. At busy times everyone will have to squeeze up. If there is a queue of people waiting to sit down, be considerate and don't stay too long.

↓ Patiently waiting in a birdwatching hide may eventually produce very close views of normally shy species such as Green Sandpipers.

THE WILDLIFE CALENDAR

If you head for woodland in search of butterflies in January, you'll
be disappointed. A seabird colony that's teeming with life in
June will be silent and deserted by October, and even your
busy garden bird feeders may fall very quiet in summertime. Every species
of plant and animal has its own annual schedule, and you have to adapt to that
if you want to see particular species or behaviour. Working out where to go and
when can be frustrating, but the wider your range of interest, the more you'll
find to see wherever and whenever you go.

↑ Severe winter
weather increases the
chances of your seeing
certain species, such
as Bittern, in areas
where they don't
normally occur.

WINTER

This is the 'survival season' for most of our
wildlife. Deciduous trees and shrubs have dropped
their leaves and become woody skeletons, while
herbaceous plants have died back to their roots
(or died completely in the case of annual plants).
Many animals are hibernating, including almost
all insects, which may winter in their egg,
immature, pupa or adult stage. Few mammals
are active – bats, most rodents and Hedgehogs all
hibernate and others, such as Badgers, become
much less active. Reptiles and amphibians sleep,
while fish sulk on the lake or river bed.

Many of our breeding birds migrate south in
winter, but their places are taken by an influx of
winter visitors, escaping colder weather further
north and east. This is the season for wildfowl, for
noisy flocks of thrushes and finches, for bird tables
to seethe with hungry visitors, for upland birds to
move to the lowlands and it's also the best time to
see birds of prey.

SPRING

Butterflies that hibernate as adults, such as Peacocks and Brimstones, start to
seek out others of their kind on the first warm days of late winter. Early-flowering
trees and other plants are pollinated by early-flying bees and moths, while as
plants generate new foliage, insect larvae wake up and begin to eat it. Reptiles and
amphibians begin their year with a mating frenzy, Common Toads making their
pilgrimages to spawn in the ponds where they were born. March sees the hectic
courtship chases of Brown Hares.

The dawn chorus really picks up its pace in spring. This is also the season to see dramatic courtship displays. Some birds nest as early as February, while by April the summer migrants are pouring in. The winter visitors will be departing, too, and passage migrants (birds which spend neither summer nor winter here but stop off on migration in spring and autumn) work their way northwards.

← One of the earliest of our summer visitors to arrive is the Sandwich Tern, which will be back on its breeding grounds before the end of March.

SUMMER

This is the peak season for insect activity, with most of the winged species having a short flying season in the summer months in which they mate and lay their eggs. Damselflies gather alongside lakes and streams, while dragonflies hunt over open water and dry land alike. Butterflies and moths work the day and night shifts, busy pollinating a colourful array of summer flowers.

With the shorter nights, summer is a good season to see nocturnal animals in daylight. Barn Owls may begin hunting in mid-afternoon, and nocturnal mammals may also have to forage before it's quite dark. Many birds keep a low profile after the song-and-dance of spring as they rear their broods, but later in summer there are suddenly fledglings everywhere. Passage migrants will be visiting on their southbound migration by midsummer, this time including juvenile birds born that year.

AUTUMN

For many animals, autumn is all about preparing for the rigours of winter. Hibernating animals will be feeding up frantically, laying down fat supplies to see them through the long months of starvation. The Peacock butterflies are no longer interested in mating but only want to eat – they gorge themselves on the sweet juices of windfall fruit, and hibernating rodents store up nuts and seeds in their nests.

↑ Some butterflies, like the rare Silver-spotted Skipper, can only be seen for a few weeks in summer, so plan your outings carefully if you want to see them.

← Insect activity dwindles through autumn, with Migrant Hawker dragonflies among those likely to be seen on the wing later in the year.

Autumn is the peak season for mushrooms and toadstools, while plants have finished flowering and are now producing seeds in profusion.

Some migrant birds also feed up before their long journeys and may gather in big flocks before departing, as winter visitors start to arrive. Autumn is the season to watch dramatic deer ruts, and to see Grey Seals with their new pups.

CLOCK-WATCHING

Just as each animal species has its annual schedule, so each animal has its daily routine. Getting familiar with animals' patterns of activity is key to seeing what you want to see. Sometimes watching the most exciting wildlife behaviour will require you to violate your own human preferences about when to be awake and when to sleep, but early mornings and late nights once in a while are a small price to pay for privileged insights into animal behaviour. Besides, there's plenty of interesting stuff to observe during the more civilised daylight hours too.

↑ Misty mornings mean reduced visibility, but that works both ways around – this singing Wren seemed unaware that it was being observed.

→ Large birds of prey like Buzzards need thermals to help them soar, and so are most likely to be seen on the wing in the warmest parts of the day.

DAWN

Most of us don't find it very easy to crawl out of bed while it's still dark outside, therefore most of us don't. So if you are one of the few who do, you can enjoy both solitude and wildlife for a couple of hours – even a town park can seem like a tranquil haven for nature if you're there in the early morning. Dawn is a great time for wildlife-watching. Nocturnal mammals may still be out and about, while most birds rise early and are intensely active at first light. In spring, this means lots of singing, while in autumn dawn is a great time to look for newly arrived warblers and other migrants, feeding hungrily in hedgerows. Most insects and other warmth-dependent animals are less active in the cool of the early morning, but if you are observant you might find them resting on vegetation and waiting to warm up.

MIDDAY

Birds and mammals are generally less active in the middle of the day. Exceptions include raptors, especially the high-soaring species which need rising warm air currents (thermals) to gain height. In the warmer months, insects are at their most active in the hottest hours, and this is also a good time to look for reptiles basking in the open. Some flowers, like Scarlet Pimpernels, only open up in the warm hours, closing their petals later in the day or if the weather worsens.

EVENING

This can be nearly as good as dawn for wildlife-watching, though there tend to be more people around. Birds have another burst of activity before sunset, making sure they've eaten enough to last the night. Nocturnal animals may come out to begin foraging before dark, especially

in summer, and butterflies often bask in the last sun of the day, making for great photographic opportunities. Many bird species roost communally in winter, and watching them fly in to their roosts against a glowing sky is always exciting – the dazzling pre-roost aerial swirls and tumbles of Starling flocks are rightly famous.

NIGHT

The obvious problem with night-time wildlife-watching is the difficulty in seeing anything. You can use artificial lights, but these may disturb the wildlife, and night-vision gear is expensive. However, on well moonlit nights in the right places you can enjoy views of animals you are unlikely to meet in the daytime. Night-time can be good for garden wildlife-watching – sit quietly in your garden and you might hear a Hedgehog come snuffling along. Nocturnal animals can get used to permanent lights, and if you feed your local Badgers or Foxes you might find they are happy to come up to the house and give you good views in your outside lights.

↑ In summer evenings there are hours of beautiful evening light, and mammals like Rabbits will be active well before dark.

TIME AND TIDE

Animal behaviour isn't just governed by night and day. For animals that live and feed along the coasts, the state of the tide can be very important. Wading birds which feed on sandy and muddy shorelines arrange their daily schedule around the tides, feeding when the tide is out and resting elsewhere when the incoming sea covers up their feeding places.

If you want to get good views of winter waders on the coast, you should consult your local tide table and plan your visit to coincide with high tide. At low tide there's just too much good feeding ground exposed, and the waders will be spread out, but as the sea comes in they are pushed further up the beach. At some places a very big high tide will force the waders off the beach completely and they will move to a nearby field or other safe place. At some RSPB reserves, such as Snettisham in Norfolk and Frampton Marsh in Lincolnshire, there are hides sited to overlook traditional wader high-tide roosts. The biggest (or 'spring') tides happen twice a month, but often occur very early in the morning – so go in autumn rather than winter (when it will be too dark).

RAIN OR SHINE

We Brits might complain non-stop about the weather, but we – and our wildlife – generally have it pretty easy compared to some other parts of the world. However, just as the weather has a dramatic affect on humans, so it does on animals. The seasons dictate a plant's annual growth pattern and an animal's development and behaviour cycle, but day-to-day changes in the weather can have a dramatic effect, and can really make a difference to your chances of seeing a given species on a particular day. Get used to checking weather forecasts and learning what the clouds can tell you about imminent weather changes – it will all help you plan for success.

TEMPERATURE

↓ A female Adder basks on a log to warm up. Reptiles spend much time basking, as it keeps their body temperatures high enough for rapid movement if necessary.

For cold-blooded animals that need warmth to move about, the temperature will determine whether they are out and about, basking to get warm or hiding and inactive. Adders, for example, emerge from their underground hibernating holes when the temperature reaches about 10°C, while a hibernating Brimstone butterfly won't get out of bed for anything less than 14°C. When the temperature is only just above the minimum that allows activity, butterflies and reptiles alike will bask, sitting motionless with as much of their bodies exposed to the warming air as possible (for butterflies, this usually means resting with wings fully open). On warmer days, animals like these will reach their optimum body temperature – this means butterflies will be very active and reptiles will be able to move like greased lightning. If things get really hot, both may become inactive again.

The amount of cloud cover affects the air temperature. Things warm up more quickly on sunny days, but in summer a bit of cloud cover won't keep the air from getting warm enough for butterfly activity.

WIND

In general, windiness is bad for animal activity. It makes flying difficult, so birds and winged insects tend to avoid getting airborne. It also discourages small birds from moving to the outer twigs of trees or the tops of reed stems, so they hunker down out of sight among denser vegetation. However, windiness at sea means that birds moving over the water will come closer to shore, so if you want to see lots of seabirds you should pick a day when there are onshore winds pushing the birds closer to where you are. After very big storms, such as the 1987 hurricane, seabirds are sometimes found along rivers and around reservoirs far from the sea, having been driven well inland.

Overnight easterly winds during spring and (especially) autumn push migrating birds towards the east coast of the UK, while westerly gales are responsible for driving migrating American birds (and the occasional flying insect) to western 'rarity hotspots' like the Isles of Scilly.

↑ Even in a serious downpour, there still may be wildlife to enjoy through the window. Woodpigeons are among the species that will 'bathe' in falling rain.

↓ Blue Tits and other small birds will visit garden feeders in increased numbers after a snowfall, as natural food becomes difficult to find.

RAIN

Getting cold and wet isn't fun for wildlife either, and you probably won't miss that much if you stay in during a rainstorm. Straight after rain, though, can be good for wildlife-watching. Rain encourages mushrooms and toadstools to sprout, and gets slugs and snails active and brings earthworms to the surface (which may attract other animals). If migrating birds were grounded by a storm they may be taking the opportunity to do some feeding. Rain coming after a long dry period may encourage birds like pigeons to sit openly in the downpour with their wings spread, taking a shower.

SNOW

For animals that are active through winter, snowfall can be extremely bad news. Freezing temperatures mean it's imperative to eat enough, but foraging on snow-covered ground is difficult. Both birds and mammals may temporarily lose their fear of humans as they desperately search for food.

Garden bird feeding really comes into its own at times like this, and the RSPB received numerous reports during the cold snap of unusual garden visitors, such as Meadow Pipits, Skylarks and Woodcocks. Snow and ice can also make notoriously shy and skulking birds, such as Water Rails, easier to see, as they are forced to search more widely for food. And if the weather is even worse on the near continent, birds like Bitterns will migrate here for a slightly easier time.

SETTING TARGETS

Whether you're a newcomer to wildlife-watching or a veteran with 50 years' experience under your belt, you'll still have a wish-list of animals or plants that you want to see. Just seeing the species isn't necessarily enough, either. A split-second glimpse of a bolt of blue powering down the river means you can put a tick next to Kingfisher in your book, but you're still going to hanker for a longer sighting of another one, perhaps a bit closer, perhaps sitting rather than flying, perhaps even catching a fish. Finding a Smooth Newt hiding under a stone in winter is exciting, but you'll still want to see a male in spring with his glorious colours and showy crest. You'd need several (hundred) human lifetimes to see all there is to see in nature, so save time now and plan how you're going to start ticking off those wish-list targets.

→ In the 1970s, you would have had to visit Wales to see Red Kites. Now they are more widespread, thanks to introduction schemes, and could turn up almost anywhere.

↓ Rare Bird Alert publish an online map, updated through the day, showing the real-time whereabouts of rare birds throughout the British Isles.

DO YOUR HOMEWORK

Field guides are not always very helpful when it comes to telling you exactly where to find an individual species. While most do have distribution maps, these will only give you a vague idea. The kinds of books which give you specific places to go for particular species are called 'site guides' – the *Where to Watch Birds* series published by Christopher Helm, for example, covers several counties per volume and gives comprehensive lists of the best birdwatching sites and what you'll see at them at different times of year. However, some field guides, such as Helm's *Orchids of Britain and Ireland*, do include a site guide. For RSPB reserves, *RSPB Where to Discover Nature* (also published by Helm) tells you which plants and animals live on RSPB reserves throughout the UK.

The internet is also a helpful resource for site-finding. Try a Google search for your target species plus your home county. Many regions have local wildlife groups, whose websites may include a gazetteer of good places to go with a list of which species are likely to be found. They may also include the more specific details you'll sometimes need to home in on a very localised species.

ASK THE EXPERTS

You can't beat a bit of inside information. Join your local birdwatching or wildlife-watching group to meet more like-minded people locally and exchange knowledge. If you're out at a nature

← You are unlikely to 'just bump into' scarce butterflies like Silver-studded Blues – a planned trip to the right spot at the right time will be necessary.

→ Scotland is the UK's stronghold for Red Squirrels, but a few colonies survive elsewhere too – including Brownsea Island in Dorset, and Formby in Merseyside.

reserve, try chatting to other visitors – you may find out about new sites to try or get some valuable tips on exactly when and where to look for your most coveted species. You can also make the human connection online. Websites with message boards, such as the RSPB's community pages (**www.rspb.org.uk/community**), Birdforum (**www.birdforum.net**) and Wild About Britain (**www. wildaboutbritain.com**), enable you to post questions which will be answered by other community members.

TWITCHING

Maybe you've flicked through your field guide and decided you want to see a Bee-eater, say, or a Monarch butterfly, neither of which normally lives in Britain. You could go to France for the Bee-eater or the US for the Monarch, but once in a while both of these species do appear on our shores. When lost animals which don't normally live in Britain turn up here (usually birds, but occasionally flying insects and even the occasional bat or seal!) it's often possible for interested members of the public to see them, as long as the person whose land they are on is agreeable.

Knowledge of what rarities are about can be found on certain subscription websites or pager services. Going to see an individual rare animal at a specific place is called 'twitching' – most wildlife-watchers do it from time to time but for for some it is the main interest. There are nearly 600 species of wild birds on the British List, many of them with only a handful of records, and the keenest twitchers have seen in excess of 450 of them.

CARELESS TALK COSTS LIVES

In general, swapping knowledge with other wildlife enthusiasts is harmless. However, in a few cases, it's best not to reveal the whereabouts of a particular animal or plant. Although we generally have a quite enlightened and positive attitude towards wildlife in this country, there are still a few bad apples out there who would uproot and steal a rare plant, take birds' eggs from their nests, or poison and shoot birds of prey or predatory mammals. Sometimes, though, access or viewing facilities can be arranged, as with the Purple Herons that nested at RSPB Dungeness in 2010.

MAKING THE MOST OF IT

It's not always easy to make the most of a wildlife-watching trip. You might opt to walk the 'red trail' at a nature reserve and see next to nothing, only to bump into someone at the crossroads who took the 'blue trail' and saw all manner of wildlife wonders. Or you might pay a quick visit to a place new to you while you're travelling, and be faced with an overwhelming amount of choices about where to go and what to look at – how can you be sure you won't miss the best stuff? Because wildlife-watching is inherently unpredictable, there will always be days when you'll kick yourself for not pausing a little longer at point A or hurrying a bit more quickly to point B, but there is plenty you can do to help squeeze more enjoyment out of every day.

A MATTER OF FOCUS

↓ High vantage points are great places to stop and just watch what goes by, especially in migration season where you may see large flocks of birds on the move.

If a photographer wanted to go out with every bit of kit they could ever possibly need, they would need a team of Sherpas to carry everything and they'd make pretty slow (and noisy) progress. They might have all the equipment to exploit any opportunity, but managing the sheer bulk of that equipment would seriously limit the opportunities they encounter.

It's the same with wildlife-watching, to a certain extent, though what limits you is usually time rather than weight of gear. If you give yourself an hour to visit a large nature reserve and you're determined to walk the full length of every path, you'd have to do it at a brisk jog. So you need to plan and decide beforehand where to concentrate your efforts. This will be largely dictated by the time of day and year, and the weather, but also by what you want to see. Looking for insects requires a very different search strategy to looking for mammals. If you are at a specific site to see a specific individual bird, for example, you might just have to walk straight past other interesting-looking things to reach the right place.

The other side of the coin is that wildlife is unpredictable. Sometimes opportunities will be thrown in your path, and your reactions will determine how things pan out. Stay alert and be prepared to freeze or edge behind a tree trunk or other piece of cover if you bump into an animal at close quarters.

What happens next? If you arrive at a hide overlooking a wetland area teeming with all kinds of birdlife, it can be difficult to decide what to look at first. Some of those birds might stay there all day, but others might pay only a transient visit. Look around and see which birds are resting and which are actively feeding – the former are more likely to move away sooner. Smaller birds are generally more restless than large ones. Flocks of terns will often take off en masse and circle around for no apparent reason, but if the waders join them that probably means a bird of prey is around. Experience will help you to hone your skills in anticipating behaviour.

↑ A surprise encounter with a mammal like this Fox cub when out in the countryside is a moment to be treasured – keep very still and you may prolong your views.

↖ One moment these Black-tailed Godwits were feeding peacefully on a lagoon, the next they had erupted into flight – a sure sign that a bird of prey is nearby.

Tricks of the trade

Sometimes you can take a closer look at an animal, or persuade it to take a closer look at you, by attracting its interest or curiosity. Many birdwatchers use 'pishing' (making a squeaky sound by kissing the back of their hand) to coax a shy bird out of cover. 'Pishing' can also work with certain mammals – Weasels and Stoats are particularly curious about squeaky noises, so if you spot one running away, stop walking and start squeaking – it may well come back to inspect you.

Providing food attracts wildlife to our gardens, but in the wider countryside offering water can have more dramatic results, especially when the weather has been dry. Try pouring water into a dry hollow and waiting somewhere out of sight. Birds may come to drink and bathe, and insects may be attracted as well. And loading a plant mister with water sweetened with sugar and spraying the leaves of a tree may coax down treetop butterflies such as hairstreaks.

TOO CLOSE FOR COMFORT

Every wildlife watcher will, sooner or later, encounter a situation where they aren't sure whether just sitting back and watching is the right thing to do. Wild animals may fight violently, get injured or get sick, and baby animals may appear to be lost and abandoned. Should we always let nature take its course, or are there sometimes occasions when it would be right to step in and do something to help? In general, we should leave nature to take care of itself. However, every situation is different, and this section aims to help you decide when to take action and what that should be.

↑ A newly fledged young Robin is very vulnerable. It will soon become much stronger and warier.

INJURED AND SICK ANIMALS

Sometimes you will see an animal with a visible injury – a mammal walking with a limp, a bird with a trailing wing. However the injury occurred, the value of trying to catch and then treat the victim has to be weighed up against the risks to its health from the trauma of being caught and handled, and also its chances of recovering or surviving if left alone. With birds with wing damage that renders them flightless, it is often worth catching and treating them. However, if they have a leg injury they will easily evade capture by flying away. Young animals are more likely to heal well and adapt to temporary captivity than old ones. If you find an injured bird which you think could be caught and treated, contact the RSPCA or a local wildlife rehabilitator. If you need

NOT EVEN A FLESH WOUND

Not everything that looks like an injury is one. Here are some examples.

■ **Deer with a missing antler** Deer shed and regrow their antlers every year. It's common to see mono-antlered deer in autumn to early winter.

■ **Bird with one leg** Birds habitually rest standing on one leg, and may not bother to put down the resting leg but instead hop when moving short distances.

■ **Flightless wildfowl in summer** Wildfowl moult all their flight feathers at the same time in the summer, so are temporarily flightless. Male ducks moult into a female-like 'eclipse' plumage at this time to camouflage them while they are at their most vulnerable.

■ **Birds with missing tails** Bird tails, unlike mammal tails, don't contain bone, just feathers. Sometimes a bird will lose all its tail feathers in a failed predator attack, but they will soon grow back.

to catch an injured bird or mammal, the safest way (for you and the victim) is to drop a soft towel over it. Be aware that most mammals and larger birds can and will injure you if you handle them carelessly.

Animals with an illness often give themselves away by being unusually approachable. Often the eyes look dull, the posture hunched and the fur or plumage ruffled. Some illnesses are treatable, and again this is a job for the RSPCA or a wildlife hospital. If you notice ill or dead birds in your garden, the cause may be an infectious disease, such as trichomonosis, and you should take down your bird-feeding equipment and sterilise it to curtail the risk of spreading the infection.

ABANDONED?

Every spring and summer, wildlife rehabilitators are handed dozens of pathetic-looking baby birds and a few baby mammals too, brought in by well-meaning individuals who thought the youngsters needed help. However, most of the time they're wrong. When fledgling songbirds leave the nest, they are often unable to fly properly for a few days, and spend their time on the ground, waiting for

↑ In areas where they are used to people, even normally shy animals like Fallow Deer can become extremely approachable, especially if they associate humans with food.

← This Bank Vole is clearly either injured or sick, but there is little that can be done to help such a small, fragile and highly strung animal.

← This Bar-tailed Godwit is only using one leg, but that doesn't mean there's something wrong with the other one – birds habitually rest on one leg.

food deliveries from mum and dad. Any uninjured, fully feathered young bird should therefore be left where it is unless it is in immediate danger (for example, it's on a busy pavement) in which case it should be moved to a safe sheltered spot. Featherless youngsters found on the ground are a different story – they should still be in their nests. If the nest can be found the baby should be returned to it. If not, it should be passed to a wildlife rehabilitator for handrearing.

Mother deer often leave their offspring alone in a well-hidden, sheltered place, and if you find one you must leave it well alone. Baby Brown Hares (leverets) may also be found apparently abandoned, but they too are just waiting for their parents' return.

THE GREAT INDOORS

Just because you've closed the door on the outside world, that doesn't mean your wildlife-watching has to stop for the day. Of course, there's no substitute for being out in the open air having face-to-face encounters with animals, but thanks to the wonders of modern technology, you can enjoy as-it-happens wildlife spectacles that you'd never be able to experience in the usual way. As long as you have an internet-linked computer, you can enjoy a veritable cornucopia of wonders, from your own back garden to the furthest corners of the Earth.

CCTV

→ This nestbox, available from the RSPB, comes with mini cameras inside which link up to your computer, so you can enjoy live views of the birds inside.

↓ In winter a live streaming webcam films feeders at the RSPB's Abernethy Forest reserve in the Highlands, giving views of Red Squirrels and various birds.

We use closed-circuit tv to deter criminals (and to gather evidence against them if the deterrent didn't work). However, CCTV also has its role in wildlife-watching. Set one up overlooking your garden and you can see exactly who's visiting when you're not looking. This is a great way to see if nocturnal wildlife like Foxes or Badgers are visiting your camera, and also to show younger members of the family (with earlier bedtimes) what goes on after lights out.

Bird nestboxes with built-in cameras that you can link to your computer offer a great opportunity to observe the whole process of nest-building, egg-laying, incubation, hatching and care of the chicks until independence. At the time of writing, some quite affordable 'nest-cam' packages are coming onto the market. Of course, you cannot guarantee that your box will be used, but you can improve the chances by siting it carefully (perhaps replacing a previously used box) and well ahead of early spring. Do bear in mind, though, that some broods will fail at the egg or nestling stage, which could make for upsetting viewing.

WEBCAMS

Who needs *EastEnders* and *Coronation Street* when you can watch in intimate detail the personal lives of real-life glamorous couples like EJ and Odin at RSPB Loch Garten or Marge and Frank at the Loch of the Lowes? There are many other webcams around the world pointing at well-known Osprey nests, some offering live video streaming so you can watch the birds' lives unfold minute by minute. The RSPB has also set up webcams to view Hobby and Goshawk nests, while in winter there are 'feeder cams' at various reserves. Never seen a Red Squirrel? Tune into the Abernethy Forest cam and you soon will – you could also spot a Crested Tit, alongside legions of Siskins and Coal Tits. It's not quite the same as being there, but it's not the same as watching edited and scripted tv either – the excitement of not knowing what's coming next is just as real as if you were standing there.

A look around the internet will provide numerous other options for 'virtual' wildlife-watching, and the quantity and quality of this 'reality tv' is increasing all the time. You could watch hummingbirds coming to a feeder in a lush Costa Rican garden or tune into 'waterhole tv' and wait for Leopards, Impalas and assorted African eagles to come and drink at a Botswana lake.

↑ The Africam webcams enable you to watch animals like Impalas live, with footage streamed from Nkhoro Pan in South Africa, and various other locations.

↑ The RSPB's Osprey tracking pages include a Google Maps display of the migratory paths taken by satellite-tagged young Ospreys as they travel from Loch Garten.

PLAYING TAG

Even in the most lavish wildlife documentaries, not every wildlife drama can be captured faithfully on film. For one such drama – bird migration – we can have the next best thing. Satellite-tracking technology means that birds tagged with the appropriate equipment (usually in the form of a tiny lightweight 'backpack') can have their travels accurately mapped. In 2008 and again in 2009 the RSPB fitted tags to two Osprey chicks from the Loch Garten nest, and many of the people who had watched these chicks grow up via the Loch Garten webcam could now follow their first migration to Africa. The data gathered provided valuable insights into Osprey behaviour, though there were many moments of anxiety – and heartbreak in the case of the one youngster of the four which did not make it to Africa – for those following the young birds' perilous journeys. Other satellite-tracking projects are under way involving Honey-buzzards, Woodcocks, Hobbies and, further afield, endangered species like the Northern Bald Ibis, as well as several animals that travel by sea such as whales and Hawksbill Turtles.

BEST DRESSED

We touched on the general principles of what to wear when wildlife-watching on page 39 – that clothes need to be quiet (both soundwise and colourwise) and comfy. Now it's time for a more detailed, head-to-toe examination of the ideal outdoor attire. As with so many things, you get what you pay for, and it's perfectly possible to blow a small fortune on your clobber, but by careful shopping around, you can pick up some bargains.

↑ Tough cotton trousers in dull green are a must for any wildlife-watcher, and the pockets on the thighs provide handy extra storage space.

BEST FOOT FORWARDS

The standard wildlife-watching footwear is the trusty walking boot. It doesn't let the water in, comes up high enough to support your ankles when you're on uneven ground and has a grippy sole to cope with all manner of underfoot surfaces. When buying your boots, try them on while wearing the same kinds of socks you'll mostly wear in the field (normally thick walking socks) and have a good stomp around in them to check whether they cause any incipient 'hot spots' on your feet (which will quickly turn into blisters when you hit the trails). By choosing last year's colour scheme and going to the shops at sale time, you can pick up a bargain.

If you are negotiating very muddy places, Wellington boots offer the extra protection you'll need. They've undergone something of a renaissance since the very cold winters of 2008/09 and 2009/10, with a much wider choice now available.

TOPS AND BOTTOMS

Sports shops sell a wide range of breathable T-shirts and long-sleeved tops, which you can layer on for colder weather. For trousers, try an outdoor or mountain-walking shop, or a specialist retailer such as Country Innovation. Trousers designed for outdoor walking often come in suitably dingy colours and tend to have lots of useful pockets. It's wise to cover your legs when walking in long vegetation to reduce

FOOT CARE

Your feet may carry you thousands of miles over the course of a long wildlife-watching career, so it pays to look after them. A foot file and moisturiser will help deal with painful thickened skin. Break in your new boots with shorter walks, and it's always wise to take blister plasters with you, such as those made by Compeed – they work far better than ordinary plasters to take away the pain of rubbed skin and to curtail blister development.

← When you're seawatching (observing birds flying past offshore), you'll need a notebook to keep track of their numbers.

→ With apps such as *Moths of Britain and Ireland* (Birdguides), you can turn your smart-phone into a portable mini-library of useful wildlife information.

The same restriction, of course, doesn't apply to what you keep on your shelf at home – but human memory being what it is, having some kind of guide with you at the time you observe your mystery plant or animal can be very helpful. When choosing a guide, check out the illustrations of species that you know well to assess their accuracy.

↑ An A5 spiral-bound notebook fits easily into a jacket pocket, and you can safely stash your pen in the spiral.

TAKE NOTE

Making handwritten notes in the field is no longer the only way to keep a record of your sightings, but it does have the personal touch. It's a joy to read back through old notebooks and to see where your handwriting goes a bit unsteady when recounting particularly exciting wildlife encounters. Notebooks are also the easiest way to record notes and sketches together, for times when your camera just doesn't have enough reach for a decent photo, or for when the animal you're watching has disappeared and you need to record as much detail as you can before the memory fades away too.

For a notebook to use in the field, look for something that will fit in the pocket of your usual jacket, with a sturdy enough binding to stay in one piece over prolonged use. Continuous spiral binding is good, but the 'tongue and groove' style can unravel itself over time. If you can find one, a pad with blank pages on one side of an opened spread and ruled on the other is ideal for notes and sketches. Whether you use a pen or pencil, make sure it's one that won't smudge.

WHERE TO WATCH

Another genre of wildlife books which you'll often find yourself turning to are the site guides: books which list and describe good wildlife-watching places by region. Most of these are specific to particular wildlife groups, such as the Christopher Helm *Where to Watch Birds* series. For some groups there are books on the market which combine a field guide and a site guide – for example, *Orchids of Britain and Ireland: A Field and Site Guide*, published by A&C Black. Conservation bodies that manage reserves have their own site guides – for the RSPB, there is *Where to Discover Nature in Britain and Northern Ireland*, with visitor information for RSPB reserves and guides to what you'll see at each. Keeping a collection of site guides in your car can help you discover exciting new places when you're on the road.

TAKING THE BINS OUT

Ask 100 birdwatchers which piece of kit they'd most hate to lose, and 90 of them will say their binoculars. Bins aren't quite as essential to plant-lovers, but for anyone who watches wildlife that moves, they are absolutely essential. A good pair will last you a lifetime, but don't hold out until you can afford the very best – optics technology continues to improve so fast that even budget bins can be really excellent tools. For newcomers, the first task is to get to grips with binocular terminology, before getting the hang of actually using the things.

↑ Using binoculars takes practice. It's important to keep your eyes relaxed and try not to squint or keep one eye closed.

NUMBER CRUNCHING

Every pair of binoculars is defined optically by two numbers. Common combinations include 7x21, 8x42 and 10x50.The first number describes their magnification power, and the second is the diameter of their objective lenses (those are the big lenses at the 'far end' of the bins, as you hold them up) in millimetres. So a higher first number means more powerful magnification, while bigger second numbers mean the binoculars gather in more light and so give a brighter view.

Pros and cons of different bins

Therefore the best bins will be 10x50s, right? Well, maybe. But the extra glass compared to the compact 7x21s means more bulk and weight – perhaps too much, especially as it can be difficult to hold more powerful binoculars steady. For magnifications of 12x or more, this can make for bins that are seriously difficult to use, as well as extremely heavy. Besides, powerful bins need their bigger objective lenses to gather an equivalent amount of light to less powerful bins with smaller objectives. There is more to light-gathering than objective lens size, too – the quality of the optics inside are important as well, and they also determine things like depth of field (how much stuff at different distances from you is in focus at the same time) and how close the bins will focus.

Binoculars come in roof-prism or porro-prism designs – the latter have barrels of even thickness, while porros widen towards the objective lens. Roof prisms are more compact and lightweight, but porros often give a brighter image.

USING YOUR BINS CORRECTLY

First of all, get the strap length right. Ideally your bins should sit fairly high on your chest, with the tops at about armpit height, but see what's comfy for you.

If your bins come with an uncomfy strap, replace it sooner rather than later – wide neoprene straps are the most comfortable. If you wear glasses, fold or twist the eyecaps down. Invest in rain caps if your bins don't come with any.

Binoculars are designed to be used with both eyes, but many people try to use them with one eye closed. Correct use may take practice, but getting the distance between the barrels right and keeping your gaze 'soft' and relaxed helps.

↑ A fast-flying Jay. Keep your eyes on the bird as you raise your binoculars and you should be able to 'lock on' to it quickly.

Getting the adjustment right Most binoculars have a dioptre adjuster on the right-hand barrel. This is there to help you 'match up' the two sides of the bins, and for most people with normal eyesight the right dioptre position will be 'o', but if you have better vision in one eye than the other you might need to tweak it. To adjust, start with it at the 'o' position. Close your right eye, look through the bins at a distant object and get it in sharp focus using the central focus wheel. Now open your right eye and, while looking at the same object with both eyes, move the dioptre adjuster slowly one way then the other to see if you can improve the sharpness.

↑ Porro-prism binoculars (a) give a more 'three-dimensional' image than the straight-barrelled roof prisms, though they are also heavier and bulkier. Roof-prism binoculars (b) have parallel barrels, making them lighter and easier to use than porro-prisms. Most top-end binoculars now are roof-prisms.

CHOOSING YOUR BINS

Think about what you want to use your binoculars for, to help you draw up a checklist of the most important qualities you'll need. For example:

- **Watching distant wildlife** Powerful magnification
- **Wildlife-watching late in the day** Good light-gathering powers
- **Watching insects** A short close-focus distance
- **Seawatching** Good depth of field, so you don't have to refocus when switching between near and distant birds
- **Taking anywhere and everywhere** Lightweight, good build quality and perhaps rubber armouring.

Armed with some clues as to what you want, and how much you're prepared to spend, hit the shops. Or, even better, go to an RSPB reserve with an optics shop or to a special 'optics day' at a reserve. This will enable you to try out a range of different bins in field conditions, looking at real wildlife.

↘ The right-hand eyepiece of most binoculars has an independent focusing control or dioptre, allowing you to match up the focusing on both sides.

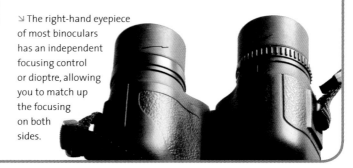

SCOPE FOR IMPROVEMENT

Having a telescope lets you in to a new world of, well, faraway stuff. With a scope, you can enjoy much closer views – up to 60x magnification versus the 8x or 10x of most binoculars – and see far more detail. This may be overkill if you are mainly interested in plants or insects, but for birdwatchers, scopes make a huge difference. They also enable you to indulge in the hobby of digiscoping – a clever way to take good photos of very distant wildlife without splashing out on a DSLR camera and super-powerful lens. When budgeting for a scope, remember you'll need a tripod as well.

↑ Using a scope to get views of a small and restless bird, like this Melodious Warbler, can be difficult, so it's always worth carrying binoculars too.

→ A tripod is a must when using a scope. Secure attachments mean you can carry the tripod over your shoulder without fear of the scope falling off.

BODIES AND EYES

The magnification of a scope is provided by its eyepiece, which in most scopes is interchangeable. So when you choose your scope, consider not only the size of the objective lens (usually 60mm or 80mm – 80mm means more light but also more weight and more money), but the kinds of eyepieces available. Eyepieces come in fixed focal lengths (such as 30x) or zooms (such as 20–60x). Many birdwatchers own two for their scope, to be used in different situations. For general birdwatching a zoom is useful – you can scan around at 20x and zoom in on anything that warrants closer examination. At the long end, image quality tends to deteriorate a little (or a lot in cheaper scopes), and it gets more difficult to maintain a steady image. Some of the shorter fixed-length eyepieces offer a wide-angle view – useful when watching for passing birds over a wide area.

An alternative to a standard full-size scope is a miniature model like Opticron's Mighty Midget. Scopes like this are much lighter and smaller (though you'll still need a tripod) and work best with less powerful eyepieces.

CHOOSING AND USING

As with binoculars, the best way to choose is to try out a variety of models at a nature reserve. You'll also find that other birdwatchers are usually happy to let you take a look through their scopes. It is worth holding out for the scope you really want

STRAIGHT OR ANGLED?
Scopes come in two basic designs. Straight models are just that – the eyepiece is lined up with the body so light follows a straight path. In angled models, the eyepiece sits at an uptilted angle to the body. Angled models give you a neck position that's more comfortable over long periods, so tend to be more popular, but straight ones have their advantages too – they may be easier to use in hides, for example.

at the price you can afford – higher-end scopes (and binoculars for that matter) come with a lifetime guarantee, taking some of the risk out of buying second hand.

Get the hang of your scope by working at the shorter end of your zoom eyepiece at first – focusing becomes much fiddlier at 60x. With telescopes, the actual moving-it-around process is a function of the tripod, so it's often a good idea to try to buy both at the same time.

THREE LEGS GOOD

Your scope comes with a tripod collar with a threaded hole in its base for attachment to a tripod plate. When choosing a tripod, bear in mind its height, weight and the type of head. If you are very tall, you might have to shop around for a tripod that extends high enough, particularly if you have a straight rather than angled scope. A heavy tripod is hard work to carry around, but one that's too light may blow over and send your scope crashing groundwards. Foam padding on tripod legs makes them more comfy to carry around.

Consider the head
Tripod heads are interchangeable in higher-end models, so you can upgrade if you want. More expensive heads will be sturdier and have smoother panning (side to side) and tilting (up and down) movement. Try out different heads to see whether you like the way the levers work together. Some tripods come with a fully flexible ball-and-socket head rather than a pan-and-tilt head, but these are better for photographers who may want to frame their shots from weird and wonderful angles – for birdwatching pan and tilt is the way to go.

↑ Telescopes give you views of distant wildlife, and with the addition of a compact camera they can be used as long telephoto lenses too.

CATCHING CAMERAS

With the advent of the digital camera, photography suddenly became a lot more affordable and, you could argue, a lot more fun. It's a rare wildlife-watcher these days who doesn't head out with some form of camera on their person, whether it be a humble camera-phone or a bells-and-whistles DSLR. Chapter 6 is entirely dedicated to the art and craft of wildlife photography, including advice on choosing the right make and model for you, but here we take a quick preliminary look at the camera options out there.

↑ Most 'smartphones' come with very good built-in cameras, certainly adequate for 'record shots' of approachable wildlife.

YOUR PHONE

Since the mid-noughties, mobile phones with built-in cameras have become commonplace, and the quality of these cameras is constantly improving. It's wise for a wildlife-watcher to always carry a mobile phone anyway, especially when heading out into the wilds alone, so choose one with a good camera, too, and you'll never be without an easy means to get a visual record of the wildlife you see. You can even create a makeshift telephoto lens, by holding your camera lens up to the eyepiece of your binoculars or telescope.

COMPACT CAMERAS

A basic compact camera may be very small and eminently pocketable. If you want to point it at wildlife, choose one that has some degree of optical zoom to give you some magnification for those faraway subjects (but ignore whatever the specs say about digital zoom – that works by just digitally enlarging the image, just like you can do on a computer screen, and reducing the image quality accordingly). Compacts can't match the standard of more sophisticated bridge or DSLR cameras when it comes to telephoto images, but they are often very effective for close-up work. You can also use them for digiscoping, using an adaptor (shop-bought or home-made) to attach the camera to your telescope. The telescope then functions as a long telephoto lens, and, depending on the camera and scope involved, the image quality can be surprisingly good.

WHERE TO BUY

When you have worked out which camera you want, it pays to shop around to get one at a good price. The website Camera Pricebuster (www.camerapricebuster.co.uk) is a great resource, giving regularly updated 'best prices' on a wide range of cameras and lenses. However, there's a lot to be said for supporting your local camera retailer too, even if this means paying a little more as you will get personalised help and support.

BRIDGE CAMERAS

These offer a halfway house between ordinary compact cameras and DSLRs. They are optically better than most compacts and have a larger lens with more powerful magnification – 18x or more, which is enough reach for most of the wildlife you're likely to encounter. They have more complex control options than standard compacts, meaning you can (if you want) get more creative and experiment with a wider range of settings. They are also bigger, heavier and more expensive than compacts but offer a great compromise between the convenience of a small compact and the image quality and versatility of a DSLR system.

DSLRS

SLR is short for 'single lens reflex' – a camera type that has a particular way of forming its images and, more significantly for most of us, has interchangeable lenses. The D just means digital. With a DSLR, you buy a camera body and as many different lenses as you want (or, more realistically, can afford). Depending on the camera body you could choose between hundreds of lenses, suitable for landscapes, portraits, close-up work or wildlife. DSLRs are the professional's choice because of the creative flexibility they offer and the image quality they deliver, but a growing number of amateurs use them too. The obvious downsides are expense and weight, and, less obviously, the fact that you won't necessarily have the right lens on the camera body at the right time, and so risk missing opportunities while changing lenses.

↑ Entry-level DSLRs are not only cheaper than semi-professional models, but are smaller and lighter, ideal for beginners.

← Many compact cameras have excellent macro modes, but a DSLR with a fast macro lens was needed to achieve the blurred background in this Germander Speedwell shot.

SPREADING THE LOAD

By now, you might be forgiven for thinking that you'll need a wheelbarrow in which to cart all that gear around. Luckily, there are alternatives, specifically designed to help you carry optics, camera gear, lunch and a whole host of other bits and bobs in comfort. When figuring out how to carry your stuff, you'll need to consider things like easy access to the things you'll need most, weatherproofing and making sure you're balanced and comfortable from the start of your day to the end.

↑ For longer walks, or when you have a lot of things to carry, a rucksack spreads the load evenly and comfortably across your shoulders.

PLENTY OF POCKETS

This is why you need that jacket with the big pockets. There are certain things that you'll want to be able to locate quickly without having to rummage in a bag. If you're a light traveller with a well-thought-out jacket, you won't need a bag at all – you'll have more than enough 'on board' room for compact binoculars (which will be around your neck most of the time anyway), compact camera, a notebook, phone, keys and wallet. Ideally, pockets will be securable with a zip and will have an overhanging flap to protect your belongings against downpours.

RUCKSACKS

The hikers' choice, a rucksack is the most comfortable way for the human body to manage a heavy load. The weight is spread across your shoulders and both hands are free for more important stuff, like using your binoculars. Rucksacks come in a bewildering variety of styles. In general, go for something with wide straps for comfort, made from good weather-resistant material and with several easy-access pockets. Zip or drawstring fastenings are your choice, though zips may break with heavy use.

Female-specific rucksacks are a good option, especially for shorter women, as standard rucksacks are designed for longer bodies and may sit uncomfortably on the top of your bum. Open side pockets are good for carrying a water bottle, while 'hydration backpacks' for runners and cyclists come with a bladder, which you fill with water, and a tube through which you can drink without taking the pack off.

You will probably not want a rucksack with a metal frame unless it's seriously big – the frame will add a fair bit to the weight. However, rucksacks that incorporate a little folding chair are well worth the extra weight. Out-curved

↑ A shoulder-bag is a comfortable way to carry your stuff, and you can easily access the bag without taking it off your shoulder.

→ Several companies manufacture specialised backpacks that can accommodate a tripod, meaning you can have your hands free as you carry your scope or large lens.

THE TRIPOD PROBLEM

Many birdwatchers and wildlife photographers will have a tripod with them at all times, with scope or telephoto lens permanently attached. How to carry this cumbersome arrangement around? Many keep the tripod legs fully extended but pushed close together and carry it upright, the top resting against one shoulder (this is where padding on your tripod's legs comes into its own). Carrying it this way means the whole thing can quickly be put down and set up. You can also buy special tripod-carrying rucksacks, such as the Mule or the Scopac, which are comfy and will free up your hands, though the penalty is a longer set-up time.

rucksack designs will hold the load off the middle of your back, preventing things from getting too sweaty.

The main disadvantage of rucksacks is ease of access – you have to take it off to get at anything or ask your companion to open it and extract what you need. Some rucksacks have a 'swivel-round' bottom section to get around this problem.

OTHER BAGS

A shoulder bag with a long strap can be comfy to carry and leave your hands free if you loop it over your neck, though you'll need to keep the load pretty light. A bag like this will give you easy access to the contents.

↙ On a busy boat trip, photographing seabirds like these Great Black-backed Gulls, find somewhere to stow your bag to keep it out of the way.

SWEATING THE SMALL STUFF

Remember how you needed a jacket with lots of pockets and maybe some multi-pocketed trousers too? It's now time to think about what to put in those pockets. Besides the things you take with you everywhere – your keys and mobile phone for a start – there are various handy little bits and bobs which can help you with your wildlife-watching. Some are specific to particular kinds of wildlife study, but others are useful for everyone to carry.

GETTING A CLOSER LOOK

↑ A simple home-made reflector can be used to shine light onto resting butterflies like this Brown Argus and encourage them to open their wings.

One of the simplest and most rewarding additions to your pocket collection is a hand lens or loupe. This will enable you to examine in detail the smallest objects you encounter – the structure of flowers, the appendages of insects, the gill arrangement of mushrooms. Unlike the optics you need for seeing faraway birds, a hand lens is extremely portable, and you can buy very good ones for a fraction of the cost of your binoculars. They come in various magnifications, with 6x, 10x and 20x being popular – it will be easier to hold the lens steady and see a clear image at less powerful magnifications.

You may also want to buy a collecting pot or two with an inbuilt magnifying lens, which will enable you to examine an insect without worrying about it escaping from view. For examining plants and fungi, a soft paintbrush is useful for removing debris, and it's often wise to wear thin latex gloves if you're handling a plant that may irritate your skin.

SAFETY KIT

Your mobile phone is your key safety item if you're going out on your own – if you have an accident or get in trouble with sudden bad weather you can call for help. Other useful kit to have if you are venturing away from civilisation include a whistle to attract attention, a pocket torch (wind-up torches bypass the need to also carry batteries), and a Swiss army knife with its array of useful miniature tools. It's always wise to carry drinking water if you're out for any length of time. And a simple first-aid kit should be considered a necessity if you're really going off the beaten track and if you are out and about with children.

BUG-CATCHING

The pooter is a beautifully designed simple device for easily catching small invertebrates. You can make one at home if you're so inclined or buy a ready-made version. The photo above left shows how a pooter is put together. You position the mouth of the open-ended tube over your insect and suck through the mesh-ended tube. The insect ends up inside the jar, and the mesh means there's no danger of you accidentally inhaling it yourself. You could then transfer your catch to a small collecting pot with an inbuilt magnifying lens, which will enable you to examine an insect without worrying about it escaping from view.

A white sheet that folds up small is another useful tool for the amateur entomologist. To use it, unfold it on the ground under a bush then gently agitate the bush's branches. Any insects that fall out will be easily spotted when they land on the sheet. A simple white hanky has its uses in a similar capacity, providing you with a clean, bright backdrop on which to examine an object.

↖ A pooter can be made from a jar, two wide straws and a piece of muslin for the end of the 'sucking' tube. The lid must be air tight to create the vacuum

↑ A hand lens reveals fine details in small animals like this Red Spider Mite.

↓ You probably won't want to touch a Stinging Nettle – to remove an insect from one of the leaves, use a soft paintbrush.

OPTICAL ASSISTANCE

Whatever optics you use, you should carry a proper glass cleaning cloth to keep their lenses clear of dust and smears. Wiping your lenses with the ends of your sleeves won't always clear away dirt and may damage the coatings on the glass. Glass-cleaning cloths, available from opticians or camera shops, are ideal. An air blower with a soft brush fitted is another useful optics-cleaning tool.

A home-made reflector is another helpful tool when it comes to looking closely at small plants or animals and is useful for the macro photographer too. To make yours, just tape silver foil (shiny side out) over an A7 or larger piece of card. You can position this to reflect extra light onto whatever you wish to examine, making for a better view or a brighter photograph. A mirror will do the same job, of course, but is heavier and more expensive.

TECHNICAL DETAILS

One of the beauties of wildlife-watching is that you can go as high- or low-tech as you like. Many a birdwatcher takes nothing into the field except their binoculars, while those interested primarily in plants don't even need those. However, there is also a wealth of technology available to help make your wildlife-watching easier and more enjoyable. Some of the kit belongs at home, next to your computer, but some of it can join the more prosaic hand lens and handkerchief in your pocket.

DIGITAL FIELD GUIDES

As enthusiasm for ebooks grows, it's becoming more feasible to carry around a library of reference material in digital form. There are several advantages to a digitised field guide – you can search the content for keywords, there can be click-through cross-referencing and, of course, you can store a vast amount of information in a very small physical space. The guide can also include sound and video, immensely helpful for birds and some other animal groups.

Using digital guides

Software like this comes in several forms. You could run it on your home computer, but you can also take it out into the field on a hand-held PDA or palmtop computer. Smartphones like Apple's iPhone, the BlackBerry range and phones running Google's Android operating system now offer a huge range of downloadable applications (apps), including some suitable for wildlife-watchers.

↑ There are several wildlife-related interactive DVD-ROMs on the market, such as browsable back issues of the magazine *British Birds* (a), and the authoritative *Birds of the Western Palearctic* from Oxford University Press.

WILDLIFE SOUNDS

Getting to grips with birds' songs and calls is a real challenge and listening to recordings can help a lot. There are many CDs on the market, covering bird sounds from almost every country in the world, and you can transfer these to a simple and inexpensive MP3 player for easy listening whether you're at home or out and about.

A CD of bat sounds won't be much use to you as most are too high-pitched for human ears to detect. However, a bat detector will pick them up, play them back at a frequency you can hear and assign them to species. You can also use your bat detector to generate digital sonograms – graphical representations of the

a

b

sound waveforms. Bat detectors are expensive but a vital tool for those seriously interested in this enigmatic mammal group – and they will also help you pick up high-frequency insect sounds.

KEEPING IN TOUCH

It isn't just doctors who carry pagers. Super-keen birdwatchers do as well. Companies such as Rare Bird Alert collate news about rare and scarce birds in the UK and distribute it to their subscribers via the internet and personal pagers. A pager message will name the bird and give detailed directions to its location. These information services are really only for genuine twitchers (birdwatchers who go out of their way to see as many new species as they can), but Rare Bird Alert and other services do provide a general summary of rare bird news for free on their websites.

If you are out with other people and the group has to split up from time to time, you might find it helpful to use walkie-talkies to stay in touch, as they offer a more immediate means of communication than mobile phones. One situation where they can be useful would be when your group is travelling in more than one car, and the group in the leading car wants to alert the cars behind to an interesting sight on the roadside.

↖ ↑ Come spring, a birdsong CD will be invaluable to help you learn the songs of confusing species like Blackcap (a) and Garden Warbler (b).

↓ A simple bat detector is reasonably affordable and will open your eyes (and ears) to these amazing and fascinating animals.

Paperless note-taking

The most straightforward digital substitute for the trusty notebook would be a dictaphone, enabling you to record spoken notes. Your phone may well have a built-in microphone and recording capability. Some smartphones come with a stylus, and with handwriting recognition software, you could handwrite notes to be translated into digital form – this is probably quicker than using your phone's keyboard unless you are very dextrous. You may also be able to use the stylus to make digital sketches.

SPECIALIST STUFF

For general-purpose wildlife-watching, you really don't need much stuff. However, if your interest starts to grow in a particular direction, you may want to invest in some extra gear. If funds and storage space allow you could easily shop from dawn till dusk for a week and end up with the ultimate store cupboard of goodies for every wildlife-watching eventuality.

HIDING IN A HIDE

↗ Using a portable hide enables you to get very close to normally shy species like Great Spotted Woodpecker – and shelter from inclement weather at the same time.

↓ A portable hide of your own means you can set up a private wildlife-watching spot anywhere you like (as long as you have the landowner's permission).

If you've visited a few nature reserves you'll know just how great hides can be for giving you close views of wildlife. The next stage is to invest in a portable hide of your own, which you can set up anywhere. Birds and mammals quickly get used to non-human-shaped, non-moving new additions to their surroundings and with a little patience a well-sited hide can give you brilliant views and great photo opportunities. Those on the market include dome-shaped, tent-like hides, tubular ones to be used lying down, or a bag arrangement over a chair – all with camouflaged patterns.

Do not disturb Setting up and using your own hide in the field requires care, sensitivity and common sense (see Chapter 8). Be aware that, without an appropriate licence, it is against the law to do anything that may disturb certain bird species when they are at or near their nests, whether for photography or any other purpose.

MOTH TRAPS

With more than 2,000 species out there, moths in Britain offer lots of opportunities for rewarding study. Unfortunately, their nocturnal ways make them difficult to study. Moth traps exploit many moth species' attraction to light – a powerful mercury vapour bulb draws them in, and when they enter the main box part of the trap via a funnel there are broken egg boxes inside on which they can safely rest. Commercial moth traps come in various shapes and sizes, though all are rather expensive. You can make your own moth trap (and some suppliers sell a complete set of suitable electrics separately so you can build your own box), but for safety reasons you must be extremely careful about weather-proofing the electrics.

↑ When out camping or walking, you could try 'being your own hide' with a complete camouflage outfit – these can be astonishingly effective.

↙ For long hikes or camping trips you'll need a sturdy and capacious rucksack – ideally in a wildlife-friendly, unobtrusive colour.

HAPPY CAMPING

Here we venture into outdoor-living territory, for those who wish to make overnight stays out in the wild. In England and Wales, you should not camp independently without the landowners' permission (though plenty of campsites will place you well within good wildlife habitat), but in Scotland 'wild' camping is fully legal. The wildlife-watcher's tent should be one that doubles as a hide, so go for dull colours and built-in viewing 'windows'. When you sleep, keep expensive optical gear in the main part of the tent close to you, if you don't have a car in which you can lock it.

 **Sleeping** The comfiest way to sleep in a tent is probably on an airbed, but a lightweight option is a roll-up foam camping mat. On top of this place a sleeping bag appropriate for the seasons. Use a silk liner inside the bag – it can be washed and dried very quickly and easily, and on hot nights you can get rid of the bag and just sleep in the liner. An inflatable pillow will be more comfy for your head and neck than the usual substitute, a rolled-up bundle of clothes.

■ **Cooking** Use a gas or meths-powered stove for cooking, and always have a torch handy – it will help you spot wildlife after dark as well as enabling you to see what you're doing.

■ **Head-torches** are ideal for working around your campsite after dark as they keep your hands free.

■ **Folding chairs** are invaluable for comfort around the campsite and can be taken on excursions too.

WHY ID?

One of our most primal human urges is to categorise things, including living things. You can see how it would have been helpful, at the dawn of language, to have one word for the delicious berries and another for the deadly ones. Today, learning how to identify different species will greatly enhance the value and enjoyment of your wildlife-watching.

GETTING TO KNOW YOU

A distant musical burbling announces the approach of a great skein of geese, silhouetted against the dusk sky. For a moment their calls and the rush of their wings fills the air, then they are gone. A wonderful wildlife moment – why spoil it by delving into the prosaic matter of what kind of geese they are? The answer is that once you have a name, you instantly have the means to find out a whole lot more about what you've just seen. The book tells you they're Pink-footed Geese and they come here in winter from the high Arctic. You've already gained an insight into their way of life and made a closer connection with the individual birds you saw. Also, because the book tells you whereabouts the geese tend to spend their day and where they roost, you now know where to go to see them heading off again at dawn – you can have another wonderful experience.

THE FILING CABINET OF LIFE

We all know that we're related to monkeys, and, if you go back far enough, to all other living things to some extent. The science that works out which species is which by looking at the degree of 'relatedness' between them is called taxonomy, and through taxonomy we give different species their scientific or 'Latin' names, which express the species' true relationships to all other species.

The first principle of taxonomy is that everything is classified by a series of levels, which are arranged in the form of a 'nested hierarchy'. Animals, plants and fungi are divided at the top, into three kingdoms. Each kingdom is further divided into several phyla (singular: phylum). Each phylum contains several classes, and so on, down to individual species. Let's look at the classification of a couple of familiar species.

← From wild roses like Dog Rose, people have selectively bred garden roses in a huge variety of colours and shapes, just as natural selection has shaped all wild organisms.

Taxonomy

	Stoat	Chaffinch
KINGDOM	Animalia (animals)	Animalia
PHYLUM	Chordata (animals with a spinal cord)	Chordata
CLASS	Mammalia (mammals)	Aves (birds)
ORDER	Carnivora (meat-eaters)	Passeriformes (perching or songbirds)
FAMILY	Mustelidae (weasels and their relatives)	Fringillidae (finches)
GENUS	*Mustela*	*Fringilla*
SPECIES	*Mustela erminea*	*Fringilla coelebs*

← [Opposite] The Swift (a) and Swallow (b) look and behave similarly, but a look at their taxonomy reveals they are not closely related, just adapted to the same general way of life.

From this, we can tell that an animal with a scientific name that begins with *Mustela* will be very stoat-like, and a bird with the generic name *Fringilla* will be a kind of finch. We can also tell that Badgers, which belong to the family Mustelidae, are more closely related to Stoats than Foxes (family Canidae) are to either. Modern genetic studies help us to work out exactly how close these relationships are – you can't always tell just from physical resemblences.

It's important to realise that these divisions are for our convenience – reality is a little more confused than this. Evolution is a constant process, and at any given time one species may be in the (very slow) process of dividing into two. Taxonomists attempt to allow for this by including subspecies within some species, as well as subdivisions between some of the higher levels. However, for most purposes, if you can get your head around the taxonomic divisions in the table, you'll understand how different species are related.

↓ Beetles are the most diverse animal group on Earth, with several hundred thousand species. This is one of the more distinctive, a Spotted Longhorn.

A WORD ABOUT NAMES

All known species have a scientific name. (You'll sometimes hear it called a 'Latin' name but that's inaccurate as the words are not always Latin.) The scientific name is always written in italics. The great thing about scientific names is that they are universal. What we in the UK call a 'Great Northern Diver', the Americans call a 'Common Loon', but call it *Gavia immer* and everyone knows what you're talking about. This allows us to hang onto the familiar English names that we have used and loved for years. There's no need to change 'Blackbird' to 'Black Thrush' – we can tell by its scientific name that it is a kind of thrush.

TAKING THE EVIDENCE

Identifying an animal or plant is like solving a murder mystery. You are presented with a number of clues – not always all the clues you might want. Some of the clues will immediately rule out a number of possible suspects, and may be enough to pinpoint the right one when you compare your notes to the information in your field guide. It's important to be aware that some field guides are more complete than others, and if you have no luck with one, it's always worth trying another.

↑ Not every animal will oblige you with a clear view, but enough of this bird is visible to allow identification as a male Reed Bunting.

PUT YOURSELF ON THE SPOT

When confronted with an unfamiliar animal, the pressure is on. It's not so bad with a plant or mushroom – at least that is not going to fly, run, swim or crawl away before you've finished observing it. In all cases, though, you need to record as much detail about your mystery life form as possible. The quickest and easiest way to do this is to take a photo – or several. If your camera has a movie mode, making a film can give extra clues that a still image won't provide.

Besides images, whether still or moving, it's very worthwhile noting down your thoughts about what you see. If you don't have a camera, hopefully you'll have a notebook and pen or a voice-recording function on your mobile phone. Whether you use a notebook or record spoken notes, the more detail you can get down, the better the chances are that one of the notes will be the clue you need to make a successful identification.

Don't delay

Think you don't need any pictures or notes but can just check the books at home because the sight (or sound) of your mysterious animal is indelibly engraved on your memory? Think again. Human memory is incredibly untrustworthy, despite all your good intentions. Not only are vital details likely to escape, but what you do recall can be distorted. You may be unconsciously influenced by other things that you see in between making your sighting and consulting the field guides, adding erroneous new characteristics to your remembered sighting.

You can also unwittingly become biased in favour of what you would *like* to have seen. That large circling bird of prey over a Highland mountain becomes twice the size of the crows that were flying nearby rather than just 20 per cent bigger, because you want it to be a Golden Eagle rather than a Buzzard. For many reasons, eyewitness testimony is unreliable, so take notes on the spot and don't rely on memory alone.

KNOW YOUR LIMITS

We humans are better at getting some types of details right than others, and it's wise to be aware of this when you're taking your notes.

■ **Size** People are generally bad at estimating the size of something unfamiliar, especially from a distance. Unless you see your mystery animal alongside another animal that you do know well, or some other familiar object, allowing for accurate size comparison, don't set too much store by how big you think it is.

■ **Colour** Again, this is difficult to assess objectively. The appearance of colours changes hugely with the light – our brains automatically compensate if we're looking at something familiar, but be wary of colour assessment on something completely unfamiliar.

↑ When taking photos of plants like this Ground Ivy for identification, try to include leaves and stems as well as flowers.

■ **Pattern** We are good at patterns – and they often provide really accurate clues for identification. You should always focus on patterns ahead of colours.

■ **Proportions** This is another area where we do quite well. The size of one body part relative to another is easy to judge accurately, and can help greatly with identification.

←↑ Light conditions can change an animal's apparent colour quite dramatically, but pay attention to shape and pattern and you'll see these are both Dunnocks.

TIME AND PLACE

As we saw in Chapter 2, all animals and plants have their own annual and daily schedule, as well as their particular habitat requirements, and this has very important implications for what you're likely to see and when. Time and place are also important when it comes to identification – they can help you to eliminate several possibilities from consideration.

↑ This Green Shieldbug nymph is mobile and active on its six legs like an adult, but has a different shape and colour scheme.

↓ Fritillaries like this Silver-washed can be difficult to identify, but if you see one in August you can immediately rule out several species.

TIME OF YEAR

Many species, from mammals to plants, change their appearance from season to season, sometimes quite drastically. When trying to track down your mystery species in the field guide, this is one of the first things you should check. Butterflies, for example, tend to have short flying seasons of only a couple of months. However, some of the commoner species have multiple generations so may be seen right through spring and summer – more time on the wing per year gives the species more opportunities to disperse to new habitats. So if you think you've seen an unusual butterfly, check first of all whether it is supposed to be on the wing at the time you've seen it. Flowering plants also may have short seasons – if your plant isn't in flower, you will need to rely on other clues like its leaves or fruits to help identify it but you should always note these details anyway.

For longer-lived animals, seasonal change isn't so marked, but many bird species have distinct and different plumages at different times of the year. From late spring through to autumn young birds in juvenile plumage often look confusingly different to their parents, and to make things worse these plumages are not always shown in field guides. Some mammals develop a distinct winter coat as well.

TIME OF DAY

The day-to-day routine of animals – and of plants – can also help to provide identification clues. The commonest owl in Britain is the nocturnal Tawny, but if you spot a brown owl

out hunting in broad daylight, it is much more likely to be a Short-eared Owl as that species is diurnal. Some flowers close up without fail after midday, while others only open at night.

PLACE

Animals and plants can show up where they're not expected. Mobile species like birds and the larger, strong-flying insects are especially likely to wander out of their usual haunts. However, checking the distribution map for your candidates will certainly help inform you of the likelihood of it being what you think it is.

↑ Rare migrating birds, like this juvenile White-winged Black Tern, are likeliest to appear in the autumn months.

↓ A young Shelduck goes through various confusing plumage states before developing the adult's distinctive pattern.

BIRD IDENTIFICATION

Birds are our most-watched wildlife group, and with getting on for 600 species on the British List, there is plenty out there to keep you guessing. Some species are unmistakable, but many others have lots of very similar-looking close relatives, and particularly difficult groups like warblers and waders can easily drive you to distraction. However, the key points that will help you distinguish them are quite predictable, and knowing exactly where to direct your attention when studying a strange new bird is extremely helpful.

↑ Birds of prey like Kestrel (a) and Sparrowhawk (b) can be hard to identify in flight even when they are actually quite different in size. Note the Kestrel's narrower, more pointed wings and proportionately bigger head.

SHAPE AND SIZE

The first thing to focus on is the general shape of the bird. How does it compare to other species that you know well? Is it like a thrush but dumpier, about the size and shape of a Magpie but with different colours and a shorter tail? Does it have long or short legs for its body size? If there are other birds around which are familiar species to you, how does its size compare to theirs?

A more detailed analysis of its shape should focus on its body proportions. How far beyond its wingtips does its tail reach? How long is its bill relative to the length of its head? If it is flying, do its feet project beyond its tail, how wide are its wings relative to their length and is the bend of its wing close to its body or more like halfway along its length? Do its eyes look large in its head or small? If it is a long-legged bird, how much length of leg is visible above the ankle bend (what we sometimes think of as the 'knee' although the fact that it bends the wrong way reveals it's really the ankle) before it reaches the body?

COLOUR AND PATTERN

Judging colour can be tricky. It can also vary a lot between individuals. Feather staining through dirty water or flower pollen can create confusion, as can fading of an 'old' coat of feathers prior to the moult. Then there are genetically caused plumage colour abnormalities such as leucism (when some or all feathers are white rather than their normal colour) or melanism (excessive dark pigmentation). So don't set too much store by colours. The colours of a birds' 'bare parts' – the eyes, bill, legs and any areas of bare skin on the face – are often more reliable than feather colours and more useful for identification.

Songs and calls

Sound can greatly help with bird identification. Sometimes, it's all you have as the bird sings from an invisible hiding place. Rather than trying to transcribe the sounds as words, pay attention to the number and length of notes, whether they rise the scale or fall, and whether they recall any other sound, such as bubbling water, a squeaky gate, the notes of a flute or a croaking frog.

Use pattern instead

Pattern is altogether more helpful for identification. Look for any contrastingly coloured areas that show in flight – a white rump patch, white outer tail feathers or light-coloured wing-bars. The bird's face pattern is also helpful, and if you don't have a camera it can really help to make a quick sketch of where any stripes on the face are positioned and their shape and size. Many birds have a dark stripe through the eye (eyestripe) and a paler stripe above it (supercilium). How extensive and prominent these markings are is very helpful for identification.

I LIKE THE WAY YOU MOVE

Observing behaviour is another vital part of the puzzle. Some birds creep mouselike on the ground, others rarely descend to ground level at all. Some wading birds walk around purposefully, others make rapid dashes interspersed with pauses. Waterbirds may feed by diving or by taking food from the surface. Flight style is important too – does the bird bound in undulating flight or hold a straight line? Does it soar effortlessly or flap frantically? Even tiny behavioural details like a tail-bobbing habit or the exact angle of the wings when gliding can help.

↑ Many birds reveal distinctive markings in flight. These Black-tailed Godwits show white rumps and wingbars, the latter lacking in the similar Bar-tailed Godwit.

↓ Is it a Carrion Crow or a Raven? This time it's a Raven – look for the proportionately huge bill and wedge-shaped tail.

MAMMAL IDENTIFICATION

As Britain has far fewer mammal species than birds, identifying a mammal seen here should be an easier task. However, mammals are less likely to allow you to study them at length, so you may have only the briefest of sightings on which to try to build your identification. However, it's usually possible to easily narrow it down to a group, and from there other clues can help.

DEER

↓ Fallow Deer have a distinctive rump and tail pattern, although white individuals (which are common) lack the dark stripes.

In the UK we have seven species of deer, though only two (Red and Roe) are native and of the others, one (the Reindeer) is only semi-wild. To identify a deer, pay attention to its size, its antlers if present, coat pattern and what its backside looks like. The combination of some or all of these characteristics should lead you to the right deer. Unique traits include the tiny size of the Muntjac (no bigger than a Labrador), the flattened antler shape of Fallow Deer, the large white rump patch of the Roe Deer and the long, prominent tusks of the Chinese Water Deer.

CARNIVORES

Everyone can recognise a Fox or a Badger, but the smaller members of the weasel family can be confusing. The trickiest are Stoat and Weasel, and American Mink and Otter. Stoats and Weasels are small, lithe, long-bodied and bright brown animals. The Stoat has a solid black tail-tip which the Weasel lacks; it is also larger with a more 'developed' shape while the Weasel resembles an attenuated mouse. Both the introduced American Mink and the native Otter are often seen in water, but Otters are much larger, mid-brown in colour and lighter below, while minks are squatter and fluffier-looking, and most have black fur. Scottish Wildcats, which are very rare, resemble oversized domestic tabbies, with thicker, fuller tails.

SMALL FURRIES

To identify your small furry, look at the size of its eyes and ears, the shape of its muzzle and the length of its tail. Mice and rats have large eyes and ears, tapering pointed snouts and long tails – the tiny Harvest Mouse has slightly more vole-like proportions. Voles are blunt-nosed, with smaller eyes and ears and shorter tails. Shrews have tiny eyes and ears, long narrow snouts and fairly short tails. The rare Dormouse has honey-gold fur and a long and fully furred tail.

SEA MAMMALS

Two species of seals live around our coasts. Common Seals are the smaller, with dog-like faces, while Greys have arching 'Roman noses'. Identifying whales and dolphins can be very difficult – look for the shape, relative size and position of any visible fins, and the height and angle of the 'blow' (air exhaled through the blowhole) is also important.

BATS

Another very tricky group. By far the most reliable way to identify them is to analyse their sounds using a bat detector. A few species do have some useful 'field marks' – the Long-eared and Grey Long-eared Bats' huge ears may be visible, Noctules are very large with a low squeak that many people can hear and Daubenton's Bats are closely tied to watery habitats, often hunting over lakes.

... AND THE REST

Telling a Rabbit from a Brown Hare is easy with good views – the hare has amber rather than dark eyes, longer black-tipped ears and is taller, leggier and brighter brown. A rabbit-like animal with greyish and/or white fur and black ear-tips seen on an upland moor will be an Mountain Hare.

Hedgehogs are unmistakable, and so are Moles. Our two species of squirrel are usually easy to tell apart as the Grey is grey and the Red is red... but beware some Greys which can develop a tawny tint to the fur on their backs. Most Reds show long ear-tufts which Greys lack. The rare and introduced Edible Dormouse is like a miniature Grey Squirrel – grey-furred with a luxuriant bushy tail.

↑ To tell our two seal species apart, look for the rounded head and dog-like muzzle of the Common Seal (a), versus the Roman nose of the bigger Grey Seal (b).

↓ The Rabbit (a) has darker eyes and much smaller ears than the Brown Hare (b) as well as different overall colour and proportions.

REPTILES AND AMPHIBIANS

Unlike warmer countries in mainland Europe, the British Isles has very few native reptiles and amphibians. We have augmented their numbers with several non-native introduced species, though most of these are (at least for now) extremely localised so unlikely to be encountered unless you go out specifically to look for them. Identifying these animals is usually not too difficult if you get a good look.

SNAKES

We have three native snakes in Britain, and luckily all are quite distinctive. The smallest and commonest is the Adder, which has a bold dark zigzag pattern down the length of its back. The Grass Snake is largest and mossy green with a striking yellow 'collar'. Rarest and plainest of the three is the Smooth Snake, which is grey-green with a subtle darker chequered pattern.

LIZARDS

↓ Adders have a broad and bold dark zigzag stripe the length of their backs, standing out less on the browner females than on the paler males.

There are three native British lizards, too, though one, the Slow-worm, lacks legs so may be mistaken for a snake. It is smaller than any of our snakes, tubular with no obvious neck, and very small neat scales which give its brownish body a beautiful polished gleam. The Common Lizard is a small and dullish-coloured lizard, while the rare Sand Lizard is considerably larger with a proportionately bigger head and stronger pattern. Males develop bright-green body sides.

FROGS AND TOADS

We have two of each, though the rare Pool Frog, with its striking yellowish back-stripe, was until recently thought to be introduced. Common Frogs have a smoother skin than toads and usually have a dark eye-mask. Toads, which prefer to walk rather than hop and have warty skin, also possess large, bulbous, venom-producing paratoid glands on their head-sides. The rarer species, the Natterjack, is smaller and more warty than the Common Toad with a thin yellow back stripe.

NEWTS

Our three species of newts can be difficult to tell apart. The most distinctive is the Great Crested, which is much the largest and darkest species. Smooth and Palmate Newts are very similar but occur in different locations. The Palmate has webbing between the toes on its hind feet which the Smooth lacks – other clues include the Smooth's spotted throat and the male Palmate's less developed crest.

↑ A surfacing female Smooth Newt, showing the hind feet with clearly separated toes – webbed hind toes would make it a Palmate Newt.

↖ The Marsh Frog's brilliant green skin and larger size, with proportionately smaller head, help separate it from the Common Frog.

NON-NATIVES

Of the many non-native amphibians and reptiles that have been deliberately or accidentally introduced here, several have established themselves. The Wall Lizard, a large and strikingly patterned species, occurs on the Isle of Wight and in Dorset. The Aesculapian Snake from southern Europe is a long, slim, tree-climbing snake, plain golden-brown or dull green in colour, which has established two small colonies here – one in Wales and the other in London. The large, bright-green Marsh Frog is common in southern wetlands now, and easily found by its very loud and persistent squeaky croak.

Other introduced species include the Red-eared Terrapin, a swimming, tortoise-like animal, the Green Lizard which is related to the Sand Lizard, and a small selection of exotic toads and newts. Most of these animals descend from liberated pets – the terrapins are largely the result of pets bought during the Teenage Mutant Ninja Turtles craze; they outgrew their tanks and their owners' interest. As with all introduced species, there is a risk that they will harm native species by outcompeting them for food or by preying on them – adding a non-native predator to an ecosystem often causes catastrophic declines in certain vulnerable species. Attempts have been made to eradicate some non-natives, such as the huge American Bullfrog.

← Non-native reptiles like Red-eared Terrapins are now found in various parts of the UK.

WATER LIFE

Just seeing animals that live under water is a challenge, never mind identifying them. Don't let that put you off though. There's a wealth of interesting wildlife living in fresh and sea water, from fish and crayfish to anemones and periwinkles, and becoming familiar with some of the more common and easily observed species isn't too difficult if you're in the right place.

→ Three Carp of three different forms – from the top a scaleless 'leather', a partly scaled 'mirror' and below a fully scaled Common Carp.

FRESHWATER FISH AND CRAYFISH

Observing fish in their natural state is easiest in clear fresh water, whether a river or a lake. Sunshine draws fish to the surface to bask and feed on the insects that are more active at this time. Using sunglasses that polarise light and thus reduce reflections makes it easier to observe activity under the surface.

When you're trying to identify a fish, note its approximate size, its length relative to width (and the same for its head alone), the size and prominence of its scales and whether the fins are a contrasting colour to the body. Assessing colour is very difficult but look for any contrasting body markings. If views permit, try to check the tail shape, and whether there are any barbels (fleshy 'whiskers') around its mouth. Habitat is also helpful with fish identification, as some species prefer still water and others only thrive in fast-flowing rivers.

Crayfish, which resemble small lobsters, live on the beds of lakes and rivers, so you're only likely to spot them

DISCOVERING MARINE WILDLIFE

There are some places in the UK where you can snorkel in clear seas and get wonderful views of an array of wildlife, much of it more dramatic-looking than you might expect to find in British waters. If you're a newcomer to this and seriously interested in identifying what you see, you may want to carry a waterproof camera to record your sightings. You could encounter colourful sea-slugs, dramatic coral formations, a huge variety of seaweeds, remarkable fish including seahorses, assorted molluscs and crustaceans, and dolphins and basking sharks.

in shallow water. Two species live in the UK – the native White-clawed, and the larger, introduced Signal Crayfish which has replaced the native species in many areas. The Signal Crayfish also carries a disease which has killed many of the White-claweds. Size is the main difference between the two, with the Signal reaching 30cm long and the White-clawed less than half of that.

ROCKPOOL LIFE

The easiest way to observe a range of marine life is to explore rockpools, where the trapped water often hosts a lively community of small sea animals. With rockpool fish, the same principles given previously apply. Anemones' body shapes and tentacle length differentiate the species. Most molluscs you'll see in a rockpool are either gastropods, with a single shell like a snail, or bivalves which have a pair of half-shells held hinged together. The proportions, texture and pattern of the shells will help you to identify molluscs.

PONDLIFE

Pond-dipping is a great way for everyone to discover the small creatures that live on the lake or riverbed. When you join a pond-dipping session, you or your child will be given a net which you gently sweep through the water, then you empty out any catches in a white container holding a little of the pond water and take a look at what you have. Common catches include dragonfly and damselfly larvae – six-legged, long-bodied animals with bulbous eyes, and a triple tail-fin in the case of the damselflies. You might also net pond snails, tadpoles (or toadpoles, which are blacker), caddisfly larvae in their tubular shelters, or adult aquatic insects like Water-boatmen or Pond-skaters. Many RSPB reserves organise pond-dipping sessions, with experts on hand to help you identify the animals you catch.

↑ Tidelines reveal many marine treasures, such as these Dogfish egg-cases which resemble tightly packed beads of foam.

↙ Pondskaters (a) use their long legs to spread their weight so they can literally walk on water. Water-boatmen (b) are aquatic 'true bugs' which often come to the surface. They propel themselves along with their powerful hindlegs.

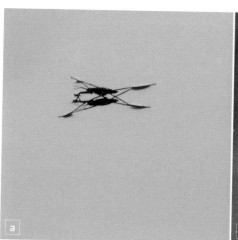

a

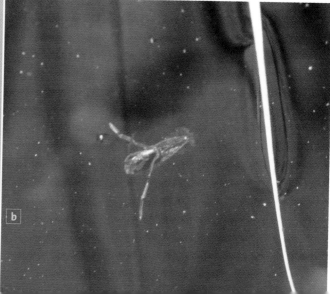

b

BUTTERFLIES, MOTHS AND DRAGONS AND DAMSELS

The most eye-catching insects around are the large, winged ones – butterflies, moths, dragonflies and damselflies. These insects attract particular enthusiasm from wildlife-watchers because of their beauty, conspicuousness and (generally) their ease of observation, so we treat them separately from the other insects. The British Isles has well under a hundred species each of butterflies and dragons and damsels, but more than 2,000 moth species, making this group by far the most challenging to identify.

↑ To identify 'brown' butterflies, pay particular attention to the 'eyespots'. The round black spot with a double white pupil helps identify this as a Gatekeeper.

BUTTERFLIES

These beautiful day-flying insects are easy to observe and, by and large, quite easy to identify. Several of the British species are unique and unmistakable, but there are other groups which present some conundrums. The most difficult are the blues, the fritillaries and the 'golden' skippers. The underside wing pattern tends to be more important for identification than the upperside. With blues, the shade of blue, presence and thickness of any dark borders, and the underwing pattern are all important. With fritillaries, identification comes down to sometimes subtle differences in pattern, particularly on the underwings. Our two most similar butterflies, the Small and Essex Skipper, can only be reliably told apart by the colour of the underside of their antennae tips (brown in Small Skipper, black in Essex).

CATERPILLARS

When you find a caterpillar that you want to identify, the first thing is to establish which species of plant it's on – many species only eat a single type of plant. Then, look at its colour, pattern, hairiness, any bumps or tufts, and how it moves.

MOTHS

Now we enter tricky territory. There are so many species of moths, and so much similarity between some of them (not to mention individual variation within a species), that even the experts are sometimes stumped. For a beginner, working out which family of moth you are dealing with is the first stage. Here are some of the main moth groups (see chart *top right*).

As with butterflies, pattern is more important than colour. Also check the shape of the antennae and the palps (the projections at the front of the face, protruding between the eyes).

Varieties of moths

- **Hawkmoths** Usually large, with long, narrow wings and often colourful hindwings..
- **Noctuid moths** A large family. Many are medium-sized with dull forewings and brighter hindwings, rest with wings held close to the body and often have hairy tufts on the thorax (middle body section).
- **Geometrid moths** Another large family. Many are small with slim bodies. Some rest with the wings fully opened.
- **Plume moths** Unusually shaped moths, with the wings held in tight, narrow rolls, so that the resting moth looks shaped like a capital T.
- **Burnet moths** Striking day-flying moths, large-bodied and usually black and red.
- **Clearwings** Moths with transparent wings and large bodies, often marked to resemble wasps or hornets.
- **'Micromoths'** This grouping covers lots of unrelated species, which are similar in that they are all very small.

DRAGONS AND DAMSELS

Collectively known as the Odonata, these insects have four wings, long, slim and often colourful abdomens, and hunt other insects. Dragonflies fly strongly and are large with round heads, their huge eyes close together. Damselflies are smaller, with a more fluttering flight, and have heads shaped like dumb-bells with widely spaced eyes. For the more confusing species, the patterns on the thorax and abdomen are important for identification, and so is eye colour, the colour of the pterostigma (a small opaque 'cell' on the outer tip of the forewing) and the presence of any dark patches on the wings.

↓ The Grizzled Skipper is very moth-like with its grey and white wings and relatively large head and body, but the clubbed antennae identify it as a butterfly.

→↗ The black marking on the segment of the abdomen nearest the wing bases is a U shape in Azure (a) Damselflies, and an oval on a stick in Common Blue (b).

BUTTERFLY OR MOTH?

It's not always straightforward to tell whether you're looking at a butterfly or a moth. Some moths fly by day, while some butterflies are as dull in colour and buzzing in flight as any moth. The most reliable trait is antennae shape – butterfly antennae have enlarged, club-like tips, while moth antennae may be simple and straight, or fringed like tiny feathers. A handful of moths do have somewhat clubbed antennae, but the ones you're most likely to see are the highly distinctive burnet moths, which don't look like any butterfly species.

MORE MINI BEASTS

Well over half of the animal species in the world are insects. Add on the other land invertebrates and you have an amazing wealth of life. For the amateur wildlife-watcher, getting to grips with all of this diversity is a huge challenge, but an immensely rewarding one. Identifying species may be almost impossible – sometimes you can only get as far as a genus or family – but there are plenty of distinctive individual species out there as well.

↑ Shieldbugs are often eyecatching insects with distinctive shapes and patterns. The Dock Shieldbug has a 'waisted' body and prominent dark wings.

↗ Scorpionflies are smallish insects with chequered wings and beak-like mouthparts. The female lacks the bulbous, scorpion-like 'tail' of the male.

INSECT TYPES

Insects all have six legs, attached to their thorax which is the middle of their three body sections. They may have two, four or no wings, and they usually have a more or less obvious pair of antennae on their heads. We have already looked at two taxonomic orders of insects – the Lepidoptera (butterflies and moths) and the Odonata (dragonflies and damselflies). Here are some more.

Orders of insects

■ **Hymenoptera** Bees, wasps and ants. All except worker ants have four wings, the front pair often much larger. Many live in colonies and show very sophisticated social behaviour; some are armed with stings or large biting jaws. The colours and patterns on the abdomen help with identification.

■ **Coleoptera** Beetles. They have four wings, the front pair modified into hard wing cases (elytra). A hugely diverse group, principally identified by the shape, texture, colour and pattern of the elytra.

■ **Hemiptera** True bugs. They have pointed, piercing mouthparts to suck the juices from plants or animal prey. Many look superficially like beetles.

■ **Orthoptera** Grasshoppers and crickets. Long-bodied insects with powerful hindlegs for jumping. Many produce sound by rubbing body parts together. Wing length and type of sound made can help with identification.

■ **Diptera** True flies. They have just one pair of wings. The group includes many biting insects and also the hoverflies which mimic bees and wasps. Colour, pattern and body proportions help with identification.

■ **Ephemeroptera, Trichoptera and Plecoptera** (mayflies, caddisflies and stoneflies) are all four-winged insects which spend their immature months living in water. Wing size, pattern and shape are key to identification.

Once you become familiar with a few examples of each of these orders, you'll be able to assign most new species you encounter to the correct taxonomic order. Then it is a matter of working downwards, to determine which family and then genus your mystery insect belongs to. Getting the hang of insect identification will be much easier if you have some understanding of how the different groups can be broken down.

MORE THAN SIX LEGS

With multilegged animals, the number of legs is key. If it has eight, it is an arachnid, probably a spider (though it may also be a harvestman, mite or tick). The type of web your spider has made is as important as the appearance of the spider itself for identification. However, not all spiders spin webs – some chase down or ambush their prey. Invertebrates with more than eight legs include woodlice, which have armoured, domed bodies, centipedes, which have sprawling legs and large jaws, and millipedes which, with two legs per body segment, are the leggiest of all.

NO LEGS

Legless animals you may encounter include various kinds of worms, slugs, snails and certain insect larvae. Snails can usually be identified by the shape and pattern of their shells. Slugs are easy enough to recognise with their long 'feelers' – shape, colour and size should help you determine the species. With worms and other long, wriggly things, note whether the body has visible segments or not, whether the shape thickens or tapers at any point and the kind of habitat in which you found it.

↑ To identify bumblebees, note the position of the coloured bands on the head, thorax and abdomen. This is a Buff-tailed Bumblebee.

↓ Harvestmen are not true spiders, lacking a 'pedicle' connecting the head and body, though they are classed as arachnids and possess eight (very long) legs.

FLOWER IDENTIFICATION

We're all attracted by the beauty of wild flowers, but identification isn't always easy. The British Isles has thousands of species of flowering plant, and the potential for confusion is increased by the fact that some show much individual variation and others are inclined to hybridise at the drop of a hat, producing peculiar intergrades. As with birds and insects, the way to find the right identification is to get familiar with some of the main plant groupings.

LOOKING AT A FLOWER

↑ Wild Thyme bears small flowers in clusters – look closely to see the fine detail of individual flowers.

The structure of your flower is the first clue to narrowing down an identification. First of all, what is its general shape – is it flat, bowl-shaped, tubular or bell-shaped? Next, is it symmetrical in multiple directions, like a rose, or does it only have symmetry on the vertical plane, like an orchid? Does it have a large centre surrounded by a circle of thin petals, like a daisy? How many petals does it have, and do all flowers on the plant have the same number?

Once you've assessed an individual flower, look at how it grows on the plant. Are the flowers on individual stems, or do they grow close together in a cluster or up a stem in the form of an elongated spike? With these details, you should be able to work out which family your flower belongs to – here are some possibilities.

LOCATION, LOCATION, LOCATION

Each plant species tends to have a favourite soil type. Some species like heavy soils, some prefer chalky or sandy conditions. There are plants that only grow close to fresh water, and others that thrive in sea air. So where you see your flower is as important for identification as what it looks like.

← The number of petals, whether or not they are divided and if so how deeply are all clues to help identify this as Greater Stitchwort.

Flower families

■ **Rose family** A diverse group of plants in terms of size. The flowers are flat and symmetrical with (usually) five fairly large rounded petals, in pink or white.

■ **Daisy family** These flowers are composed of a central cluster of tiny 'disc florets' surrounded by a ring of 'ray florets' which each bear a single large petal, so what appears to be a single flower head is in fact a cluster of tiny individual flowers. Most are all or partly yellow but other colours, including blue, occur too.

■ **Carrot family** These are usually tall plants which bear their flowers in flat-topped, umbrella-like clusters. The individual flowers are very small, four-petalled and symmetrical, and are usually white, yellow or light pink.

■ **Orchid family** The flowers form a spike. They are symmetrical only on the vertical plane, and often have an enlarged central lower petal. They are usually purple, pink or white in colour.

■ **Pea family** The flowers may grow individually, in clusters or in spikes. They are symmetrical only on the vertical plane, and have a bulbous double petal at the bottom of each flower with a 'hood' above and a pair of 'wings' at the sides. They are usually purple or yellow.

Buttercup family These have simple flat flowers with (usually) five large petals. Most species are yellow.

LEAVES AND STEMS

The flower on its own is not always enough to allow you to identify the plant, so when making your notes or taking photos, make sure you include details of its leaves and stems as well. The crucial things to note about the leaves are: how are they arranged on the stem (in pairs, in rings, individually); what is their width/length ratio; are they smooth or hairy; are they simple or divided into lobes; and are their margins straight or jagged (toothed)?

With the stems, make a note of how hairy they are (if at all) and their shape in cross-section. You don't need to pick the plant, just feel whether the stem is rounded or square.

DON'T PICK!

Tempting though it can be to pick or uproot wild flowers, try to resist. Like all wild things they should be left where they are to complete their life cycles – if picked they will not be able to form and set their seed. Several wild plant species have had their populations depleted or even wiped out by this kind of activity. Some scarce species are protected by law and you could be prosecuted if you damage them or remove them from their habitat.

→ The distinctive Bee Orchid is much easier to identify than some of its relatives.

TREES AND SHRUBS

Trees and shrubs are the cornerstones of most of
our dryland ecosystems. Therefore, if you want to
gain some real understanding about the wildlife
in your garden or local area, they are probably
the first species you should be seeking to identify.
If your interest is more casual, you're still likely
to be faced with trees or shrubs so beautiful that
you just have to know what they are.

A PLETHORA OF CLUES

↗ Some trees and
shrubs have very
inconspicuous flowers.
Elder is not one of
them, producing large
umbrella-shaped
clusters of strongly
scented white flowers.

Unlike soft or 'herbaceous' plants, which die back to their roots or die altogether
in winter, trees and shrubs (or 'woody' plants) maintain an above-ground
presence all the time, making them about the only living things you can always
see, no matter what time of year. This means you'll have plenty of time to study
them, although the number of clues on show will vary from season to season.

↓ The long leaves
with their coarsely
toothed margins,
coupled with the
bright green and very
spiny fruits, mean
this has to be Sweet
Chestnut.

Leaves As with herbaceous plants, the shape, size and texture of the leaves
is important. First, decide whether you are looking at individual leaves (one per
stem) or pinnate leaves (multiple separate 'leaflets' per stem). Pinnate leaves may
have the leaflets arranged along the leaf stem, as in Ash trees, or radiating out
from the same central point, as in Horse Chestnut trees. Individual leaves may
be oval, diamond-shaped, heart-shaped or lobed, and if lobed the lobes could be
rounded or pointed. Measure a few different leaves (length and maximum width)
to give you an average size.

With coniferous trees, many of which grow simple needles, note whether the needles grow singly or in pairs, and how long they are on average.

Flowers

Most woody plants produce flowers, though some are very inconspicuous. Examining these may be tricky if the tree is tall with few low branches, but if you can see the tree is bearing flowers, look for fallen ones on the ground. Shrubs often produce profuse and strongly scented blossom – noting your impressions of the smell can help with identification.

Fruits

Flowers mature into fruits, and these are among the most distinctive parts of a tree or a shrub. More people would recognise an acorn than the leaf of an oak tree, and several trees and shrubs bear fruits that we are eager to spot come autumn, when it's time to make blackberry jam, rosehip jelly, roasted chestnuts and sloe gin.

If your mystery plant is bearing berries, record their colour, size and whether the berries are borne individually or in clusters. If the fruit is concealed in some kind of protective fleshy casing, open it up if you can to see what it looks like. Some tree seeds come with a fibrous 'wing' to help them catch the wind and travel away from the parent tree – record the shape of this wing and how it causes the seed to move when 'in flight'.

↑ Because of its mainly white bark, the Silver Birch is one of our most distinctive tree species at all times of year.

↓ Many shrubs bear berries in autumn. This is Common Hawthorn, identifiable by the shape of the leaves as well as the fruit.

Bark

This can vary quite a lot within a species, but the texture and colour of the bark is sometimes very helpful for identification. Silver Birch bark is distinctive, as is the variegated bark of London Plane trees, produced as small, round-edged chunks of bark peel off, leaving a contrasting patch of fresh bark beneath. Some trees have deeply fissured bark, others are very smooth. If the tree has a wound which is colonised by a fungus, identifying the fungus may help you identify the tree – and vice versa.

Round or pointy?

A cone-shaped pine tree offers an outline completely unlike that of a classic English Oak. However, identifying trees by their overall shape is tricky, as the shape is influenced by many other factors. Trees that grow up in isolation can spread out a lot more than those in dense woodland, and accidental or deliberate damage affects the shape, too, as can a run of poor growing seasons. However, it's another thing to bear in mind, just don't set too much store by it.

SIMPLE PLANTS AND FUNGI

Besides lofty trees, colourful shrubs and herbaceous flowers, there are hosts of less showy plants out there, from horsetails and ferns to mosses and liverworts. There are also the fungi, and bridging the gap between the plant and fungi kingdoms are lichens, which are essentially a working partnership between a fungus and an alga. Identifying these mysterious organisms is difficult but worthwhile, as it will give you insights into their curious biological heritage and ways of life.

FERNS AND HORSETAILS

These are primitive, non-flowering plants. Horsetails have straight stems with rings of simple, filament-like leaves running up their length, while ferns are quite variable but often exhibit delicately fringed fronds like the most familiar member of the group – Bracken. Some other ferns have simpler, tongue-shaped leaves.

To identify these species, make measurements of the leaves and stems as well as photographing or sketching their shapes and branching patterns. Quite a number of species have exacting habitat requirements and/or restricted geographical ranges, which should simplify your search.

MOSSES AND LIVERWORTS

These are tiny, simple plants with no stems, true leaves or flowers. From a biological point of view, the important thing about them is that they have no vascular system – the network of vessels used to transport water and nutrients around in higher plants. Typical mosses grow in dense, carpet-like clusters, looking like a velvety or shaggy green growth. You'll find them on a wall, piece of dead wood or on the ground. Liverworts resemble tiny, fleshy lobe-like leaves, and tend to grow on surfaces that are permanently damp. Both will sprout, in certain circumstances, reproductive spores, which usually look like tiny balls or cups on stalks.

← New growths of Bracken, probably our most familiar fern species, appear in early spring with the fronds tightly coiled.

FUNGI

From our human perspective, fungi are plant-like because they don't move around. However, biologically they are distinct and belong in a separate kingdom to plants. The main part of a fungus is usually out of sight – a network of tiny root-like fibres called a mycelium, which grows deep into the ground, rotting wood or other substrate. The mushrooms we observe in autumn are just the 'fruiting bodies' of the fungus, which release tiny reproductive spores into the air.

Mushroom and fungi identification

To identify a mushroom, measure the width of its cap (ideally, take an average from several specimens), note the cap colour and texture, and look at the underside of the cap to see where the gills join the stem. If you leave a mushroom cap on a piece of white paper for half an hour or so it will leave a 'spore print', the colour of which may help with identification. The smell of the mushroom can be important, too, as well as the colour of the flesh when bruised or broken. With bracket fungi, which grow in a shelf-like shape on dead or dying wood, the species of tree they're growing on will help you identify them.

↑ The Shaggy Inkcap belongs to a group of fungi whose fruiting bodies disintegrate around the cup edges with age, dripping a black, inky goo.

LICHENS

These fascinating organisms are two for the price of one – each is a 'dual organism' formed from an intimate association between an alga (a very simple plant) and a fungus. The cells of the two components are completely intermingled and interdependent. Often the component species can live independently, and look totally different in this state.

← Lichens are very diverse and difficult to identify. This one is of the 'leafy' type and is a member of the family Parmeliaceae.

Lichen identification
Lichens come in three basic forms – crustose (forming a crust), foliose (leaf-like shapes) and fruticose (forming branches). There are more than 1,500 forms in the British Isles, but some of the commoner ones are quite distinctive in form and colour. Habitat and geographical location will also help you narrow down your options when trying to identify a lichen.

← Identifying seaweeds involves noting the colour, shape of the 'leaves' and presence of any extra structures, like the air pockets in this Bladder Wrack.

WHY YOU SHOULD DRAW

Gone are the days when every wildlife-watcher needed to produce 'field sketches' as a visual record of what they had seen, for identification later. With digital cameras so readily available and easy to use, field sketching is in danger of becoming a lost art. However, there are still good reasons for taking pencil to paper from time to time, and the activity remains as rewarding and enjoyable as it has ever been.

SKETCHING FOR IDENTIFICATION

You won't always have a camera with you, and even if you do, the animal you want to photograph may not wait around for you to line up your shot. It's even possible that a plant you want to photograph is out of reach of your lens. That's why it's worth carrying a notebook, so you can quickly draw your impressions of what you've seen, either while you are looking at the subject or soon afterwards. You don't need to be an accomplished artist to produce a useful field sketch, although the more you do it, the better your drawings will get.

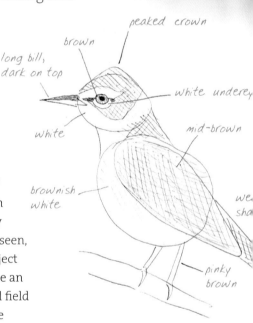

peaked crown

brown

long bill, dark on top

white undereye

white

mid-brown

brownish white

we sha

pinky brown

↑ Even a simple field sketch (a) complete with annotations, can be enough to identify a mystery bird – in this case a Reed Warbler (b).

WILDLIFE ART FOR PLEASURE

The other reason to draw is sheer enjoyment. If you loathed art class at school with a passion, you might be tempted to skip the rest of this page... but think back to when you were much younger – too young to turn an overcritical eye upon your own work. Most of us lost interest in art when we started to become disappointed with the results of our efforts, rather than losing any enjoyment in the actual process of creating artworks. If you can silence your inner critic effectively, you can recapture all the fun of drawing, painting and other art forms, and what subject matter could be more inspiring than the natural world?

← To overcome 'fear of getting started' on a new piece of artwork, try 'warming up' with some rough sketches on an equally rough piece of paper.

THE TYRANNY OF THE BLANK PAGE

When it comes to actually making the first mark upon a pristine sheet of paper, the anxiety about whether you'll 'get it right' can become paralysing. One way to get around this problem is to use 'rough paper' for your sketches, perhaps printed on one side with stuff you no longer need, so you're working on paper which is already marked. You can turn this into a sketchbook with a fold and a couple of sketches. To practise just getting the feel of moving your pencil over the paper, you could also try drawing a simple shape on the page, say a circle or a cross, then building your sketch around that.

ENCOURAGING CHILDREN TO DRAW

If you have young children, you'll know how much they enjoy creating pictures. Inevitably, with time they will start to expect more of themselves, and this is the vulnerable time when the enjoyment in producing art can evaporate. As well as heaping praise and encouragement on your children to continue to draw, now is the time to get them to really value the practical usefulness of their work. Encourage them to draw the wildlife they see, perhaps by creating 'identification charts' or by making a scrapbook combining notes and drawings. In this way you can help your children develop real artistic skill. Not everyone is destined to become an accomplished artist, but the ability to produce recognisable drawings of things you observe is a genuinely useful skill. Far too many children lose a genuine early gleam of artistic talent through a lack of encouragement.

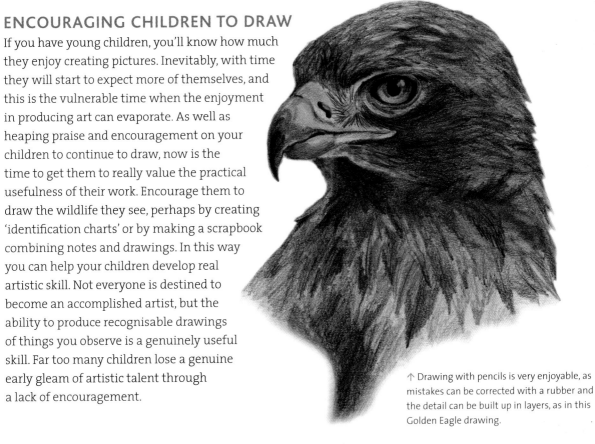

↑ Drawing with pencils is very enjoyable, as mistakes can be corrected with a rubber and the detail can be built up in layers, as in this Golden Eagle drawing.

SKETCHING FOR IDENTIFICATION
MAMMALS, REPTILES AND AMPHIBIANS

All too often, you spot a mammal or a reptile too late – it has already seen you and is beating a hasty retreat, and if you don't recognise it and want to identify it, that obviously presents you with a problem. Amphibians are more approachable, but they too can disappear if startled. If you have a camera and the animal isn't too far away you could try to grab a shot, but you may be better off just watching, taking in as much detail as you can, then producing a sketch to check against the field guide later.

MAMMALS

Depending how skilled you are as an artist, accurately capturing the shape of a mammal varies from very difficult to virtually impossible. However, the mammals you'll see in the UK can be divided into groups with quite similar 'body plans' and the fine details within these groups are not generally helpful for identification, so you can draw a quick and rough approximation of the shape and then get on with adding details of pattern and the proportions of the extremities, which are more helpful.

Particular details you may want to record (if you manage to observe them) include the rump and tail pattern of deer, the ear and face shape of bats (if you're lucky enough to discover a bat at rest in the daytime), and the position of the fins on a whale or a dolphin.

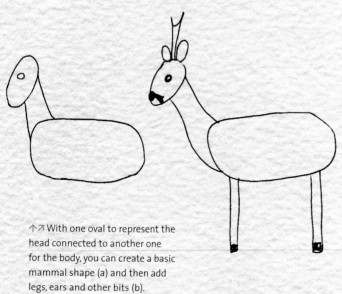

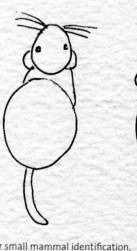

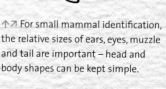

↑↗ With one oval to represent the head connected to another one for the body, you can create a basic mammal shape (a) and then add legs, ears and other bits (b).

↑↗ For small mammal identification, the relative sizes of ears, eyes, muzzle and tail are important – head and body shapes can be kept simple.

REPTILES

Snakes are easy to draw if you imagine them stretched out rather than in coils as they usually are in life. Draw your snake outline as a simple cylinder, add a narrower neck and simple wedge-shaped head, then get to work adding the markings as these are what will help you identify the snake. Annotate your drawings with your impressions of the colours. For a lizard, you can draw a snake shape and just add short sticks to represent legs, on either side for a top-down view or all at the bottom for a side-on view.

AMPHIBIANS

The body shape of a frog or toad can be represented by a circle with a triangular bulge at one end representing the head. Rather than drawing the legs in their natural but confusing folded position, draw them as if they were fully extended for simplicity, and don't worry about adding the toes. It is the colours and patterns on the body that you need to concentrate on to produce an identifiable sketch.

For newts, you can use a similar method to the one described for lizards. If your newt is a male in breeding regalia, try to draw it side on to show the shape of the crest that grows along its back and tail, as there are quite marked differences in crest shape between some species.

↑ Lizards (this is a Common Lizard) and snakes don't naturally assume poker-straight postures, but for a quick ID sketch it's easier to draw them that way.

↘ For a snake, a simple straight tube shape is sufficient – concentrate on getting the markings right (such as the collar pattern on this Grass Snake sketch).

↖↑ If you're drawing a lizard or newt, just add legs to the snake 'tube' (a). If you're drawing a newt with developed 'crests', a side-on view will be helpful too (b).

SKETCHING FOR IDENTIFICATION
BIRDS

It's amazing how bad a bird photograph has to be before the bird in it becomes unidentifiable. However, just as with mammals there will always be times when you just can't focus on the bird in time, or it's too far away for your lens (though perhaps not for your binoculars). Luckily, it's quite easy for anyone to produce a passable field sketch of a bird as, despite the number of species, there isn't that much variety in their body plans.

OUTLINES

↓ As with mammals, two ovals can represent a bird's head and body (a). Connect them up and add a bill, eye and leg (b), then finish with wings and tail (c). Now you can erase the connecting lines if you like, and add colours (d)

Producing the beginnings of a bird outline is simple. You need an oval shape, with another smaller (about half the diameter) and rounder one placed close to the first at about the ten o'clock position (or two o'clock if you want your bird to be facing right). Then connect the two ovals with lines and you have the head and body of your bird. You can then add the bill, legs and tail, and start adding in the patterns you can see in the plumage. There is no need to draw in the wings in detail, just the rough position of markings. As the illustrations show, this basic bird outline can be modified to make a bird in flight or a swimming bird.

↑ Every bird field guide has diagrams like this, showing the main feather tracts. Learning their positions will help make your field sketches more accurate.

←When sketching a swimming bird, note how high it 'sits' on the water. Herring Gulls (b) are very buoyant, but the back of a swimming Cormorant (a) barely clears the surface.

GOING INTO THE DETAILS

Birds' feathers are arranged in lines or 'tracts', some of which are very obvious, especially those in the wing. Once you have the hang of the rough outline, you could try drawing in the wing tracts. This can be helpful for identification, as these tracts tend to be where distinctive contrasting markings are placed. There's no need to draw individual feathers, just mark out the tracts in blocks.

DRAWING MOVEMENT

Sometimes, a sketch representing the way a bird flies can really help you pin down an identification. Some species fly with deep or shallow undulations, while others perform dramatic courtship flights involving climbs, dives and even barrel rolls. The easiest way to express this is with arrowed lines. You could also show the position of the bird's wings at different points in the flight pattern.

→ From the basic two-ovals start, you can make almost any bird shape, such as a duck (a) or a wader (b). Changing the position of the wings gives you a bird in flight (c), or by lining up the head and body ovals you can have a top- or bottom-down view of a flying bird (d).

Come prepared

If you're keen on exploring bird sketches for identification, you can take a short cut by drawing your outlines before you go out, so they are ready to fill in when the bird is in front of you. If you go for quite elaborate and 'finished' outlines with feather tracts marked out, you may not have the right shape of outline for the mystery bird you see, but this isn't necessarily a problem – you can easily draw the markings of a finch on an outline of a duck, as long as you remember to make a note that that's what you've done!

SKETCHING FOR IDENTIFICATION
INSECTS AND OTHER INVERTEBRATES

Because their bodies are symmetrical in our usual view of them (looking down onto them), insects and other invertebrates can present a tricky sketching challenge. However, as with other groups there are short cuts you can take to make things simpler. They also (usually) tolerate closer approach and more prolonged study than larger animals, and often where you find one individual of a species you'll soon find more, so if your first model flits or scuttles away a replacement may soon appear.

WINGED INSECTS

Wing shape and size relative to the body can be important for insect identification. The good news is that you don't have to draw both wings or sets of wings on each side of the insect, as one's a mirror image of the other. So instead, just draw one side and get the details as right as you can, rather than wasting time trying to get the other side to match up.

If you have the time and the inclination, drawing some representation of the wing veins can be worthwhile. In butterflies and moths, using the wing veins as a framework can help you to place the markings in the right place. If you know you are going out looking for butterflies or moths, it may be worth preparing some outlines (complete with veins) in advance, to fill in later.

↑ The pattern on this Marbled White butterfly is very clearly dictated by the position of its wing veins.

→ It's worth making a simple diagram of the veins on a butterfly's wings, as this will help you place the wing markings exactly where they should be.

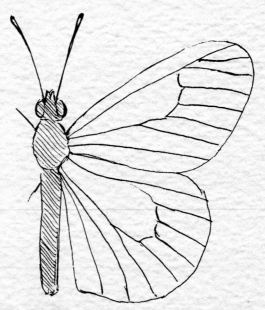

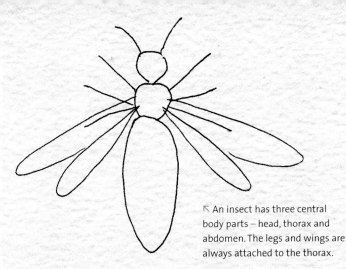

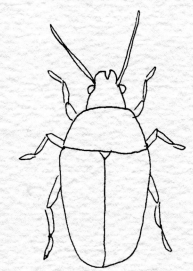

↖ An insect has three central body parts – head, thorax and abdomen. The legs and wings are always attached to the thorax.

INSECT BODIES

Insects have three distinct body parts: the head, thorax and abdomen. The head has a pair of antennae (though they may be tiny) and sometimes some quite noticeable feeding apparatus, such as the 'beak' of a weevil or the elongated palps of some moths. The legs (six of them, though in some species one pair may be reduced to stubs) and wings are attached to the thorax. The final body part, the abdomen, is usually the largest bit and may have colourful markings (or be hidden under the wings). Some insects have visible reproductive equipment at the abdomen tip, such as the paired claspers on male dragonflies or the threatening-looking pointed ovipositor (egg-laying tube) on wood wasps.

Maintain the discipline of drawing all the right body parts, with the appendages attached to the right bits, and your chances of making an identifiable sketch are much improved. Because of insects' handy modular body design, it's easy to do, and you can also isolate one body section and draw it on its own if it merits particular attention.

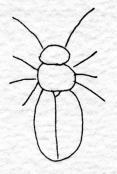

↑← A more detailed drawing of a beetle might be more pleasing to the eye, but often a much simpler shape will suffice for identification, once you've added the markings.

OTHER INVERTEBRATES

If you are drawing a many-legged invertebrate with repeated and clearly divided segments, it might be worth drawing one segment on its own in detail, to ensure you have the right number of legs per segment, the right pattern and so on. With legless animals, getting the body shape right (how it swells and tapers from one end to the other) and the position of any 'extra bits' (for example, the saddles on earthworms or slugs) is about all you can do. You may not be able to figure out which end is the head, but that doesn't actually matter.

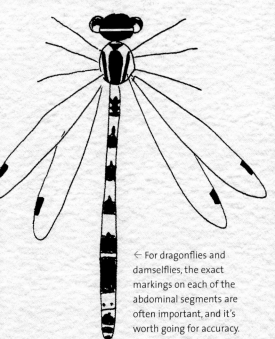

← For dragonflies and damselflies, the exact markings on each of the abdominal segments are often important, and it's worth going for accuracy.

SKETCHING FOR IDENTIFICATION
PLANTS AND FUNGI

With plants and fungi, you won't have the problem of them disappearing before you can whip your camera out, but there may still be times when you left your camera at home or just want to challenge yourself to use pencil and paper to capture enough detail for identification. Sketching flowers, leaves, mushrooms and so on is also a great way to get you used to the feel of wielding a pencil – practice that will help when you take on more lively subject matter.

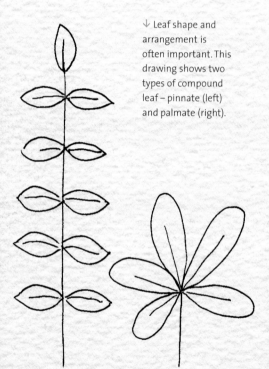

↓ Leaf shape and arrangement is often important. This drawing shows two types of compound leaf – pinnate (left) and palmate (right).

LEAVES

Sometimes, a drawing can express more clearly the essential points about leaf arrangement and structure than a photograph, because you can create a simplified 'plan' version of what may in reality be rather difficult to visualise. Concentrate first on drawing the leaf arrangement on the stem, then go into the shape of an individual leaf. If the leaf has a complicated margin, you can draw just a short section of it, separately from your main leaf picture. You can also actually trace around the outline of the leaf itself, which will give you an exact scale representation – and you don't need to remove the leaf from the plant to do this.

→ The leaves of Silverweed are pinnate in structure, with small, tooth-edged 'leaflets' arranged in pairs on either side of the main leaf stem.

FLOWERS

As with leaves, try to get down a representation of how the flowers are arranged on the stem – singly, in clusters or in the form of a spike. You can do this in a very simple, diagrammatic form.

When drawing individual flowers, try to be rigorous about drawing the correct number of petals if there are fewer than ten of them, as this can be important for identification. You can also use a little gentle manipulation to expose and then draw parts which are normally hidden. Several flowers keep their stamens and stigma (the reproductive parts) concealed behind a closed pair or cluster of petals, only to be exposed when the weight of a pollinating insect comes down on the right part of the flower.

Don't ignore the parts at the 'non-business' end of the flower, either. The sepals (leaf-like structures which protect the flower when it's still in bud, and may support it and its fruits afterwards) often have a characteristic shape and arrangement. The length of the flower 'tube' or corolla, before the petals open out, should also be sketched.

OTHER PLANT BITS

Even if you don't know exactly what you're looking at, any part of a plant that strikes you as unusual is worth sketching. Fruits at all stages of maturity, what a broken stem looks like in cross-section, the shape, size and arrangement of thorns on the stem – all are possible clues to identification.

FUNGI

Once again, the devil's in the details. Most mushrooms have the same essential shape – a cap on a stalk – so for identification your sketches should include the way the gills are arranged, whether there is a ring or other membranous stuff on the stem, and give an idea of the pattern (if any) of the cap.

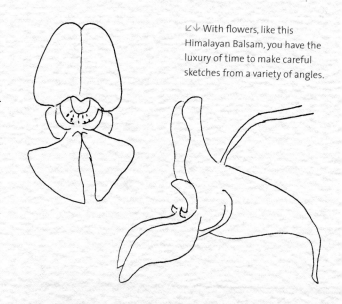

↙↓ With flowers, like this Himalayan Balsam, you have the luxury of time to make careful sketches from a variety of angles.

↑ A mature Parasol Mushroom assumes a distinctive inverted shape, like an umbrella which has blown inside-out.

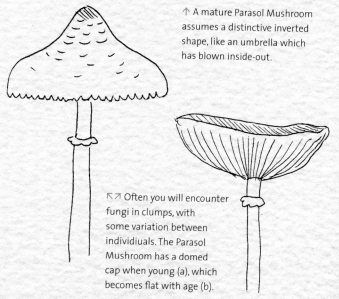

↖↗ Often you will encounter fungi in clumps, with some variation between individiuals. The Parasol Mushroom has a domed cap when young (a), which becomes flat with age (b).

FROM SKETCHER TO ARTIST

Some of the world's most accomplished artists and illustrators of the natural world started off as keen naturalists making identification sketches in their notebooks. Whether through talent or practice, their early sketching skills blossomed into an enviable ability to create beautiful and useful pieces of artwork. The path from wildlife observer to wildlife artist is a natural one, and if you enjoy being creative, that's all the excuse you'll ever need.

↑ Detailed and accurate field sketches like this Marmalade Hoverfly coloured pencil drawing begin to blur the line between sketch and artwork.

ACCURACY OR EXPRESSION?

Some of us long to create perfect representations of our subjects, others aspire to a more personal and impressionistic look. The best way to explore both is through drawing – a lot of drawing. A pencil and paper provides you with a cheap, simple and forgiving creative playground. Whether you are drawing from life or using photos as reference, use your drawing to explore your impressions of your subject. This might be attempting to capture its contours as naturalistically as you can or to convey a sense of the way it moves. Either way, you'll find that practice and more practice will produce increasingly pleasing results.

You may find that precise and meticulous work suits you best. If you are going for naturalistic representation, though, remember to sit back and look at the

INSTANT INSPIRATION

When you sit down to create a fully realised painting, you probably have a detailed plan of what you want to produce already in your mind's eye. That is fine, but it can be discouraging when you're just getting the feel of using a pencil and really studying your subject. Few of us ever produce the kind of image we would like to at the first touch of pencil to paper, so try to put aside all your hopes for what you want the drawing to be like and engage on a more instinctive, reactive level to your work as you go.

When we plan, we are already racing ahead in our minds to the next stage, but when you're learning to draw you really need to immerse yourself in the moment. This means achieving as complete a detachment as you can from thoughts of both past and future. If you manage this, you'll be completely absorbed in what you're doing, time will fly and you'll find that the real joy lies in the process rather than in the results.

↓ Capturing something of the subject's character is the artist's challenge. A singing Sedge Warbler is restless, striking many poses (some more pleasing than others).

←↓ Same subject (a Stoat) – two very different interpretations. One is a detailed and careful line drawing (a), the other a much looser and more expressive drawing in coloured pencils (b).

bigger picture from time to time rather than getting 'tunnel vision' as you work on a small detail, to keep the whole subject correctly proportioned. Artists who work this way will generally make a complete outline first, and then begin to work on the component parts. To master a looser and more impressionistic style, you need to shed your inhibitions somewhat and let your pencil move in longer and perhaps swifter strokes. Work on general shapes and keep things dynamic.

There's no need to limit the way you work, especially not at the outset. The more confident you become at accurate and meticulous drawing, the better this will translate into more expressive work, and allowing yourself a bit of free rein will help you capture essential details more quickly.

THE WORLD THROUGH ARTISTS' EYES

Once you develop a serious interest in making your own wildlife art, you'll start to look at nature in a slightly different way. The effect of light upon a surface, whether the ruffled plumage of a bird, a swaying meadow of seeding grass-heads or the transparent wings of a dragonfly, begins to capture your attention. Watching an active animal, you'll see it move through a series of postures, some more beautiful to you than others, and through a series of compositions as it moves through its environment. Scenes and species that may have started to become dull and familiar gain a new life as you begin to see the art in them.

DRAWING MATERIALS

For identification sketches, any old pencil (or pen) and piece of paper will do. However, there is a lot more to drawing than HB pencils, and as your interest grows you'll probably want to start exploring some of the other options out there, as there will be some that suit your style and that you find more enjoyable to work with than others. There's also a distinction to be made between good drawing materials for when you're outside, and the materials you might want to use when working at home with lots of desk space.

↖ An ordinary HB pencil is an inexpensive and user-friendly drawing tool, ideal for quick, rough sketches like this female Banded Demoiselle damselfly.

PENCILS

↓ Zoo animals give you the chance to make lots of sketches, from which you can build up a detailed final artwork, using a variety of pencil grades.

Standard pencil 'leads' contain no actual lead. They are a combination of clay and graphite. Pencils with more clay (the 'H' series) have harder 'leads', so you need to apply more pressure to make a heavier line. They are ideal for making accurate, light outlines. If there's more graphite (the 'B' series), the line will be blacker and the 'lead' softer and more easily smudged, so they are good for creating intense shading. With HB marking the central point, pencils are graded in increasing numbers in both directions, so B is a little blacker and softer than HB and H a little harder, 2B/2H a little softer/harder respectively, and so on. You'll rarely need a pencil softer and blacker than 6B, or harder than 6H.

That's the monochrome pencils covered. There are also coloured graphite-type pencils available, as well as standard coloured pencils with their more waxy 'leads'. Coloured pencils vary a great deal in quality, and you'll be better off buying a small set of good ones than a huge array of colours in a cheaper set. Some coloured pencils are water-soluble, meaning you can create watercolour-like 'washes' of soft, even colour by shading with the pencil and then using a brush to mix water with the colour on the paper.

DRAWING GEAR FOR THE ARTIST ON THE MOVE

If you're drawing outdoors, you'll need a streamlined set of kit so you don't have to carry too much and you can get access to what you need quickly. A sketchpad with thick, heavy covers will be resilient and somewhat weather-resistant. Choose just a few pencils to work with, plus a good rubber and sharpener. If you're taking coloured pencils too, you should be able to limit yourself to perhaps 10 or 12 shades – blending colours together will enable you to create the rest. A simple pencil case is fine for carrying them around. You can fit all of these things into a shoulder bag which can sit open on your hip, ready for you to grab what you need.

If you want to draw birds and own a telescope, you'll find your scope a real boon and not just because of the magnified views it gives you. With a tripod or hide clamp you can use your scope hands-free, and so move quickly between looking and drawing – this is much more tricky to do with binoculars.

Charcoal sticks provide another drawing method – they produce very strong shading so can be used to create dramatic monochrome images. As with drawings done with softer pencils, you may need to apply a spray fixative to protect your drawing from getting smudged. Ink pens give you a much more precise means of drawing.

PAPER

Paper comes in various thicknesses, expressed as 'gsm' (grams per square metre). To give you an idea, normal printer paper is usually 80gsm, and most paper made for drawing is thicker, between 100 and 200gsm. Papers also come in different textures, with 'smooth' being very smooth indeed, and more textured types going by names like 'fine-grain' or 'medium-grain'. Some people like the look of rougher paper, which 'catches' the mark of the pencil in a slightly more unpredictable way, while smooth paper is better if you're going for maximum accuracy. You can buy art paper in individual sheets or in spiral-bound or glue-bound pads, some of which will have hard covers for durability when using outside.

↑ A Baikal Teal – one of many appealing subjects at an exotic wildfowl collection. Coloured pencils come in a huge array of shades, and some ranges are water-soluble.

↓ Pens, from inexpensive biros to fine-nibbed fountain pens, are great for making strong drawings. This White Admiral butterfly swas drawn with a rollerball pen.

PAINTING MATERIALS

Are you ready to splash out and try some painting? This is where you can really start spending some money (though your hobby will still probably be a lot less tough on your wallet than if you become a photographer). The array of paints and brushes out there can be bewildering, but for the beginner artist certain types do offer clear advantages, and once you've chosen your paints, choosing your paper is relatively simple. We also cover painting with chalk and oil pastels here.

WATERCOLOUR AND GOUACHE

These two paint types are similar in that both are water-soluble. They are different in that watercolours are transparent and may come in a hard 'pan' form or in tubes, while gouache paints are opaque and only come in tubes. Both are good for wildlife artists because you only need water to mix them, but watercolour in particular can be a difficult and unforgiving medium to master as the transparency makes it difficult to correct mistakes. Beginners often find gouache easier as mistakes can be painted over. A cheap set of hard watercolour paints in their little individual 'pans' provides as good a way as any to get used to working with a brush. However, the semi-liquid tube paints give more vibrant results and mixing is easier. If you're using liquid paints (whether gouache or watercolour) you'll need something to mix them on – a plastic or ceramic plate will do fine.

↑ Gouache paint is water-soluble – you can use white gouache to add highlights to a watercolour painting as in this one of a Bonaparte's Gull.

→ Paper for watercolour paintings often has a pleasing rough texture, and can be bought in tinted shades which show through the transparent watercolour washes.

Watercolour paper
Paper used for watercolour or gouache work needs to be quite heavy or it will warp when it gets wet and lose its shape on drying. Most watercolour paper is at least 300gsm. It is usually quite a textured paper, though hot-pressed paper has a smooth surface (it is, however, more expensive than the rougher cold-pressed paper). You can use lighter-weight paper for watercolours if you stretch it first – this means soaking it thoroughly, then taping it down flat to a piece of board while it's still wet. It will then dry flat and and you can paint on it.

ACRYLICS AND OILS

These two paint types are more challenging and less widely used by wildlife artists in general. Acrylics are water-soluble and dry to a hard, plastic film rather than soaking into the paper like watercolours and gouache. This gives a distinct glossy look to an acrylic painting. Most oil paints need to be mixed with a thinning solvent like turpentine, and linseed oil is mixed in to keep the paint flexible as you apply it in repeated thin layers. Oils in particular are slow to dry, and so can be manipulated a great deal on the paper or canvas to produce a very textured, almost sculptured effect. Specialist paper is available for both acrylic and oil painting.

PASTELS

A sort of evolved version of the chalk and crayons we used at school, pastels are sticks of colour, usually used on thin, rough-textured and sometimes tinted paper. They come in two forms – chalk, which has a powdery texture, and oil, which is more waxy. Chalk pastels smudge very easily, an attribute which can be useful when blending colours but means you need to use them carefully to avoid ruining your work. Oil pastels are a little less smudgy, and so easier to use, though working in fine detail is difficult with either – they are more suited to looser, colourful interpretations. With both types, you'll need to seal your work with a fixative spray to prevent smudging.

↓ A typical pastels set contains a great many colours, and they can be blended together to make more (though the pure colours will always be more dazzling).

Mixing your media

As if that weren't enough, many artists have fun combining two or more different painting or drawing media in the same artwork. Some classic combinations include line and wash, where a drawing in ink is coloured with watercolour washes, or using pastels to add opaque highlights to a transparent watercolour work.

← Red Grouse in pastels. Chalk pastels are fun to use and offer vivid colours, though precise detail can be hard to capture unless you work at a very large scale.

DRAWING FROM LIFE

If you're drawing something from life just to help you identify it, you can (and often should) use cheats, short cuts and other tricks to ensure you get down the salient features as best you can in the time you have. If you're drawing from life to improve your artistic skills, the rules change completely. You're no longer looking for a record of fine details, but you're seeking to capture something of the essence of the subject. The good news is that it doesn't really matter what the subject is – everything is fair game.

↗ When drawing from life, give yourself lots of space on the page. It helps to choose a fairly settled-looking subject, like this Woodpigeon.

SKETCHING MOVING ANIMALS

This can be hugely challenging. Watching a party of small garden birds coming and going around a bird feeder, for example, you'll struggle to see more than a moment of stillness. However, you don't need stillness to make a meaningful sketch. What you need is time, patience and a readiness to work fast when the moment is right. Get yourself settled and comfortable, and wait. First of all you might only get a line or two before your chosen bird has moved or gone. Don't worry, start a new sketch on the same page, and another. Soon you'll see a different bird has assumed the same pose as the one you've already started to draw, and you can add a bit to that sketch.

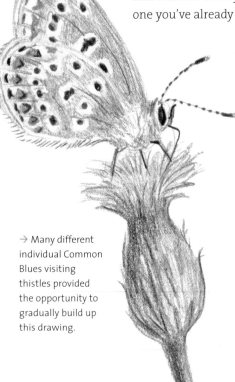

→ Many different individual Common Blues visiting thistles provided the opportunity to gradually build up this drawing.

ARE YOU SITTING COMFORTABLY?

If you don't have one already, now's the time to invest in a folding seat of some kind, as you're likely to want to sit in one spot for a long time. A simple folding stool is light and cheap – for a little more weight and money you can have a more evolved folding chair with a proper back and even armrests with built-in drinks pockets. I've already mentioned rucksacks with built-in folding chairs in Chapter 3 – there are also specialised 'seat bags' available for artists, which may not be as comfy to carry as a rucksack but have storage space designed for art materials as well as a comfy seat. For working in birdwatching hides, the built-in seats and shelves will usually suffice, and often you can just sit on the ground. If you carry a small waterproof bag or mat with you, it won't matter if the ground in question isn't completely dry.

Also, with time, your mind's eye will hold onto each moment a little longer and allow you to add more detail.

Slow it down
The garden feeding station is possibly the trickiest place for your life sketching that you could have picked. You might prefer to start with something more sedate. If your local park has a pond, chances are there will be a number of larger birds like ducks and geese around, which are much less flighty and will give you some longer poses. You could also visit a zoo, where you'll be able to draw a variety of animals on the move (or not) at easy viewing ranges.

CHOOSING PAINTS AND BRUSHES
For outdoors painting from life, you need to hone down your kit for portability and ease of use. Take only a few brushes – perhaps a large round brush for washes, a small square one for filling in smaller areas, and a fine round brush for detail. When choosing paints, a set of hard watercolour pans is easier to manage than tubes of paint, and the lid of the tin will serve as a mixing palette. Carry your mixing water in a lidded beaker.

WHAT'S YOUR BACKGROUND?
If you're hoping to be making pictures of animals within their natural habitat, you're going to have to draw parts of that habitat as well. If you're sitting around waiting for an animal to come along so you can draw it, use that time profitably and try your hand at sketching some of the natural details around you. That could include plant foliage, bare branches, bark textures and patterns, reflections on water, clouds or even details of the built environment. Then when you're making your finished piece, you can put together the most pleasing combinations of subject and background – a trick that many photographers wish they could emulate.

← No animals around? Don't ignore the plants, and rocks, and other static habitat elements. Your sketches will be useful references for future artworks.

PAINTING AND DRAWING FROM PHOTOS

How often have you taken a photo that looks great apart from one thing – it's a bit out of focus, or a bit too dark, or the composition is spoilt by an intrusive bit of litter or other distracting element? Photo-editing software helps deal with these problems, but another option if you're artistically inclined is to use your imperfect photo as the basis for an artwork. Many artists work almost exclusively from photos and learn camera skills just to provide themselves with material. Your interpretation of a photo need not be completely literal either – it can be the basis for a very free and stylised artwork.

↑ One of the advantages of painting from a photograph is that you can leave out the unwanted elements, like the distracting extra twigs in this House Sparrow photo.

COPYING

Trying to do a faithful drawing from a photo is a good discipline to try, as it will really focus your powers of observation. Some artists clip a small printed photo to the corner of their canvases, but in today's digital age you can display your photo on screen at whatever size you like.

A time-honoured method of copying a photo is to overlay a grid of squares on it, and draw a corresponding grid (scaled up or down as appropriate) on your paper. Then you can see exactly which parts of the image should go in which square, so that everything will stay in the right proportions. You can use image-editing software to add a grid to a photo (in a new layer so it doesn't affect the original photo file), and then draw the corresponding grid lightly on your paper so you can erase it once all the outlines are in place.

INTERPRETING

If meticulous copying isn't your thing, photos can still be helpful references. You can take as much or as little from a reference photo as you like – just the colours, just the shapes or use the photo to get a small detail right. Then let your imagination do the rest.

TAKING PHOTOS FOR ARTWORKS

Not every photo has what it takes to be the basis of a pleasing artwork. However, sometimes if you combine elements from several, you can pull together exactly the sort of image you want. If you like working from photos, take lots of them, so you have a decent library of reference material. If you see a beautiful lakeside view that just needs a Kingfisher darting over the water for perfection, take a photo – you can add the bird yourself when you do the painting. A photo of a flower and another of a butterfly can be combined in a single painting to show off the beauty of both. There's no need to splash out on a pricey camera for this, as it doesn't matter if your photos aren't brilliant; you only need certain elements to work for them to be a useful reference for you.

Authenticity

Whether you want your paintings to accurately reflect real life – both in their subject matter and the fine details of how you capture the subjects, that's up to you. If this is important to you, take care when building an artwork using a variety of photos as references, or you may end up with a butterfly found only in the south of England on a flower that only grows in the Scottish Highlands.

↓ This portrait of a Fallow Deer buck is not especially inspiring, but provides a good artistic reference of the species' head shape and antler structure.

HIGH-SPEED SKETCHING

Here's a way to imitate the challenge of drawing fast-moving animals from life while sitting in front of your computer. Collect your favourite digital animal photos in a folder on your computer, then set your screensaver to display a slide-show of the images, changing randomly every 10 or 20 seconds. When the screensaver displays an image, try making lightning sketches of each one – sometimes trying to capture an idea of the whole animal, sometimes focusing on a single small detail.

↖ These lightning bird sketches were drawn from a slideshow of photos on the computer screen, each image shown for 15 seconds.

DRAWING TECHNIQUES

Pick up pencil, apply pointy end to paper... is there much more to drawing than that? There doesn't have to be. However, as you get more experienced and confident you'll find lots of new ways to create the effects you want with pencils, charcoal, coloured pencils and other drawing materials.

LINES

A simple, lightly drawn line with a hard pencil is ideal for creating outlines, as it's faint already, and can be removed with a rubber if you want to, once the next layer of the artwork is in place. Simple, lightweight lines are also good for creating the textures of fur and feathers. You can build up the lines in areas of darker colour or shadow, and omit them in areas where strong light takes away the details of texture.

USING SIMPLE SHAPES TO BUILD COMPLEXITY

Earlier in this chapter, we looked at how you can create a creditable outline of an animal using a couple of oval shapes joined together. You can break down pretty much any object into a collection of simple geometric forms – circles, ovals, triangles, single lines. When you're making your initial outline, try to see the shapes that fit together to make your subject's complete form. With the outline of a bird, you can begin with the two ovals for its head and body, join them up with lines, then add a triangle for its bill, a circle for its eye, an oval for the main part of the wing, a triangle for the wing tip, then small overlapping ovals for the wing feathers, and so on, building up finer and finer detail until you have the whole shape expressed as a collection of simpler shapes.

↗ Drawn very lightly with an H pencil, this accurate drawing of a Meadow Pipit was used as the basis for the gouache painting overleaf.

→ Using cross-hatching is a neat and tidy way to build up depth of shading in line drawings, like this of a Four-spotted Chaser dragonfly.

SHADING

If you angle your pencil so the 'lead' hits the paper side-on you can made a softer and broader mark, ideal for quickly creating areas of soft, even shading. Using a softer pencil will help you build up the shading more quickly, though your pencil will wear down rather fast. With coloured pencils, overlaying shading of two colours will produce a third colour.

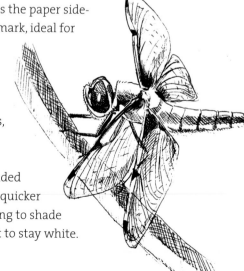

You can recover highlights from shaded areas by using a good quality rubber, a quicker and sometimes neater option than trying to shade around the area of paper that you want to stay white.

Using lines to create shading

You can also build up areas of shading using lines, with cross-hatching. Start off by filling in the area you want to be shaded with lots of fine lines, all angled the same way. Then go over the area again with more fine lines, this time at right angles to the first set. You can repeat this as often as you want to create the required depth of shading – just make sure you keep your sets of lines angled the same way for a neat effect.

↑ Pencil shading can be created in many ways. This Marbled White butterfly was shaded using the pencil tip, but the background shading was done with the edge of the 'lead'.

→ Combining coloured pencil shading with ink drawing is a good way to produce strongly outlined colour artworks, as with this Bearded Tit.

Using watercolour pencils

These pencils work just like coloured pencils until you apply water to them, when the colours dissolve into the water and can then be moved around with a paintbrush. This means you don't have to shade in the colour too precisely, as you'll be able to even it out when it's wet. If you want your picture to be a mixture of strong lines and softer watercolour washes, you could use your watercolour pencils in combination with inks which aren't water-soluble, so the ink lines remain intact when you start applying the water.

← Watercolour pencils make marks like any coloured pencil, but apply water to the marks and you can create smooth washes of colour.

PAINTING TECHNIQUES

You only have to look at the array of paintbrushes on sale in your local art shop to get an idea of how many different ways there are to paint. Brushes are just part of the story. There is an array of other accessories to help achieve different effects. When you're starting out you'll probably just want to use your paints in a similar way to how you would use pencils, but you're bound to get more adventurous with time and practice.

↑ Gouache paint was applied over the line drawing on the previous page, with washes used to build up background shades, and a small brush to 'draw on' the fine detail.

→ With just black, white and grey pastels, you can make very quick paintings of monochrome subjects like this juvenile Kittiwake.

BUILDING UP COLOUR AND DETAIL

The standard way of creating a watercolour or gouache painting goes like this. First you draw very light outlines of the subject matter with a hard pencil. Then you use quite diluted paint and a large brush to apply the first washes of colour. With watercolours, you need to work quite fast at this stage. If you start painting a blue sky and stop halfway, returning to it when the first half is dry, you'll find that smoothly blending the second half in will be almost impossible. However, this quality of watercolours can be used to your advantage. A wet wash on top of a dry one blends the two shades evenly, while two wet washes of different colours will swirl together in somewhat unpredictable but often beautiful ways.

From here you'll progressively add more and deeper washes of colour over smaller areas, using progressively finer brushes, finishing with the final details in the darkest tones, as it's much easier to make a colour darker than lighter, especially in watercolour. With the opacity of gouache paints, it's easier to apply light tones over dark, and you can even use white gouache paint as an 'eraser', painting over mistakes or creating highlights.

Protection

Watercolour and gouache paintings should be protected from dust and dirt by keeping them covered (in a plastic document sleeve) until they are framed. Pastel paintings need a coating of fixative spray (or hairspray) to stop smudging, while oils and acrylics are often varnished for protection. Keep all artworks, especially watercolours, away from direct sunlight as this can fade them.

USING MASKING FLUID

This pale whitish fluid dries to a rubbery consistency. If you begin your artwork by painting masking fluid over the parts that you want to stay white or pale and then letting it dry, you can paint over the whole thing with impunity rather than having to carefully work around the edges of the bits that need to stay white. When you have finished, you can remove the dried masking fluid by rubbing it off, and you'll be left with pristine white highlights of unpainted paper.

↓ In the Sika Deer pastel painting (a), the colours were blended together, smoothing out the shades. In the Rabbit painting (b) the pastels were used unblended for a rougher texture.

PAINTING WITH PASTELS

Because a pastel is a stick of solid colour, you can either use its tip to make fine details, or use it on its side to make a broad sweep of colour. Overlaying one colour on another blends the two shades – with chalk pastels you can blend them further by using your fingertips to rub the colours together. If you don't want to get your hands too dirty, use cotton wool to do the blending or wear a latex glove.

↓ This Whinchat on its thorny perch was drawn with a pen, then painted over with watercolour washes, and finished with coloured pencil shading.

OIL AND ACRYLIC TECHNIQUES

You can use oil and acrylic paints as thickly or thinly as you like, and both can be built up in progressive layers. Let each layer dry before you begin the next. Oil paint needs to be mixed with linseed oil to keep it supple, and because the oil will sink through towards the canvas or paper, you need to use progressively more linseed oil with each new layer that you add to your painting. If you don't, your painting could crack when it's dry. For large oil paintings you may need to use coarse, hogshair brushes or a palette knife to apply the paint effectively.

CHOOSING A CAMERA

Photography has become everyone's favourite hobby since digital cameras took away the need for expensive rolls of film and the long wait to see how your pictures turned out. Wildlife-watching brings such wonderful moments that it's only natural to want to capture them permanently, and now it's possible for everyone to achieve this – whatever their experience and equipment.

WHAT ARE THE OPTIONS?

There are two main kinds of digital cameras – compacts, with a single built-in and (usually) zoom lens, and DSLRs (single-lens reflex cameras) which come as a 'body' to which you can attach different lenses. However, within each of those two groups is a whole world of choice. Many digital devices with other primary purposes, such as mobile phones and MP3 or MP4 players, now come with a built-in compact digital camera, and some of these are very good though rather limited in terms of creative controls. Then there are very small and pocketable compact cameras with flat profiles and a lens that 'telescopes' out when in use but is normally retracted. Most have a selection of 'modes' but not too much fine control.

The next level up is the so-called 'bridge' camera. Although bridge cameras are compacts in that they have one built-in lens, they are more solidly built with more controls, giving you more creative freedom, and the lens offers a longer zoom range – in some cases approaching that of a serious DSLR telephoto lens. Naturally, they are also more pricey than basic compacts.

BUT IS IT ART?

You could easily spend thousands on a top-end DSLR plus a bushel of professional lenses and still take bad photos. Even if you do have those thousands to spare, it is well worth learning your craft on a simpler system first. Good photography is as much about imagination, an eye for a good composition and quick reflexes to capture a fleeting moment. You can begin to understand how the technical basics work with a simple compact, and transfer this knowledge when you move on to a more complex system.

← This photo was taken on holiday with a very basic compact – of course, the beautiful scenery of Sri Lanka helped to make a good photo.

↑ A DSLR with long zoom lens. A lens this size can be used hand-held, but results are often better if it is mounted on a tripod.

→ A 'bridge' camera with a long zoom range is the most affordable way to get enough 'reach' for small and easily scared-off wildlife like this Chaffinch.

↓ The Digital Photography Review is a must-read when choosing a new camera, as it offers detailed and unbiased reviews of a huge array of models.

DLSR cameras offer a big step up in image quality and creative control. The camera itself has a huge array of controls, and the lenses available from the main makers range from relatively affordable short zooms to very expensive 600mm telephotos, with pretty much everything else you can think of in between. The flexibility and quality of the DSLR system means it is the professional's choice, but it will take you more time and work to get the best out of it.

DO YOUR HOMEWORK

Once you've decided what camera you need, get online to look for reviews of models in the range that interest you. The website Digital Photography Review (**www.dpreview.com**) offers detailed, reliable and unbiased reviews of a huge range of cameras and accessories. Read the photography sections of wildlife forums such as the RSPB (**www.rspb.org.uk/community/forums**), Wild About Britain (**www.wildaboutbritain.co.uk/forums**) or Birdforum (**www.birdforum.net/forum.php**). You should be able to find out on these sites how the camera or cameras you have in mind perform for people primarily interested in wildlife photography.

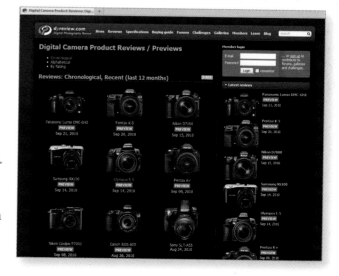

SORTING OUT THE JARGON

Whatever your camera, there are some technical basics which apply across all systems, and it's a good idea to get your head around the fundamental terminology and what it means sooner rather than later. Space only permits a quick introduction here, but the deeper your interest in photography becomes and the more pictures you take, the more you'll come to understand how it all fits together.

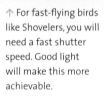

APERTURE AND SHUTTER SPEED

When your camera takes a photo, light passes through a small hole behind the lens, and reaches the sensor where the light is converted into a digital image. Like the pupil in our eye, this hole can be made larger or smaller to admit more or less light – its size is controlled by the camera's aperture ring. Therefore the size of the hole is called its aperture, and it is described by a number preceded by the letter f. High numbers relate to small apertures, so f2.8 means a much bigger hole than f22. It will take the same amount of light longer to get through a f22 aperture than an f2.8 one.

Speed and light The shutter normally covers the aperture ring, but when you press the shutter button on your camera it opens and allows light to go through. A shutter speed, or exposure, reading tells you how long the shutter will be open, and it's expressed as a fraction of a second – 1/1,000, 1/500 and so on.

Therefore, how much light reaches the sensor depends on both of these things – the size of the aperture and the shutter speed. Too much light getting in means the image will be overexposed (too white), not enough will give you a dark, underexposed image. A small aperture (such as f22) means you'll need a longer exposure to get enough light in, but the longer the shutter speed, the more chance of blur from camera shake or the subject moving.

↑ For fast-flying birds like Shovelers, you will need a fast shutter speed. Good light will make this more achievable.

→ For macro shots, it is often good to 'stop down' to a smaller aperture for more depth of field. This shot of a female Common Blue was taken at f8, with a lens of maximum aperture f3.5.

Taking control Balancing the two factors correctly is how you'll take in-focus and correctly exposed images. Most cameras can be set to prioritise either shutter speed or aperture, so one factor is fixed at whatever your preference and the camera adjusts

Depth of field

In every photo there is a distance from the camera where the subject matter is at its sharpest focus. Everything else that's closer to you or further away in the image will be less sharp. Depth of field expresses how wide the 'slice' of good focus is, and it is affected by shutter speed and aperture. For maximum depth of field you will need a small aperture and a long shutter speed. Landscape photographers often seek this combination, and usually use a tripod to keep the camera steady during the resultant long exposure. Wildlife photographers often want a blurred background so that the subject stands out, and favour the opposite combination – large aperture and short exposure.

the other factor accordingly. In fully automatic modes, the camera makes its 'best guess' for both factors.

↑ Only a narrow 'slice' of this Common Lizard is in sharp focus. A narrower aperture would increase the depth of field, but slow the shutter speed.

↓ A slow shutter speed of two seconds was used to blur the flowing water. The camera was on a tripod for stability, keeping the rest of the detail in focus.

ISO

This is a measurement of how sensitive the camera's sensor is to light, and you can adjust it or have the camera adjust automatically. A low ISO (International Standards Organisation) number means low sensitivity to light and is suitable for bright conditions. In duller conditions you may need to increase the ISO to get the same shutter speed. The drawback to using higher ISOs is that your images will be coarser, showing a speckled effect called 'noise'. DSLRs give less noisy results than compacts at high ISOs.

METERING

This is how your camera decides on the amount of light in the scene you're photographing and works out what the shutter speed and aperture should be. Many cameras have a general metering mode where the camera looks at light in the whole scene, and spot-metering where the camera just looks at a small part of the scene that you're focusing on. Spot-metering is helpful to get the right exposure when you are photographing an image that's mostly dark or mostly pale.

THE BASIC COMPACT

You may own a camera like this already, on your phone or MP3 player if not as an independent entity. It has many advantages. You can buy one for less than the cost of a trip to the supermarket, and you can carry it around in your pocket and hardly know it's there. It obviously has limitations, but if you know what those are and respect them, there's no reason why you can't take rewarding wildlife photos with the simplest compact. If you upgrade to a more elaborate bridge camera, your options open up even more.

↑ This Poplar Hawkmoth was photographed with a camera phone, demonstrating how good even simple compacts can be with macro subjects.

↗ An ordinary compact is good for landscapes, but for wildlife you'll probably long for more reach (the speck on the rock in the centre is a Peregrine Falcon!).

WHAT YOU GET

Your compact camera will have a viewscreen for reviewing images, which may take up almost the whole back of the camera. On top will be the controls – a shutter button, perhaps a button to activate the pop-up flash, a zoom lever and a control wheel offering you a choice of photography modes. Then at the front is the lens, which will have an optical zoom range of anything between 3x and 12x (18x or more in a bridge camera). The lens may be protected behind a cover, which slides back when you switch the camera on. Bridge cameras are shaped more like DSLRs, are bigger and are designed to fit a natural grip, and with a larger and more protruding lens.

WHEN TO ZOOM

As a wildlife photographer, you'll often be wanting to photograph subjects that are far away. Anything short of an 8x zoom will probably prove disappointing in this

A MATTER OF MEGAPIXELS

When you're choosing a compact camera, it's easy to be seduced by two numbers – the zoom range of the lens and the number of megapixels. While more zoom is generally a good thing, vast quantities of megapixels aren't worth the extra money, as their usefulness depends on the size of the camera's sensor. Basically, what you want in order to shoot better pictures are bigger pixels, not more of them. If you're torn between two 12 megapixel cameras, the one with the larger sensor will give you the better image quality, and will also perform better in low light.

respect, but even if you do have enough zoomability, you should not expect too much from your compact at the extreme end of its zoom range, especially in low light. Experiment with your camera's capabilities at different light levels – most zooms will not be great at their long end unless the light is very good. You might be better off seeking a harmonious composition with your subject a little smaller in the frame.

↖ A Small Copper butterfly. One advantage of compacts over DSLRs is size and weight – it is even possible to use them one-handed.

USING MODES

The fully automatic mode on compacts is usually called 'P' for 'program' but you can think of it as P for 'point and shoot', as it works out the best settings for a sharp and well-exposed photo on its own, you just point and shoot. Aperture-priority and shutter-speed-priority modes, where you set an aperture or shutter speed respectively, are usually shortened to 'A' and 'S' or 'Av' and 'Tv', but check your manual as some cameras use different codes or symbols.

↓ With the right (and not too distant) subject and good light conditions, compact cameras can give results comparable to those of DSLRs (this is a Comma).

Instant options
Many cameras have other modes such as 'portrait', 'landscape', 'night-time' and so on, designated with little symbols. They tell the camera which settings to prioritise – for example a 'portrait' mode will seek to give you a shallow depth of field so your subject stands out from its background, while a 'landscape' mode will give you a good depth of field, and 'night-time' will give you longer exposures for dark conditions.

One mode or setting you will probably use a lot is the 'macro' mode, often designated with an image of a flower. This lets you focus on things closer than normal, so that small objects will be larger in the frame than in other modes.

DSLR CAMERAS

Most people deciding to buy a DSLR will probably already have had some experience with a simpler (and less expensive) compact camera of some kind, and will see the move up to a DSLR as a natural progression. Of course, there's nothing to stop you jumping straight in and buying a DSLR as your first camera, but be prepared for a long learning process and perhaps some disappointing results until you learn how to get the most from what is a very sophisticated piece of equipment.

↓ This full-frame Chiffchaff photo (a) from a DSLR withstands considerable cropping (b) with little loss of quality thanks to the camera's large sensor.

SORT OUT YOUR BUDGET

The first thing you need to keep in mind when buying a DSLR is how much the camera body costs on its own. Your budget needs to accommodate not just the camera but at least one lens. Often DSLRs are sold as a 'kit' with a relatively useful zoom lens or perhaps two. Everything will be a little cheaper than it would have been to buy individually, but this is a false economy if the kit lenses are not ones that you actually want. You may also need to set aside some cash for a camera bag and tripod.

WHAT FEATURES DO YOU WANT?

As with compact cameras, number of megapixels is not something to get excited about, but sensor size is, as large sensors will give you the best images. Some DSLRs have 'full frame' sensors which are the same size as 35mm film, while others have 'crop' sensors which are smaller. The full-frame camera will be better in lower light and for wide-angle photography but will be more expensive. The crop sensor will effectively magnify the image, which means this kind of camera is often preferred by wildlife photographers.

Frame rate Another important factor is frame rate. If you are photographing an action-packed scene, you will want as many photos as possible to try to capture the 'one' that reveals the action clearly. The cheapest DSLRs may offer three frames a second, with higher-end models going up to ten or more.

Higher ISOs How the camera performs at higher ISOs is something else to investigate. As

ONE SYSTEM FOR LIFE?

Choosing a DSLR can be a bit of a commitment. You might start off with only one lens, but over the years you'll accumulate more, along with other extras – perhaps a flash, a teleconverter or two, filters, extension tubes... and you could end up with thousands of pounds worth of equipment, all belonging to a single system. If you start out with a Canon DSLR, gradually buy more lenses and other equipment but then decide, a few years down the line, that you should have opted for Nikon (or vice versa), it's an expensive mistake to correct. So it's worth taking a lot of time over your choice right from the start, and you should also be thinking about what additional lenses you might want to buy later on.

a dedicated wildlife photographer, out from dawn to dusk in all weathers (well, maybe), you'll often be shooting in low light so will need to use a higher ISO rating. Cameras vary greatly in how 'noisy' their images become as ISO goes up, and it's worth perusing the internet for reviews that show sample images at a range of ISOs. Given that poor high-ISO performance is a key reason why many wildlife photographers eventually find bridge cameras unsatisfactory, this is something you'll really want to get right.

↖ For reasonably approachable wildlife like this young Grey Heron, a DSLR with a modest zoom lens is more than adequate.

USING YOUR DSLR

With all those controls, things can quickly get confusing. It really is worth reading the manual straight away so you know what does what, and how to fix things if you accidentally press the wrong button and see a display on screen that you didn't expect. Once you have the controls worked out, do some serious experimenting. Shoot the same subject at different settings, see how this affects depth of field, image noise, focus. Time spent getting familiar with your camera and what it can do in various settings will pay dividends when you're out in the field, faced with that once-in-a-lifetime opportunity to photograph something really special.

↑ A Marmalade Hoverfly on a sunflower – even if you mostly take photos in your garden, you can have a lot of fun with a DSLR and macro lens.

a

b

CHOOSING DSLR LENSES

So you've taken the plunge and bought a DSLR camera – perhaps a low-priced entry-level model, perhaps something more expensive. Now you're faced with more tricky decisions – which lenses do you need? All of the main makes of DSLR take a wide variety of lens types, some from the same maker as the camera body, others from 'third party' lens makers, and some are undoubtedly more useful for wildlife photography than others. The best ones for you depend mainly on three factors – your preferred subject matter, budget and how much weight you're prepared to carry.

↑ This Green-veined White butterfly (a) was photographed with an ordinary 70–300mm lens, and is reasonably large in the frame. However, to capture tiny details like this Speckled Bush-cricket's weird moving mouthparts (b), you'll need a macro lens.

UNDERSTANDING THE SPECS

SLR lenses are described in terms of their focal length (in mm) and their maximum aperture or 'f-number', expressed as a number preceded by 'f' – eg, 'f2.8'. As explained on page 130, the larger the aperture, the smaller the f-number. A 400mm lens magnifies about as much as a pair of 8x binoculars (but note the two systems are very different and any comparison should be taken as a rough guide only). A lens with a large maximum aperture needs a large front element (the disc of glass at the front of the lens) to admit plenty of light, and this will greatly increase the overall size and weight of the lens. For example, the Nikon 300mm f2.8 lens weighs twice as much and costs four times more than the Nikon 300mm f4 lens. However, the former lens should be able to take sharper photographs (especially in low light) as its light-gathering power will give you quicker shutter speeds.

GOING LONG

For a lot of wildlife shots you'll want a long or telephoto lens. There are many reasonably priced zoom lenses on the market which reach 300mm – 70–300mm is a very popular range. However, if you are seriously interested in bird photography you will soon long for a little more magnification. Zooms that reach 500mm should fit the bill, and there are several reasonably priced options.

Telephoto primes tend to be a lot more expensive than zooms, reflecting their superior optics – many are marketed as 'professional' lenses. You can also use teleconverters with prime lenses, increasing the magnification by a factor of 1.4, 1.7 or 2. Teleconverters and zoom lenses rarely go well together because the converter reduces the lens's maximum aperture, making it difficult to get a sharp photo. This is less of a problem with a prime lens as most have a larger maximum aperture to begin with so can withstand the loss more readily.

Getting close
Macro lenses allow you to focus on objects at very close range. You can take perfectly adequate photos of largish insects or flowers with an average telephoto lens, but for real minute detail you will need a dedicated macro lens. They come in a range of focal lengths between 50 and 200mm – for flighty insects a longer macro will be better, but for most purposes a lens in the 90–110mm range will do nicely and will be fairly affordable.

↓ These Black-headed Gulls were photographed on the same perch from the same hide with two different zoom lenses – (a) with a 150–500mm lens at 500mm, and (b) with a 300–800mm lens at 800mm. That increased magnification comes at a price though – the bigger lens is three times heavier than the 150–500mm, and seven times its price.

ZOOM OR PRIME?

A lens which has just one focal length is called a prime lens. Such lenses are often better optically than zooms, which give you a range of focal lengths. However, a zoom lens gives you flexibility to photograph a range of different subjects at different distances, and zooms are often easier to use than primes – you can find your subject in the frame with the lens at its shortest focal length, then zoom in to the magnification you want. Canon's 28–300mm f3.5–5.6 lens offers you a very acceptable wide angle for landscape photos at the short end, and a quite powerful telephoto for distant subjects at the long end, plus everything in between. Sigma's 50–500mm f4–6.3 lens gives you a fantastic optical range. Both of these lenses offer a larger maximum aperture at the shorter end than the longer end, a common trait of zoom lenses.

KEEPING IT STABLE

If the lens you're using with your DSLR is a small one, your hands will provide all the support it needs. However, the bigger the lens, the more chance there is that camera shake will affect your images, and you'll need some extra stability, especially in lower light when shutter speeds will slow down. Some lenses fall between two stools in that you can sometimes use them hand-held and sometimes not, while others are so big and heavy that hand-holding them is simply a physical impossibility.

LEANING ON A LAMP POST

↓ This Subalpine Warbler was photographed using a long lens supported on a monopod, that allows greater freedom of movement for the photographer.

The simplest extra support you can give your camera is by resting your arms or your whole body on something stable as you take the picture. You could sit on a bench and rest your elbows on your knees or lean back against a tree – small things like this can make a surprising amount of difference when you're working with biggish lenses and/or slowish shutter speeds.

BEANBAGS

Sometimes you may find a solid support – perhaps a rock, a wall or a tree branch – at just the right height, though it might not necessarily be something your lens will balance on well. Here's where a beanbag comes in handy. Place it on your chosen support then settle the camera lens onto the beanbag. It will provide a stable and protective cushion for your lens. You can buy photography beanbags but it's very easy to make your own. If you go the DIY route, make it with an outer cover and a removable inner pouch for the beans, then you can take it on holidays empty and fill it up when you arrive.

← This low-light shot was stabilised by placing the camera on the log from which the fungi grew, and using the self-timer to eliminate camera shake.

↓ Holding a long lens steady is a strain on the arms and it's hard to avoid camera shake. The solution is to use a tripod, fitted with a strong head.

TRIPODS

A tripod is the standard support of choice for most photographers using big heavy lenses, as well as landscape photographers who need support for long exposures and macro photographers who also often need slower shutter speeds to achieve enough depth of field. It has three extendable legs and (usually) a central column. The lens is attached via a thread drilled into its base. Tripods come in a variety of sizes and materials. Lightweight is good for carrying long distances, but make sure the tripod can deal with the weight of the lens you want to use on it.

Tripods used for telescopes usually have a pan-and-tilt head, for easy and smooth side-to-side movement. For photography, other heads are sometimes seen, such as the ball-and-socket head which gives almost complete freedom of movement, making it easy to switch to a portrait mode or whatever angle you like. However, manipulating a heavy lens on a ball-and-socket head can be awkward, as the weight distribution is imperfect and the whole assembly will flop over if you're not careful.

A HEAD FOR WEIGHTS

The kind of head favoured by users of seriously heavy lenses is the 'gimbal' head, which is very strong and designed to naturally and perfectly balance the lens so you can move it around lightly and easily, with no risk of 'flop'. The downside with these heads is that they are costly, but if you've already invested in a big, heavy and expensive telephoto lens, you'll probably not resent the additional cost of an appropriate tripod head for it too much as it will protect both lens and tripod, and will help ensure your photos are sharp.

MONOPODS

Monopods, as the name suggests, have just one telescopic leg, which means they are much lighter and easier to carry around than tripods. Of course, they don't stand up on their own either, but that one leg gives you a solid connection to planet Earth and often that's enough stability for a mid-sized telephoto lens.

→ This Great Tit was photographed from a car in low light. Supporting the lens on the car window gave just enough stability for a clear shot at 1/80th of a second.

THE EXTRAS

If you're using a small compact camera, the only extra stuff you'll want to carry will be spare batteries and memory cards. As you move up through more elaborate camera systems, the array of 'extras' grows more extensive. There are teleconverters, filters and external flashes available for bridge cameras, and for DSLRs you can include all of this and plenty more besides. This section looks at some of the more useful and relevant bits and bobs you might want to throw into the camera bag.

ESSENTIALS

Compact cameras generally take the smaller and cheaper SD cards while DSLRs take compact flash cards. The amount of photos a card will hold depends on the resolution of your camera, and what image quality settings you're using, so a 4GB card could hold as many as 2,000 photos or as few as 300. You should also carry at least one spare battery or set of batteries, and a lens cleaning cloth.

OPTICAL ENHANCERS

Teleconverters Teleconverters are attachments that increase the magnification of your lens. On a DSLR they go in between the lens and the camera body, and the standard sizes are 1.4x, 1.7x and 2x. Because teleconverters give your lens a smaller maximum aperture (for example, a 1.4x converter changes an f4 lens to an f5.6 lens), they work best with prime lenses that have large maximum apertures. Check before you buy that the teleconverter you want will work with your lens – sometimes using a teleconverter disables the autofocus function. Teleconverters for bridge cameras go on the end of the lens and will give best results if you use them only in very good light.

↑ Purpose-built camera bags have padded pockets for your lenses and camera body, and moveable partitions so you can adapt them to your kit.

Extension tubes Extension tubes can be used with DSLRs and also go between the camera and the lens. They contain no glass, and so don't alter the image, but allow you to focus more closely on near objects. Using an extension tube therefore effectively turns an ordinary lens into a macro lens.

Filters Filters contain a single piece of glass and go on the end of a lens. They have different effects on the image. Polarising filters reduce reflected light, so are great for photographing underwater wildlife. 'Close-up' filters work like reading glasses, enabling a lens to focus more closely. There are also various coloured filters available, to give more intensely blue skies or a sepia tint to your photos.

A UV (ultraviolet) filter eliminates ultraviolet light, making little difference to most images, but it also provides an inexpensive and non-intrusive way to protect the front element of an expensive lens from scratches.

MAINTENANCE AND PROTECTION

Besides the trusty cleaning cloth, you might also want to buy a brush blower, which has a squeezable bulb and a soft brush for blowing and brushing dust off your camera's optics. A cleaning solution especially for photographic gear can be used to remove more stubborn dirt. A plastic rain hood may be useful too, as most cameras are not truly waterproof.

... AND ALL THE REST

External flash An external flash unit is useful if you're taking shots at night or need extra light. A cable release allows you to take photos remotely – useful for 'set-up' shots when you need to stay hidden – and you can also buy remote-control units to control many of your camera's functions from a distance.

Camera bag A good camera bag is a must with delicate optical kit – well padded with compartments for each lens. Shoulder bags give easy access; rucksacks are more comfortable on long walks.

Downloading on the move

On a long trip, some portable means of downloading photos from the memory cards will be helpful. If you have a laptop with you you'll just need a card reader or a USB cable to connect your camera directly. Portable hard disks are a compact way of backing up your images, and some portable storage devices incorporate a viewscreen and simple interface.

↑ An external flash was needed for this indoor shot of a Harlequin Ladybird which appeared on the kitchen table.

↖ A 1.4x teleconverter turns a 300mm f4 prime lens into a 420mm f5.6 lens, fine for shy, smallish birds like this Green Sandpiper.

↓ A portable hard drive is an easy and fairly secure way to back up your photos, and you can connect it to any computer to view or edit the images.

COMPOSE YOURSELF

If you know what your camera's buttons do, you're on your way towards taking good photos. However, you'll also need a good eye and creativity. Some people are naturally skilled at seeing and seizing beautiful moments while for others this is a skill that needs to be learned. Additionally, there are some helpful generalities about good picture-taking which everyone should know about, even though it's good to bend the rules from time to time.

COMPOSITION

This describes the arrangement of the different elements in your photo. There will usually be an obvious main subject... and sometimes that's all there is (for example, in a photo of a bird in flight). More often, though, there are other elements – some background or perhaps some other things sharing the foreground with the subject. However much 'stuff' there is in your photo, there will always be more and less harmonious ways for them to fit together.

↑ This Pied Wagtail shot shows a simple composition, with the bird positioned roughly at the top right 'third', moving into the frame. Its reflection has equal space.

Go off-centre The rules of composition say that you shouldn't place your subject in the exact centre of the frame. The smaller the subject, the more important this rule becomes. So place your subject off-centre, but make sure it is facing into the larger part of the frame, as if you are allowing it some space into which it could move. Our eyes naturally go to the subject and then towards what the subject is looking at, so if your subject is facing out of the frame, that's where the viewer's gaze will go too. Most cameras allow you to move the point of focus to wherever you want it to be in the frame.

Rule of thirds Other general rules of composition include the 'rule of thirds', which says you should place the points of interest in your photo (such as the subject's eye) a third of the way across and a third of the way down the frame (with four possible starting points, which gives you four different points to choose from). If there's a horizon in your photo, avoid placing it dead centre but above or below the centre line, depending whether there's more to look at in the sky or on the land. When photographing a bird on water, position it high in the frame so you include its reflection. Finally, when you take the photo, make sure the point of focus is on your subject's eye. If your subject doesn't have eyes, focus on the most prominent part of it – the centre of a flower, the 'horns' of a snail. If you're photographing a bewildering mass of moving animals, it is probably best to keep your focus to the centre of the frame.

LIGHTING

Light conditions can make or break a photo. In general, have your back to the sun so its light falls on your subject. However, you can sometimes achieve dramatic effects by shooting into the light. Side-on lighting can also work well in some situations. Unconventionally lit shots work best with strong shapes that will work as outlines – if it's fine detail you want to capture, you will need the light to fall fully on your subject.

Different qualities of light

Not every day is a sunny one, and photography on dull days can be more challenging, with colours and contrast both looking rather muted, and slower shutter speeds thrown in to make life more difficult. However, it's still worth persisting. Sometimes duller and flatter light can be good for capturing more detail, especially in macro work. Light changes with time of day as well as the weather, with morning and evening light redder and warmer-looking than midday light.

↑ With frame-filling portraits, you can get away with more central placement of your subject on the vertical plane. This Grey Squirrel's eye is the focal point of the image.

↙ To get an eye-level shot of a small creature on the ground, like this Keeled Skimmer dragonfly, it may be worth carrying a plastic bag to kneel or even lie on.

Eye to eye

As relatively tall animals, we tend to literally look down on much of the wildlife we see, and the effect is magnified the closer we get. To get better photos of small, close animals, try going down to their level. You could crouch or kneel, or go the whole hog and lie flat on your belly – it's very worthwhile as eye-level photos have a lot more impact.

BREAKING THE RULES

The beauty of photography – and other creative arts – is that you can take the 'rules' of what makes a good image seriously or you can take them with a pinch of salt. With wildlife as your subject you don't have as much creative control as those who photograph inanimate (and portable) objects. However, there are always new and unconventional ways to look at any photographic subject, and investigating them is a good part of the fun of photography.

CURIOUS COMPOSITIONS

→ Positioning your subject near the edge of the frame can give an intimate feel to a photo, as with this Fallow Deer doe and her fawn.

Your subject shouldn't be in the centre of the frame, but it doesn't have to be centre-stage either. Sometimes you can use a photo to tell a story, by half hiding your subject among the other elements in the photo. As long as the eyes are visible, the photo can still have as much impact as one that shows the whole animal unobscured. You can also try placing your subject right in the corner of the frame, perhaps using natural lines across the image to draw the viewer's eye to where you want it.

You can't always get as close to your subject as you want to, but that doesn't mean you can't take a good and evocative photo of it. Stepping back and giving your subject some context can create real drama, especially if the context is especially interesting in its own right. Showing how a rare orchid is dwarfed by the other plants nearby will convey a sense of fragility. Alternately, you could go very close indeed and use a macro lens to capture the smallest details – good for plants and also for particularly approachable animals. Macro lenses aren't just for tiny subjects, after all.

BLURRED VISION

↑ Strongly backlit subjects become silhouettes, which can make striking images if they have an interesting shape, like this plume moth.

Usually, blurriness is bad. However, there are times when it is eye-catchingly, excitingly good, and that's when it's motion blur – whether a field of long grass swishing in the breeze or the fast-moving legs of a running animal. Of course, motion blur doesn't always look good, and getting it right can take a lot of practice. 'Panning' (following a moving animal slowly with the camera while taking photos) can achieve the desired effect. Motion blur looks particularly good if there

CANDID CAMERA

Amusing images of animals abound on the internet, whizzing back and forth by email and brightening many a bored worker's day. There's no reason you can't join in the fun too. Young animals, with their often bumbling movements, offer rich opportunities for comedy photos. Also look out for excited interactions in groups of animals feeding together and any quirks of the natural environment that would create an amusing prop or frame for a photo.

are some static elements in the frame, and this can be achieved by using a tripod and taking a long exposure. This is how photos of waterfalls with the water looking soft as steam are taken – you might get the same effect with animals by taking a long exposure of a moving group and hoping one or two of them stay still to provide the contrast between sharp stillness and blurry activity.

TURN OUT THE LIGHTS

Don't always go for well-lit subjects. Silhouettes can make for striking images, and if you shoot into the light on water you can get a lovely starburst effect. Backlit plants can look beautiful as their leaves and petals are often translucent, so the backlighting produces very intense and vivid colours. Sunsets are a time-honoured favourite, and can be combined with wildlife to create some wonderfully evocative images. By exploring the darker side of lighting, you can extend your photography time well into the evening, when more conventional photographers are at home wishing there were more hours in the day.

↑ Photography can reveal amusing moments that are all over too quickly for our eyes to register, like this Magpie which seems to be carelessly falling off a wooden bench.

↓ This is a bad photo from an identification point of view, as only the head of the Green Shieldbug is visible. However, the unconventional angle makes for a striking image.

SETTING THE SCENE

So far, the photographic ideas we've discussed rely heavily on good luck and your ability to make the most of opportunities. However, you can also do a little manipulation to make the images you want, and doing so doesn't need to inconvenience your wild subjects at all if you are sensitive and careful about what you do and how you do it.

YOUR GARDEN, YOUR PHOTO STUDIO

↗ Placing your garden feeders near photogenic branches which birds like Blue Tits can use while they wait their turn to feed can result in pleasing photos.

↘ This odd couple of Garden Snails were both on the wet garden bench, but were moved closer together for this photo.

If you have a garden, then you have all you need to create your own photographic sets, designed to show off your wild models to their best advantage. The obvious place to start is your bird-feeding station. Hanging the feeders close to bushes or other cover so the birds feel safe is essential, but you can also aim to place them in areas where the light will be good at the time of day you're going to want to photograph them. Make sure there are some attractive-looking twigs nearby as the birds will often perch on these while waiting for their turn on the feeder. If there is a tree with attractively bright foliage that will form a colourful blur behind the birds, so much the better.

Water features The same goes for any container of water you put down for the birds. Choose a photogenic container, like a weathered old dustbin lid, or if that's not possible try to 'landscape' it nicely so that it blends into the background. If you have a pond, you can do great things with plants and stones to make it look both natural and pleasing as a backdrop for wildlife photos – the pond itself will attract the wildlife for you.

Plants and landscape The plants you choose for your garden, and where you put them, will also play a part in creating a good wildlife photography studio. The more native plants you have, the more appealing your garden will be to wildlife, but you can still choose attractive varieties and plant them in good spots for picture-taking.

STILL LIFE

As you go about your wildlife-watching travels, you're bound to find beautiful natural objects – feathers, empty snail shells and so on – from time to time that make you think, 'hmmm, that would make a great photo'. You could photograph it where you find it or move it to a more pleasing backdrop. Or take it home and build your own collection of still-life subjects, which can be photographed on their own or used as 'props' in photos of living creatures.

MINIATURE MODELS

You can't persuade a Fox or a Robin to walk into your set if it doesn't want to – all you can do is offer food and hope for the best. Some insects and other invertebrates are not unduly bothered by being gently moved from one place to another, and for these subjects you can decide where you want them and then carefully move or coax them into place. You could photograph a glossy beetle walking across a weathered piece of driftwood or try a shot of a snail from underneath, on a piece of glass. Whatever the shot, remember to treat your models with the utmost respect. Handle them very gently, detain them briefly and return them to where they came from when you've finished.

↑ A swan feather caught on the spines of a dead Teasel head makes a pleasing photo, and it's an easy shot to set up.

↙ It's not just moths that are attracted to light. This Oak Bush-cricket came in through a lit window and was gently moved to a wall for a photo before it was released.

ANIMAL ARTEFACTS AND THE LAW

Some animals are protected by strict laws, which means that if you were found with one (living or dead) in your possession you could face fines or even imprisonment. While it's OK to take home a found feather or two, you should probably avoid making off with entire dead animals, whatever your photographic intentions. Photograph them *in situ* by all means, and report your discovery to the police if you have reason to suspect the animal did not die naturally, but leave them where they are.

DIGITAL ENHANCEMENTS

As if there weren't enough great things about digital photography already, here's another – you can use digital image-editing software to easily make numerous tweaks and improvements to the final product. That doesn't mean you can turn a disastrously out-of-focus or badly exposed image into a prize-winner, but you can certainly make dramatic improvements, and also add some artistic effects.

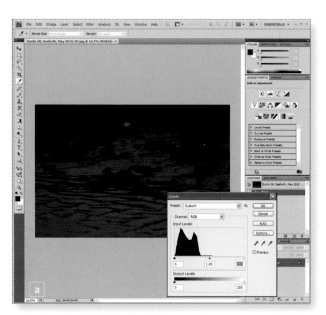

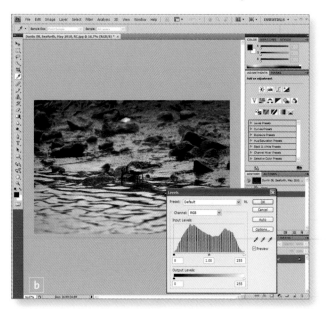

↑↓ This Dunlin photo is very underexposed, as its histogram shows (a). After levels adjustment (b), the histogram shows a much more balanced distribution of dark and light.

FINDING YOUR WAY AROUND

Although image-editing programs are quite intuitive, you'll probably need to read the manual or at least an online tutorial to begin to get to grips with them. The different programs vary in small details but once you know your way around one, you'll find the others quite easy to get along with. On screen you'll generally see a palette of tools down one side, which are for directly drawing onto, selecting from or cropping the image, and menus along the top which include actions to be applied to the whole image (or whatever part of it you have selected). These actions include things like rotating the image, applying a filter or making colour adjustments.

SIMPLE FIXES

Three tweaks you'll often want to make are cropping, adjusting contrast and sharpening.

Cropping Cropping is the simplest fix of the lot. You use your software's crop tool to select a rectangle within the frame that has the elements and composition that you want. It's an easy way to cut out intrusive elements at the sides of the image and to enlarge your subject if it's a bit small in the frame. Bear in mind, though, that the cropped image will have a lower resolution (fewer pixels and therefore less detail) when viewed at the same size as the original.

Contrast If your image looks a bit flat and grey, you can improve its contrast by adjusting the 'levels'. Selecting the levels option gives you a

graph, which shows the dark/light balance of the image. Along the bottom of the graph are sliders at the 'blackest' and 'whitest' end of the graph. When you move the 'white' slider in from its start position, the image becomes brighter (so this will help correct an underexposed image). Adjust both sliders to give you an image with more contrast.

Sharpening Sharpening works by looking for areas of contrast in the image and increasing that contrast. Therefore, if you're going to adjust the levels and also use sharpening, do the levels change first, so the sharpening process has more to work with. The most effective method of sharpening is to use the confusingly named 'unsharp mask'. Start off with the settings quite low and increase them if you need to. As sharpening can cause smooth, blurred backgrounds to go a bit grainy, it is sometimes a good idea to use the 'lasso' or 'magic wand' tool to select just your subject, and then the unsharp mask will only affect that part of the image.

FUN WITH FILTERS

As well as making your photo look better, image-editing software can make it look as though it isn't a photo at all. 'Artistic' filters can turn your photo into a watercolour painting, a line drawing or even a stained-glass window. Not every effect will look good with every photo, but you'll have a lot of fun experimenting.

↑ When photographing flying birds like this Mediterranean Gull, the composition is often less than ideal (a) but can be cropped to a more pleasing shape (b).

WHICH SOFTWARE?

The 'industry standard' is Adobe Photoshop, an amazingly powerful but also rather expensive program which does a lot more than you're ever likely to need. Its trimmed down and less expensive relative, Adobe Elements, is a popular choice for amateurs, but you don't have to spend any money at all to get your hands on a very good editing program. The GIMP (Gnu Image Manipulation Program) is free to download, runs on Windows, Mac OSX and Linux, and is very powerful, with many of the same functions as Photoshop.

VIDEO CAMERAS

Photography is addictive enough, but using video cameras to capture footage of wildlife can be even more absorbing – and challenging. This has the potential to be another expensive hobby, but many cameras now come with a video mode so you may find you already have what you need to make films. If not, there is quite a bit of choice out there.

CONVENTIONAL CAMERAS THAT FILM

↗ Many camcorders offer a powerful optical zoom, and yet are still small and light enough to be carried in a pocket.

Many cameras designed principally for taking still photographs, from compacts to DSLRS, have the capacity to take films as well. If you think this is something that may interest you, bear it in mind when choosing a new camera. If you choose a camera with good optics, it will take good, clear film footage, and footage from compact cameras often looks better than you might expect. The camera will record sound simultaneously when in video mode, unless you ask it not to.

CAMCORDERS

↓ Wildfowl such as this Gadwall family are good subjects for the film-making beginner, as they are not too fast or unpredictable.

Your standard video camera for amateur use records digital footage onto memory cards in a format called DV (top-end cameras use a different format, called DigiBeta). It is small enough to slot easily into your hand and has a flip-out screen on which you can watch what you're recording and play back footage. It will also have a zoom lens, which magnifies by anything between 10x and 60x. (The blurb may also mention additional 'digital zoom' but don't be seduced by that, as it just means the recorded image is cropped rather than optically magnified.)

THE VIDEO *!*

If your camera comes with a built-in video mode, you may well have experimented with it already. However, you may not even have noticed it was there when you bought the camera. Either way, it's well worth flipping the dial to video mode once in a while – you may be surprised by how easy it is to capture footage, and how much fun. You'll have the same zoom range available to you as you do when taking photos, and the camera will work out how to expose the footage in the same way. One uncertain factor is how quickly the films will fill up your memory card. If you're out and wanting to take both photos and footage, keep a close eye on how much storage space you're using up and have extra memory cards with you.

↑ Marsh Harriers have a rather slow and steady hunting flight and so make good subjects for working on your flight-tracking technique.

A camcorder that costs no more than a mid-spec compact still camera may well suffice for beginner wildlife film-makers.

The more you spend, the sharper and more powerful the lens should be, and you'll also start seeing extras such as image stabilisation and extra built-in storage space – perhaps even infrared capability for night-time filming. Most camcorders can also be used to take still photographs, and they come with software that will allow you to edit your footage.

EXTRAS

With ordinary cameras, you can often get away without any stabilisation as you're only opening the shutter for a fraction of a second each time. When recording on a video camera, you'll be following your subject around so you need freedom of movement, but some stabilisation is also helpful to prevent shaky footage. A tripod with a smooth pan-and-tilt head will help greatly here, and if you're already a keen photographer you may well have one already. Camcorders have built-in microphones to record sound but you can also connect a separate external microphone for better sound quality.

↓ Filming dragonflies in flight is a huge challenge. The Broad-bodied Chaser gives you some help by habitually making short flights and returning to the same perch.

MAKING MOVIES

If a picture paints a thousand words, then how about 30 seconds of video footage with sound? Filming wildlife is a wonderful way to tell the stories of the animals you see, as faithfully or creatively as you like. It is also a very difficult art to master and requires particular sensitivity to the well-being of your subjects. Luckily there are plenty of easy subjects out there to help you get the hang of it all.

↑ A moment of drama like this – a Lesser Black-backed Gull stealing a Black-headed Gull chick from its nest – can be the centrepiece of an exciting film.

PRACTICE MAKES PERFECT

Filming wildlife doesn't have to involve huge physical challenges and great practical difficulties. Start simple – pick an approachable subject. Your local park probably has Grey Squirrels and assorted waterfowl which will not object to having a camcorder pointed at them. Experiment with different zoom ranges, tracking your subject with the camcorder hand-held or perhaps on a tripod. With filming, smoothness is vital, so use the zoom slowly, and try to keep everything steady as you move the camera around.

CHALLENGING SUBJECTS

Photographing birds in flight is difficult, but filming them can actually be easier than trying to follow their movements on the ground (depending on the species). For a bit of additional challenge, try aiming your camcorder at a flying bird of prey. There are several places in Britain where Red Kites can be seen in profusion, and another ideal subject is the Marsh Harrier, which can be observed flying low and slow over reedbeds at many RSPB reserves along England's east coast. Garden birds and flying insects also offer plenty of challenge because of their very quick movements.

TELLING THE STORY

You might just want a short film of a species as an extra reference for identification. Getting film of how an animal moves can be very helpful for working out what you're looking at or 'revising' the key attributes of the species. You might also want to make a more elaborate film with some kind of storyline, which is where your editing software – and your imagination – come into play.

Experimenting with your footage

If you spend a whole day with your camcorder at a local flooded gravel pit, you'll probably come home with plenty of footage of Coots. What you do with that footage then is the fun part. You could edit together a simple story of one Coot's day, beginning with a scenic shot of the habitat and then 'introducing' the lead character, showing it feeding, interacting with other Coots, and perhaps fading out as it falls asleep and then back in to show it enjoying a preening and bathing session. Or you could dub on some heavy metal music and splice together a film that just shows a relentless stream of violent fights between rival Coots.

Supporting characters
You won't necessarily set out with a story in mind, but as you record your footage ideas will suggest themselves. Besides your main subject, it's often worth including material of 'supporting characters', and some general shots of the area, including plantlife, moving clouds and so on.

↑ Films that tell a species' life-story often work well – this one begins with a Painted Lady butterfly laying her egg on a thistle head.

↓ Don't neglect common or even unpopular wildlife for your films – Common Wasps, for example, exhibit fascinatingly complex behaviour.

Keep your distance

When filming an animal, it can be tempting to pursue it wherever it goes so you can keep capturing footage. You must always have the animal's welfare at the forefront of your mind, and avoid stressing it by chasing, crowding or obstructing it. More than any other branch of wildlife-watching, film-making requires exemplary fieldcraft. If your subject is stressed and frightened, this will be quite obvious in your footage, so it's in everyone's interest to stay quiet, stay back and give the animal no cause for alarm. You should also be aware of the law concerning protected species (see page 215) and avoid doing anything that could disturb them.

NOTE TO YOURSELF

Some people are natural diarists and enjoy making and storing proper notes about their lives or hobbies. If that's you, then you won't need to be reminded of the value of keeping a record of your wildlife-watching exploits. If you're not one of life's note-takers, this section aims to gently persuade you to give it a go, with the reasons why it can be a good idea to maintain some kind of simple record of where you go and what you see.

MAKING MEMORIES

Taking notes in the field is one thing, and we've already talked about the advantages of doing it. However, 'writing up' your day afterwards might be much more, or much less, fun, depending on your outlook. You might find it all a bit of a chore, like the compulsory 'what I did in my holidays' essay homework in the first week back at school. But there's no denying that looking back over your notes from the last month, year or decade is fun.

Reliving a wonderful day out in the countryside, perhaps seeing plants or animals that you had never encountered before, is always enjoyable, but all the more so if you have your own written words from that day to take you back. Even a routine day around your local patch will make for pleasant reminiscences,

◣ The first Cuckoo of spring – but what was the date you first heard or saw it? Does it vary year on year? This kind of information is well worth keeping long-term.

especially if you move to a new area or have some other change in circumstances that keeps you away from your favourite wildlife places.

THE SERIOUS SIDE

Maintaining a written record of your observations can have more value besides inducing some pleasant meanders down memory lane. Animal and plant numbers and distribution are changing all the time, and seasonal patterns of growth and behaviour may also be on the move in some species. If your notes record a steady change in the numbers of Small Tortoiseshells visiting your Buddleia bushes or a shift in the first date that you see a Swift over your house in spring, they could indicate a general trend, which will be of interest to the organisations that research such things.

Some observers are sticklers for detail and will amass a great wealth of information, much of which will only really be of interest to them. If your brain doesn't work that way, you might find writing up even brief notes a bit of a chore, and there's no point in forcing yourself. However, it's still worth making a few short notes of particularly interesting observations from time to time, and it needn't take you more than a minute or two.

A NOTEBOOK ENTRY

So what should you record? The simplest notebook entry would just give the date and then list the more interesting species you observed. You might prefer to write it as a journal entry with a more narrative style (which will certainly make for more enjoyable repeat reading). Background details like weather, wind direction and how long you spent at the site could also be included.

If you are in the habit of regularly visiting a 'local patch', it may help you to make a simple map of the area and divide it into sections. Then you can give each section a reference number or nickname which can be used as shorthand in your notes when recording where in the patch you made each observation. If you have a serious interest in wildlife surveying, whether for a possible future career or for voluntary work at your local nature reserve, keeping meticulous notes from your everyday observations will be excellent practice for this.

Water
Woodland
Meadow
Road
Reed bed
Hide
Car park
Footpath

↑ Using a reference like a large-scale OS map or Google Maps, it's easy to draw a simple map of your local patch, which you can then divide into sectors.

↓ It's easy to quickly build up a big library of digital photos – and there are many ways you can store and show off the fruits of your labours.

RECORD COLLECTION

What with notes, sketches, photos and maybe even video clips, you can easily amass quite a 'body of work' through your wildlife-watching. How are you going to organise all this into a coherent form that you can easily read back and perhaps show to other interested people? There are various options, depending on how much work you want to put in, and whether you're technically proficient or prefer the handwritten word.

↑ Keeping handwritten notes in a set of handsome A4 notebooks may be a bit too 20th century for some, but has a certain appeal.

↓ Spreadsheets are a great way to record bird sightings. In this daily wildfowl and wader count, bold and highlighting is used to pick out exceptional sightings.

NOTEBOOKS AND SCRAPBOOKS

When you're taking notes in the field, you can use any old notebook – in fact it's often best not to go for something cheap and cheerful as it may get a bit of a battering over the weeks. However, you can transcribe your notes to a sturdier and nicer book later on. Hardback A4 books offer an attractive way to keep your notes – if you go with a 'classic' brand like Black n' Red you can make a full shelf of attractive matching books. Or you could go for large scrapbooks, and put in them not just your notes but printouts of photographs, pasted-in sketches, and even pressed flowers and leaves. Making a wildlife scrapbook like this would be a great project for children.

DIGITAL RECORDS

Most of us use computers at home, and writing up your day's wildlife-adventuring in Word or an equivalent program (OpenOffice is a free downloadable alternative) will probably come quite naturally. You can also easily paste in your digital photos and scans of your sketches.

Organising the data One of the great advantages of digital record-keeping is how easy it is to add extra detail, if you feel so inclined. You can log your species sightings in an Excel spreadsheet (again, OpenOffice provides a free alternative), and if you're a spreadsheet whizz you can then produce graphs showing monthly fluctuations, year-on-year trends and a wealth of other visual displays.

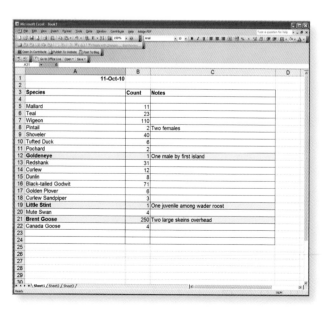

	A	B	C	D
1	11-Oct-10			
2				
3	Species	Count	Notes	
4				
5	Mallard	11		
6	Teal	23		
7	Wigeon	110		
8	Pintail	2	Two females	
9	Shoveler	40		
10	Tufted Duck	6		
11	Pochard	2		
12	Goldeneye	1	One male by first island	
13	Redshank	31		
14	Curlew	12		
15	Dunlin	8		
16	Black-tailed Godwit	71		
17	Golden Plover	6		
18	Curlew Sandpiper	3		
19	Little Stint	1	One juvenile among wader roost	
20	Mute Swan	4		
21	Brent Goose	250	Two large skeins overhead	
22	Canada Goose	4		
23				
24				
25				
26				
27				
28				
29				
30				

Another advantage of digital records is that you can quickly search your notes, so you can find out when you last saw a Willow Warbler on your local patch or what time last year the first Common Spotted Orchid came into flower. Keeping a note of such details can help you plan your future wildlife-watching trips, and will also allow you to give meaningful advice to others. You can also revisit and add in extra notes later – for example, you might not be able to identify a certain species straight away, but later on you could bump into an expert who can tell you what it is, so you can amend your notes accordingly.

When you're comfortable with the software you'll be able to use Excel or other spreadsheet programmes to produce graphs and piecharts of your data as well as to crunch the numbers and reveal interesting statistics and trends.

↑ Attractive-looking natural objects like dead leaves can be dried out and then taped into a nature scrapbook for a fun project.

↑ It's easy to add images to a Word or OpenOffice document, and they can help liven up your wildlife-watching reports.

Filing and back-up

Filing all your wildlife-watching documents in folders named by month is a sensible and straightforward way to go. Alternatively, you could arrange them by place, and include an introductory document with useful and relevant details about the place in question – perhaps a map, grid reference, details of the size of the site and who owns it.

As your library of notes grows, the importance of making back-up files increases. Word documents don't take up much space, and you'll be able to store plenty on a standard CD, though if they include embedded images they will become considerably bigger. An external hard drive is another option, and many of these have more than enough storage for a long lifetime of wildlife-watching notes. Make sure your stuff is always stored in at least two places, and ideally three, with the third somewhere other than in your house (with a friend or at your workplace perhaps) just in case.

STORING PHOTOS AND VIDEOS

When you start getting really interested in photography, you'll quickly assemble a large collection of pictures and be faced with some dilemmas about how best to organise and store them. The same goes for video clips. Without a coherent storage system, your photos and videos will start to go unseen because it's just too much hassle to look through thousands of images with no clue as to what they show, so it's worth being disciplined from the start and filing them in an organised way.

FILENAMES

The logical thing to do is to change the name of each file from the meaningless one the camera assigns it to something that explains what the image or clip is. How much or how little information you include is up to you. You could label all your Blackbird photos 'Blackbird 1', 'Blackbird 2' and so on. You might be better off including a few noughts though – eg, 'Blackbird 0001', 'Blackbird 0002' and so on, as this way the computer will organise them in the correct numerical order rather than placing 'Blackbird 1' next to 'Blackbird 11' – though you'll be in trouble if you take more than 9,999 photos of Blackbirds.

A bit more information in the filename can be helpful. You could include species and date, or species, date and location. Adding additional detail, such as the age and sex of the animal and information about its behaviour, may be helpful too (especially for videos), though there will come a point where you'll get long and unwieldy filenames, and inputting all the information will become a real chore.

↓ A filing dilemma – this image contains three different species, so it could be filed three times, or in a separate 'multi-species folder.

CLEVER FILING

The other option is to dispense with detailed filenames but instead just number all your images sequentially and rely on an accurate and 'deep' filing system to help you locate what you want. The nested filing system used by Windows

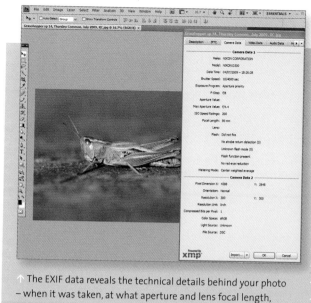

↑ The EXIF data reveals the technical details behind your photo – when it was taken, at what aperture and lens focal length, whether a flash was used and so on.

EXIF data

Sometimes you will want to remind yourself of some of the technical information about a photo. This might include the aperture and shutter speed, whether flash was used, which lens was on the camera if you used a DSLR and so on. Luckily, you don't have to bother including all of this in the filenames because it's all stored in the image's EXIF data (along with other useful stuff such as the time and date, provided this is correctly set on your camera). You can usually access the EXIF data via your image-editing software – for example, in Photoshop go to 'File info' in the 'File' menu and choose the EXIF or Camera Data tab.

and other operating systems is ideal. You could have main folders titled 'Birds', 'Plants', 'Landscapes' and so on, and have further subdivisions within them. For example, for birds and plants you could have species names and for landscapes, geographical areas. If you find you're amassing too many photos per category, just create further subdivisions. So, with those 9,999 Blackbird photos you could first divide them into males, females and juveniles, and then by behaviour being shown, and so on.

IMAGE-MANAGEMENT SOFTWARE

Besides whatever comes as standard with your computer's operating system, there are various downloadable free programs that help you organise your files. One of the most popular is Google's Picasa program, which gives you a clear interface for previewing your photos (including correcting the orientation for photos taken in portrait mode). These applications allow you to do simple image editing, too, such as converting your photos to a format suitable for publishing online.

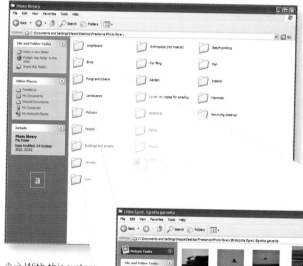

↑→ With this system, a main 'Photo library' (a) contains subfolders dividing up the main animal groups. There's even room for some non-wildlife subjects.

Within the 'Birds' folder (b), there is a subfolder for each species. The filenames list the species, location, date and photographer's initials.

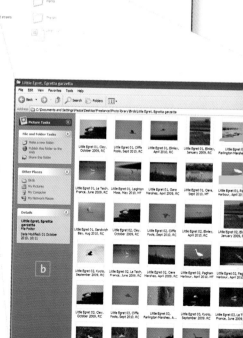

GOING ONLINE

With the internet, everyone can get their words, pictures and videos published and viewable by a potentially huge number of people. Even if you're not hungry for fame and acclaim, publishing your stuff online is an easy way to share it with friends and family, and there are lots of different ways to go about it.

BLOGGING

A blog (short for 'web log') is effectively an online diary. You make entries as often as you want, and you can include images and videos. There are many different blog providers, such as Blogger (**www.blogger.com**), WordPress (**www.wordpress.com**) or TypePad (**www.typepad.com**). All are free to use, and you don't need to have any computer expertise beyond the ability to create Word files, do simple picture editing and navigate the web – the software automatically encodes everything for you. You can choose from a range of templates, and then personalise it by adding a header and using your own fonts.

↓ It's very easy – and free – to start your own blog and share your wildlife-watching experiences with the world.

Uploading photos and other pictures to your blog is simple, but you will need to resize them first. If you make the longest side 800 pixels, the full-size version (viewable when a visitor to your blog clicks on an image) will be small enough not to spill off the edge of a small laptop screen, although you can go for bigger images if you like. However, to protect your copyright it's best to keep pictures on the smaller side.

SHARING PHOTOS AND VIDEO

If you just want to show off your images online, websites like Flickr (**www.flickr.com**) are ideal. You create a free account, and then you can begin uploading photos, which can be organised into albums for easy searching. Visitors to Flickr can search for particular images, so if you want your photos to be seen by many, give them meaningful titles and tag them with lots of relevant keywords. The most popular video-sharing site is YouTube (**www.youtube.com**), to which you can upload film clips of varying lengths once you have created an account.

ONLINE TRAFFIC

How to get people to look at your stuff online? If you just want people you know to read your blog or view your pictures, you can just email them a link. To attract the wider public, you need to promote yourself a bit. If you use

The wild side

MONDAY, 26 JULY 2010

Queendown Warren

This weekend, Team Wildside managed two butterfly-watching trips in between our other important duties (sleeping, aikido practice and, in Rob's case, watching the first and second Toy Story films so we can watch the third one tonight). This post is about the Saturday trip to Queendown Warren. I'll tell you about the Sunday trip later, when I've figured out where Rob has hidden the card reader.

So, Queendown Warren. A Kent Wildlife Trust reserve in the North Downs, off the A249 where it links the M20 and M2. We found the general area easily enough but locating the reserve car park took an increasingly frustrating half-hour of weaving around very narrow lanes. Eventually a little car park materialised and we gratefully stashed the Passat in the shade. It was a very warm, mostly sunny and quite still afternoon.

The reserve is cut up into several chunks by the aforementioned weaving lanes. The first bit we explored was steeply sloping Rabbit-cropped grassland with patches of scrub.

The general impression was of a place that looked the absolute business for downland butterflies. The rougher bits were full of flowering Teasels and Spear Thistles, the hedgerows had plenty of brambles.

social networking sites like Facebook (**www.facebook.com**) or Twitter (**www.twitter.com**) you can post links to your blog or photos, and ask your friends to share the links with their friends. If you use forums or message boards, it's usually acceptable to put up a post asking visitors to check out your blog, or you could include a link to it in your signature. Also, look around for other blogs that interest you and 'follow' them (this means signing up for notifications of when the blog is updated). Those bloggers may then reciprocate. You could also try getting your blog listed on one of the websites that list blogs with a specific theme, which carry links to many blogs featuring wildlife photographs.

↑ If you think you may have photographed a scarce species like Honey-buzzard, by posting your photos (however fuzzy) on a discussion board you can get input from experts.

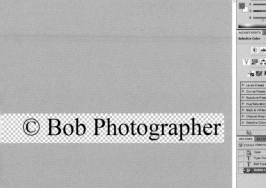

↑ You can easily create a watermark by creating a new image file in Photoshop or the Gimp with the text you want on a transparent background.

→ When using a watermark, make the text a colour that stands out, and place it somewhere on the image where it can't easily be cropped.

COPYRIGHT ISSUES

Whenever you publish anything online there's a small risk that someone else will steal it. You automatically hold copyright over all of your work, but not everyone will respect this (though profit-making companies almost always will). This is one reason why you should change your images to a fairly small size so that they cannot be used for print reproduction. You can also add an embedded watermark identifying the photo as yours – your digital editing software has the means to do this. Another good idea is to include a note asking visitors not to use your material without permission in your 'about me' paragraph on the blog front page.

The likeliest content thief would be another blogger, passing off your photos or words as his or her own. If you do encounter someone using your work online without your permission, send them an email asking them to immediately remove the content. If they do not comply, a standard 'cease and desist' letter describing the law they have violated is the next step – you can download a suitable template from the website Plagiarism Today (**www.plagiarismtoday.com**).

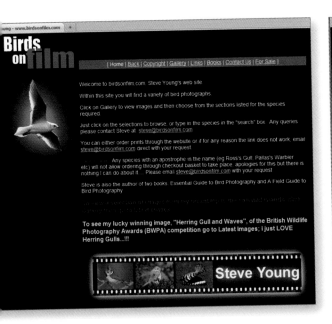

A WEBSITE OF YOUR OWN

For a lot of us, a blog offers all the website we would ever want or need. However, blogs have their limitations – they follow a simple formula, and if what you want to post online doesn't fit that formula there's not much you can do about it. If you want to promote yourself in any kind of professional capacity, a blog is not always sufficient to show off what you can offer. Many professional writers, artists and photographers do keep a blog but have a full website of their own as well.

↑ This is the website of bird photographer Steve Young, through which he can display his images but also accept orders from people who wish to purchase prints.

↗ The RSPB's website is a good example of a very large site with many pages, covering many themes and requiring frequent updating.

THE BASICS

Setting up a website doesn't come free. Even if you are computer-savvy enough to produce the design you want by yourself, you will probably still have to pay someone to host your website (in other words, to provide the slice of 'webspace' that you're going to use), and you may have to pay for a domain name – such as 'www.bobsmith.co.uk'. There are lots of companies out there which will supply both domain name and hosting, and others will offer you a complete package of name, hosting and website design. Completely free web hosting is available and improving all the time, but you will generally get more features, flexibility and support via a paid service.

WHAT'S YOUR WEBSITE FOR?

Because you pay for hosting per year, it's sensible to have a very clear idea of what sort of site you want before you dive in and start spending money. What is the main purpose of the site? What extra features do you want it to have? Will you be using it just to showcase your work or do you want to be able to sell material from it as well? What are your thoughts on how the design should look?

There is software available, such as Adobe Dreamweaver or a free open-source equivalent like KompoZer, which will enable you to build and design webpages. Getting the hang of this could save you the cost of hiring a web designer, and will also make it easier for you to update the pages yourself. You will need a bit of computer-confidence, though, or perhaps a technically minded friend at hand to help you through the tricky bits.

↑ The free website-authoring program KompoZer comes from the same team who created the popular Firefox web browser.

BECOMING FINDABLE

If you're a keen birdwatcher, you'll know that the acronym SEO means 'Short-eared Owl'. But it has a quite different meaning in internet jargon – 'Search Engine Optimisation'. If you have good SEO, your website will be among the top results produced when people perform searches via Google or other search engines for anything at all related to your site's content. To improve your visibility to search engines, make sure that your website's page headings are as relevant and precise as they can be, and use different headings on each page. Think about the sort of keywords that your potential visitors might use when they do their search and include them clearly in your page headers.

TO AD OR NOT TO AD?

Having advertisements on your website or your blog is a double-edged sword. They may distract or irritate visitors, but they can make money for you as well. If you do decide to host some ads, the key thing is to make them as relevant to your content as possible. You don't need to be well known or have a high turnover of visitors to persuade companies to advertise on your site. Joining an affiliate scheme, such as Google's AdSense, enables you to select from a large pool of potential advertisers, and once the ad is in place on your blog or website then you will earn money when people click the ad to go through to the advertiser's website.

↓ One advantage of having your own website is that you control exactly how images are displayed, and can give them as much space on screen as they need to do them justice.

CRAFTY IDEAS

Besides publishing them in some form or another, there are lots of other things you can do with your wildlife photographs and artworks. It's all too easy to just file them away and do little more than flick through them a couple of times a year, but if you're proud of your work why not show it off more widely and make it accessible to others who share your appreciation for wildlife?

FRAME-UPS

Why let your photos languish on your computer's hard drive when you could print them out, frame them up and hang them on the wall for all to see? Frames need not be expensive, and a simple design is often more effective to show off a striking photo to its best advantage. The same goes for artwork, and as well as providing decoration for your home, they can make great personalised gifts. The frame may just be a simple plastic slab with a slot for the photo, but more elaborate ones include a mount with a card border, a sturdy piece of backing board, a sheet of glass for the front and finally a contrastingly coloured wood, plastic or metal frame with clips to hold it all together.

↓ If you've put several hours in a piece of artwork, like this Caracal gouache, why not invest in a simple frame and put your work on display?

GREETINGS CARDS

Home-made cards provide a good practical use for your photos and artwork. Whether you use a comical photo and use Photoshop to add on a caption or just go for a simple image, you can easily make attractive cards with a personal touch at home. You can print straight onto a card and fold and trim it later or print postcard-sized versions of your photos and glue them onto premade blank cards (available from art suppliers). You'll need to resize the photo carefully, using your image-editing software.

DIGITAL PHOTO FRAMES

These gadgets are popular and come in a variety of shapes and sizes. You load up a selection of images, and then set the frame to display them in turn, changing the duration each image is on show to suit your preference. If you buy one of these as a gift, why not preload it with an album or two of your best photos, perhaps themed by subject or mood (while leaving plenty of room for the recipient to add their own images). There's no reason why it has to be just photos, either, any image can be used, including scans of your artwork.

← A Robin in snow is a classic festive image, and one that's easy to come by for most of us (as long as it snows). Just add text for a quick Christmas card design.

↑ Designing a calendar will take you a little while but will make an impressive, useful and personalised gift for you to give away.

If you have lots of cards to produce, you could get them printed and cut professionally – this will cost you quite a bit (though the cost per card will go down as quantity goes up) but is worth doing if you make up a large batch of cards – and leave them blank inside so they can be used for any occasion. If you're aspiring to become a professional or semi-professional artist or photographer, this is also a great way of showing off your work to existing and potential clients.

CALENDARS AND OTHER PRINTED MATERIAL

If you know a bit about making layouts on screen, making your own calendar is a fun and fairly simple project. You'll need 12 images (and perhaps also a cover image), which you can choose to convey a sense of the month in question. You could design the calendar so that the image and the dates are on the same page and are torn off as each month ends, or go for a more sophisticated leaflet design with image and dates on separate pages. Calendars make great gifts.

With a bit of help from the professionals, you can get a photo or scan of an artwork printed onto practically anything. This provides lots of scope for interesting gift ideas – you could make a mug, T-shirt, mouse mat, oven gloves, curtains – the only limit is your imagination.

MONEYMAKERS

If you've spent a small fortune on camera gear, it's only natural to want to offset some of that by making a bit of money from your photos. Many wildlife enthusiasts also boost their income from time to time by selling their writing or artwork, though making a full-time living in any of these fields is challenging to say the least. Don't be discouraged, though. You'll never know how successful you could be if you don't try.

OUTLETS FOR PHOTOGRAPHS

↓ Think topical – because the invasive Browntail moth has had quite a high profile in the news, photos of its caterpillar feeding webs could sell.

Photos of wildlife are published in books, magazines and newspapers, as well as online. Some publishers get most of the photos they use from picture libraries, and once you have taken a sizeable collection of good images you could try placing them in one of these libraries. The RSPB has an image library (**www. rspb-images.com**) of wildlife and landscape photos – have a browse through the content to see if your work is up to scratch.

You could also try approaching a publisher directly. If you have a lot of bird photos, you could send a few prints to a bird magazine publisher and direct them to your blog or website to view more – you may not have anything they want to buy straight away, but you could go on their list as a possible future contributor. If you are lucky enough to get photos of a particularly rare species or an unusual colour form, you may find you get more interest. It's often worth trying the local newspaper if you do manage to get good photos of a rarity.

GIVING YOUR WORK AWAY

You will probably find lots of people would like to use your work if they don't have to pay you anything. If you just want to see your work in print, then you might be quite happy with this. In general, though, you should avoid allowing your words or pictures to be used for nothing in commercial publications – if they are making money from your work, you should see some of that money. Sometimes you'll be offered an alternative form of payment – for example, a book publisher may offer you a free copy of the book in which your photo will appear, and this is often a fair compromise.

Things are different when it comes to not-for-profit publications, where there is often no money available. In cases like these it's up to you to decide whether you want to help out the organisation concerned – your work will reach a wider audience, so it's often worth doing it for that as well as for the general goodwill. Make sure that you insist on a proper credit, though, and see if you can squeeze in a plug for your website or blog as well.

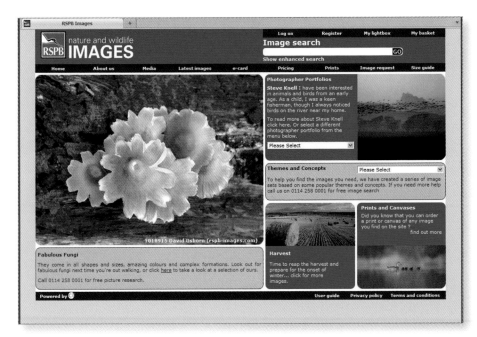

← The RSPB Images website is a photo library, selling superb wildlife and environment photographs to publishers and others.

↓ Publishers sometimes search Flickr and other online photo display sites for images, so make sure your Flickr photos are tagged with lots of helpful keywords.

Selling prints of your work is another possibility. You'd have to invest a fair amount of money up front, though, as producing large and high-quality prints is a job for a professional printer. Another option is to make your own greetings cards, though again you will have to spend a bit of money getting them printed to a professional standard first.

WRITING

Over the years, you may unwittingly become a bit of an expert at something – whether it's the wildlife of your local patch or a particular obscure group of animals or plants that captures your imagination and inspires you to research and study them. You might be surprised to learn how much in-depth knowledge like that can be sought after by publishers. If you enjoy writing and have something to say that you think might be new and interesting to an audience of wildlife readers, why not pitch your idea to the editor of a relevant magazine? If you can accompany your article with your own good-quality photos or artwork, so much the better.

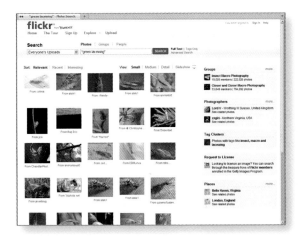

↑ The website **www.photocompetitions.com** collates details of photographic competitions of all kinds, and provides links to online entry forms.

AN ACTIVE ROLE

HANDS ON

Wildlife-watching sounds like a pretty passive sort of hobby. Even if you're making notes, sketching, photographing or film-making you're usually still very much keeping back and not getting directly involved with the natural world. There are times, though, when things can get a little more interactive. Enhancing your garden's wildlife attractability, or learning to 'talk to the animals' are among the ways to get more proactive.

HELPING OUT

We human beings have been manipulating our local environment ever since the first of our ancestors picked up a stone and used it as a tool. Of course, this has usually been to the detriment of other species that share our planet. As a wildlife enthusiast, you have the chance to redress the balance somewhat, and get more out of your wildlife-watching at the same time.

This all starts at home, of course. By making your garden a better place for wildlife, you benefit other species as much as yourself. Don't forget that your garden is just a small part of a much larger patchwork habitat though – try to encourage your neighbours to jump on the wildlife-friendly bandwagon as well.

↑ They may be small and apparently fearless, but that's no reason not to treat small animals like Ladybirds with gentleness and respect.

← Intensive conservation management, including captive breeding and tracking, has helped the shy Water Vole begin to recover from severe population declines.

The amount of habitat lost in the UK over the years to make room for houses is immense, and much of that habitat would have been deciduous woodland. Gardens, however, can be a fair substitute for the species that used to inhabit the woods, if planned and planted right.

A FINE LINE

Once you start manipulating natural environments and studying wild animals at close quarters, you run the risk of doing harm as well as good. There are several 'golden rules' to keep in mind at all times. It's fairly obvious that trapping and handling a wild bird can cause distress if you are not experienced, which is why it's illegal for you to do so unless you're a researcher or a bird ringer and hold the correct licences.

However, catching and studying an insect for five minutes doesn't cause it any apparent distress. Of course, we can't know how it feels to be a beetle, but we can observe that its behaviour seems unchanged whether it's walking about on the woodland floor or in a collecting pot. We also know by study of its nervous system that it doesn't possess the same capacity for emotional responses as a bird does. We therefore take more liberties with the 'lower animals', but that is no reason to treat them with any disrespect. To deprive any animal of the means to perform natural behaviours in a natural environment for any length of time is unnecessary as well as undesirable. However, with common sense and care there's no harm in briefly inconveniencing it for the sake of study.

↑ Human habitations have replaced extensive areas of wild countryside, but with the right planning your garden can become a veritable wildlife haven.

LEARNING FROM THE PAST

Some wildlife can be studied only from a distance, at least if you are an amateur. Other species however can safely be investigated at closer quarters as long as you're extremely careful and respectful. Not so long ago our attitude was more cavalier and our subjects suffered unnecessarily. We know now that tadpoles don't thrive in jam jars and that butterflies look better in photographs than impaled on pins, but there's still a role for amateur naturalists to increase the fund of knowledge on Britain's wildlife.

← Some animals, like Grey Squirrels, are often at ease around people which makes them ideal study subjects

FEEDING GARDEN BIRDS

The humble bird feeder has been the means by which many
people have set off on their way to becoming serious wildlife
enthusiasts. The sight of a mixed batch of songbirds vying for
position on a feeder can be thrilling, and gives everyone the
chance to watch birds at close range without even needing to
step outside. By offering the right foods at the right time, you
can increase the variety of species coming to your garden
and make a real difference to local bird populations.

WHAT KIND OF FOOD?

→ Fat balls provide
high-energy nutrition,
ideal for fledglings.
This newly fledged
Blue Tit chick (left)
has learned from its
parents where the
food can be found.

Garden bird feeding may have started
with people throwing out handfuls of
bread crusts and other kitchen scraps onto
the lawn once or twice a week, but it's now
evolved into a positive science. The RSPB
offers a huge array of food types, with
something for pretty much any species
likely to visit a UK garden. Wet and dry
varieties are both fine but with dry food
you may want to soak it first.

Raw peanuts have long been a
popular food to offer, as they are full
of fat and protein. Always buy them from a reputable
supplier who can guarantee their peanuts are free
of aflatoxin, a poison produced by fungi which can
contaminate peanuts kept in suboptimal conditions. You can offer them whole
on a bird table, or in wire or plastic feeders. Avoid offering whole loose peanuts
in spring and summer as they may cause young birds to choke.

Sunflower seeds are even more relished by wild birds than peanuts. Finches
can crack the husks, but if you go for
dehusked seeds (sunflower 'hearts')
they will also attract tits and other
species. Another good seed is nyjer,
a fine black seed that can be very
attractive to Goldfinches. You can
buy various 'mixed bird seeds' which
contain both of these types and then
scatter them on your bird table or put
them in a tubular feeder.

WHEREABOUTS?

When choosing where to put up your bird table or hang your
feeders, the most important thing to consider is that small birds
feel unsafe feeding in the open. So place them close to dense
bushy cover if at all possible. Also be wary of putting them right
in front of large windows, as birds may fly at the reflection and
injure themselves in collisions. Once those boxes are ticked,
you can put them wherever will give you the best views of the
birds, and if you are interested in photographing birds at your
feeders you can consider which spots in the garden get the most
pleasant light at various times of the day.

To please the insect-eaters like Robins and thrushes, you can buy mealworms (either dead and dried, or live and wriggling). 'Bird cake', a chunk or 'fat ball' of solid fat which may incorporate seeds and/or dead insects, is a fantastic high-energy food attractive to nearly all species, especially in winter. You can make your own bird cake or buy it premade, and there are special feeders to accommodate it. Don't forget the water, either. Some birds are frequent drinkers and bathers. If you don't have a pond, offer fresh water in a shallow container.

TYPES OF FEEDERS

The basic bird table is a flat surface on which you place the food. A high-up position will help protect the birds from cat attacks, and a roof will protect the food from getting wet or being washed away. You can put hooks on the table sides for hanging feeders. These come in two basic designs – a wire frame (the birds pull out fragments of food through the mesh) or a solid plastic tube with 'ports' on the sides where the birds perch and put their heads in to get at the food. Some types are available with suckers for attachment to window glass. Wire frames are good for bird cake and peanuts, while the solid type are better for seed. Some feeders have 'cages' around them to keep out squirrels and larger birds, and mealworm feeders are usually just simple trays.

EXTRAS

Besides proprietary bird food in feeders, you can also offer certain kitchen scraps to the birds. Fruit, such as overripe apples or spare sultanas, is usually popular, and small amounts of cheese or soaked stale cake are better fed to the birds than thrown away. Avoid offering birds any kind of oil or fat in a soft form, as it can clog up their plumage.

↑ Depending where you live, your bird feeders may attract more unusual species, such as the introduced and exotic-looking Ring-necked Parakeet.

↙ Robins are among the species which are more comfortable feeding on the ground, though they will visit bird tables and some learn to use hanging feeders.

FEEDING OTHER GARDEN WILDLIFE

Who visits your garden after dark? There's every chance that a few wandering mammals include your garden on their nightly rounds, and if you want to you can encourage some of them to stick around or make repeat visits by offering them something to eat. This is an easy way to get some great views of species which are normally difficult to observe in the wild.

↓ If you're putting out cat food for visiting wildlife, check at night to make sure that you're not just feeding next door's cat.

WHO GOES THERE?

The most likely night-time visitors (which might be interested in any food you have to offer) are Foxes, Badgers, Hedgehogs and small rodents. Foxes are especially common in urban and suburban settings – you may not even need to wait until night to see them in some areas. Not everyone is a fan of the urban Fox, as they may do unsociable things like terrorising outdoor pet rabbits and guinea-pigs, so consider your neighbours when deciding whether to feed them.

To attract Badgers you'll need to be fairly close to a sett, which usually means woodland of some description. Badgers are not athletic fence-leapers but may dig their way in if there's no easy access.

RATS

The Brown Rat is the one mammal we don't generally want in our gardens. If you know you have rats locally you should probably avoid leaving food out for other mammals, and certainly don't leave nuts and seeds on the ground for small rodents.

You may not appreciate this, so if you want to let them in and out without sacrificing your lawn, provide an entry place for them. Hedgehogs can get through small gaps and are surprisingly capable climbers. They are a real boon to the gardener because of their huge appetite for slugs. Mice and voles probably live in your garden already. You may see them hoovering up bird-table spillages or even climbing up to the table itself.

If deer visit, they may take advantage of some grain or carrots. However, be prepared for them to leave your garden in a somewhat sorry state if they start making regular visits.

WHAT FOOD?

Hedgehogs, Foxes and Badgers are all somewhat carnivorous and will appreciate dog or cat food. Wet or dry varieties are both fine, but you may want to soak the dry food first; you should also offer a dish of water. Many other foods will be taken too. Badgers enjoy whole peanuts, and if you scatter a few of these over a wide area you'll encourage the Badgers to spend longer in the garden as they sniff them out. Badgers also have a sweet tooth and enjoy fruit and even sweetened cereals. But don't ever offer chocolate or bread and milk. Chocolate is toxic to most mammals, and while Hedgehogs will eat bread and milk with enthusiasm it can give them serious stomach upsets. For the rodents, nuts and seeds are ideal. Place them on the ground or perhaps slightly elevated on a stump or brick.

A TOUCH OF THE EXOTIC

If you live in Ireland or Scotland, you stand a chance of attracting two particularly appealing mammalian visitors to your garden. Red Squirrels, their numbers beleaguered because of competition with, and disease carried by, the introduced Grey Squirrel, will readily take nuts and seeds offered for garden birds. While we aren't always delighted to have Grey Squirrels assaulting our bird feeders, it's usually a different story for Reds. You can buy dedicated squirrel feeders which aren't accessible to birds, so the two can feed peacefully side by side.

The other species is the Pine Marten, a large and beautiful relative of the Weasel. This animal is an accomplished jumper and climber and can easily access the average bird table. It has a distinctly sweet tooth and enjoys jam and peanut butter sandwiches.

↖ Rambling rural gardens may attract Rabbits – not always a good thing as they may destroy your plants, but they may also attract interesting predators like Stoats.

→ Scattering morsels of food around rather than putting it all in one place will encourage animals like this Fox cub to spend more time foraging.

NESTBOX KNOW-HOW

If you can get the birds feeding, why not see if you can get them breeding, too? Natural nest sites aren't always easy to come by, and for some species they can even be a 'limiting resource' – their availability being the main factor that puts a ceiling on the number of pairs that can live in a certain area. By providing extra ones, you can make a real difference, and give yourself the chance to witness the whole fascinating process at close quarters.

A ROOM WITH A HOLE

↓ This tit nestbox, currently occupied by Blue Tits, is made of Woodcrete which is much tougher (though more expensive) than wood.

The standard nestbox is a rectangular wooden box with a sloping, overhanging roof and a hole about two-thirds of the way up on the front face (or one of the sides). A box like this mimics a hole in a tree (whether natural or made by a woodpecker) and will attract various hole-nesters, especially tits. Blue, Great, Coal, Marsh and Crested Tits all use nestboxes (although you'd have to be very lucky and in the right place to attract the latter two). The box should be roughly 20 x 15 x 15cm (about 5cm taller at the back to allow for the sloped roof), with the hole at least 12.5cm from the box bottom. Great Tits need an entrance hole of at least 2.8cm diameter, while the smaller species can go down to 2.5cm. Small is good as it will help keep out predators.

Other species that may use nestboxes with slightly larger holes include House and Tree Sparrows and Nuthatches. Scale everything up a bit more and your box could attract Starlings. Larger hole-nesters include Stock Doves, Ring-necked Parakeets and, surprisingly, various ducks.

OPEN PLAN AND SPECIALISED

If, instead of an entrance hole, the box has a half open front like a stable door, it will appeal to Robins, Wrens, Pied and Grey Wagtails and Spotted Flycatchers.

Nestbox safety

Whether you're building a box or buying one ready made, make sure its dimensions are such that predators would have a hard time gaining access. As Great Spotted Woodpeckers sometimes drill through and Grey Squirrels sometimes chew through wooden boxes to get at the chicks, you may consider a box made of the sturdier 'woodcrete' material which combines wood fibres with cement. A metal plate around the hole also discourages predator attacks.

Other designs of wooden box have been developed to appeal to different species, such as Tawny Owls, which will use a 'chimney'-style box (a long rectangular box, open completely at one end and hung at an angle of 45 degrees or less). House Sparrows are gregarious so if you want to attract more, provide more than one nestbox. Non-wooden boxes include artificial House Martin nests, are made of a mix of sawdust and cement, and are designed to resemble the mud cups this species builds under house eaves, and 'Swift bricks' – precast masonry blocks with holes to allow Swifts to nest inside.

↑ Fix nestboxes for Sparrows high up on a wall, especially if the sparrows are already nesting in the guttering, or on a suitable tree or pole as here.

↑ Not many householders are likely to have a suitable spot for a Kestrel nestbox – you'll need to be able to give the birds plenty of space away from your house.

↓ These House Martin nestboxes go under the eaves and mimic the real thing, and if successful could form the basis of a new colony.

SITING THE BOX

Ideally, put your box well above the reach of cats or curious children, and somewhere where there is some nearby cover so the adults don't feel too exposed when approaching the box. Attaching it to a tree trunk should take care of the cover issue, but you can also fix the box to a wall. Cover is extra important for species such as Robins or Wrens, which choose the open-fronted boxes, as they rely more heavily on concealment than inaccessibility to stay safe from predators.

SITING FOR PARTICULAR SPECIES

Specialised boxes may be more limited in terms of positioning. House Martin boxes can only go under the eaves, while boxes for large hole-nesting species like Tawny Owls really need to go high up in the largest tree available. If you invest in a big box like this, make sure that your target species is indeed living locally, and be prepared for possible disappointment as these species are often fiercely loyal to their nest sites and only a newly established pair are likely to be on the hunt for accommodation.

OTHER WILDLIFE HOMES

Don't forget about the other inhabitants of your garden, big and small, when it comes to buying or making places for them to live. Most of the non-bird species we're going to look at next don't need places in which to have their babies, but do require safe and sheltered spots in which to pass the winter months. Providing winter homes for hibernating animals can be very simple and satisfying.

MINIBEAST HOTELS

↓ Part of a 'minibeast stack' – all sorts of different materials from drilled-out bricks to Teasel heads and rolled-up cardboard offer shelter for hibernating insects.

Many kinds of insects, such as ladybirds and lacewings, pass the winter in their adult form. They therefore need to find a small hidey-hole which will offer them protection from the weather and also from predators. What could be better than a hollow, broken stem of bamboo? Of course, broken bamboo stems are not a common resource in the wider countryside, but you can easily offer a bundle of them in your garden. Other options are bricks with small but deep holes drilled inside. Place them so the holes are horizontal to keep out rain.

A 'wildlife stack' is a collection of stacked-up materials offering winter shelter for insects. You can use wooden pallets as a framework. It might include bamboo stem bundles, drilled bits of bricks and wood, pine cones, clumps of hay

underneath roof tiles, woodchips and pretty much any other natural or unnatural materials offering a range of different-sized hiding places. Sited in a sheltered spot close to lots of vegetation, a wildlife stack can be as attractive to look at as it is appealing to insects.

HIDEOUTS FOR LARGER ANIMALS

Amphibians, Hedgehogs and various small rodents spend at least some of the winter months fast asleep, and it's easy to provide a place for them to snooze in peace. Frogs and newts often seek out a soggy ditch, but toads will overwinter in slightly drier places – if you have toads, you could put down some overturned plant pots, with the edge propped up on something, for them to sleep under. You can also buy specially designed ceramic toad houses.

■ **Hedgehogs** may both hibernate in and nest inside a purpose-built 'hedgehog home', which you can buy or make yourself. It should be a plywood box (12mm thick) with overall dimensions of 60 x 40 x 30cm deep, incorporating an entrance chamber of 22 x 40cm, and with entrance holes of 12cm diameter into the chamber and from the chamber into the main nestbox. Place the box in a dry, sheltered position and cover and conceal it with a covering of dead vegetation.

■ **Bat boxes** look a bit like bird nestboxes but are usually narrow at the base and have open bottoms to serve as the entrance, befitting the upside-down locomotion habits of their intended occupants. If you have bats around it may be worth fixing boxes like this to your house or to trees in the garden, where they may serve as winter roosts. Try putting several up close together at different points around a tree trunk, as they will reach different temperatures inside depending how much sun they get in the day, and offer visiting bats a choice of heating levels. The likeliest species to take advantage of them include the pipistrelles, and the spectacular Brown Long-eared Bat.

■ **Small mammals** quite often appropriate bird nestboxes in winter and stuff them with dry grasses to make a cosy bed.

■ **Certain species of bees** may also establish their colonies in nestboxes in the summer months after birds have chosen a nest site. If this happens to your box, the wildlife-friendly thing to do is to leave them to it and put up another nestbox.

↓ These Woodcrete bat boxes have been positioned close together around the same tree trunk – the heat level inside will depend on the box's orientation.

↑ This 'Hogitat' hedgehog shelter is a comfortable purpose-built home for Hedgehogs. It is available from the RSPB online shop.

GARDENING FOR WILDLIFE

Feeders, nestboxes and minibeast homes are all great things to have in your garden, but the most important element of all is the plants. As well as being a place where wild plants can be encouraged in their own right, your garden can be a miniature but complete ecosystem, with a plant community selected to support as rich a variety of animals as possible.

GO NATIVE

↑ If you're lucky enough to have an Oak in your garden, cherish it, as its leaves, branches and acorns shelter and sustain a huge number of native species.

Plants and animals which have evolved together over millennia form close interdependencies, which is why native plants will always attract and support more animal life than non-natives. That doesn't mean you can't have your favourite exotic blooms in the garden but make space for some native species too. You can buy wild-flower seed in most garden centres, but check your local countryside to see whether the species you want are already thriving in the area. If you are planting a new tree, pick a native species if at all possible, and if you already have native trees or shrubs growing in your garden then hang onto them – they are precious and will form the cornerstones of your garden's wildlife community.

Something for everyone
When choosing which plants to put in your garden, consider what the flowers can offer the animals. Animals depend on plants in a variety of ways. Caterpillars eat plant foliage, and many adult insects visit flowers for nectar. Fruits and seeds are eaten by a wide variety of animals, and the actual structure of the plant (especially if it is a tree or shrub) provides

shelter and sometimes nesting sites. Try to ensure you have a range of nectar-bearing plants that between them bloom from early spring into autumn, to accommodate insects with different flying seasons.

Shopping list
Some particularly good plants to put on your shopping list include Blackberry, Common Hawthorn, Crab Apple, Elder, Honeysuckle, Ivy, knapweeds, thistles and Teasel. If you allow a part of your lawn to 'grow wild', you will probably get wildlife-friendly flowers such as Dandelion, Lady's Smock, Ox-eye Daisy, sorrels and speedwells, along with attractive wild grasses like Cocksfoot, Timothy and Yorkshire Fog.

MANAGING YOUR PLANTS
For wildlife gardening, a hands-off approach is often to be encouraged. Don't dead-head flowers if their seeds are attractive to birds – sunflowers and other members of the daisy family produce oily seeds which finches relish. If you allow part of your lawn to become a wildlife meadow, it should be left undisturbed and only cut at the end of summer. Bushy hedges will attract more sheltering wildlife than neatly pruned ones – and at all costs avoid cutting your hedges during the breeding season (March to August) as you may disturb nesting birds.

↓ Bramble or Blackberry is wonderful for wildlife, offering nectar, tasty fruit and thorny shelter. The flowers are just as pretty as those of any rose.

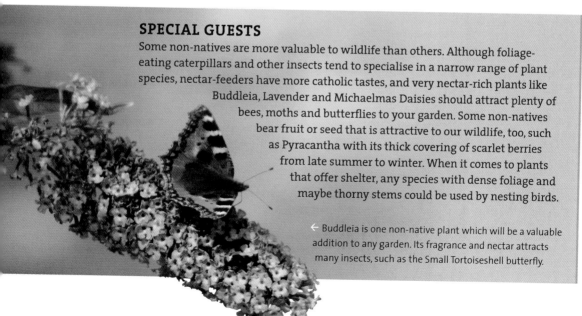

SPECIAL GUESTS
Some non-natives are more valuable to wildlife than others. Although foliage-eating caterpillars and other insects tend to specialise in a narrow range of plant species, nectar-feeders have more catholic tastes, and very nectar-rich plants like Buddleia, Lavender and Michaelmas Daisies should attract plenty of bees, moths and butterflies to your garden. Some non-natives bear fruit or seed that is attractive to our wildlife, too, such as Pyracantha with its thick covering of scarlet berries from late summer to winter. When it comes to plants that offer shelter, any species with dense foliage and maybe thorny stems could be used by nesting birds.

← Buddleia is one non-native plant which will be a valuable addition to any garden. Its fragrance and nectar attracts many insects, such as the Small Tortoiseshell butterfly.

FRINGE BENEFITS

What else does your garden need? Besides space for all the things you want to do – perhaps a play area for the children, somewhere to sit and space for drying the washing – there are plenty of other elements you can add to make it more appealing to wildlife. Most of these involve mimicking things you would find in the natural setting that's closest to the average garden – a deciduous woodland.

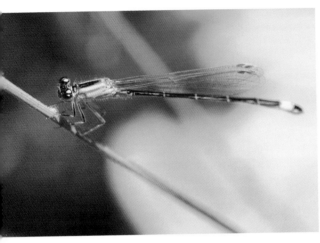

↑ Dragonflies and damselflies all need fresh water to breed. The Blue-tailed Damselfly is a common species which should be quick to colonise your pond.

PONDS

Permanent or nearly permanent fresh water is found naturally in woodlands – there may be streams, or ponds which form when hollows left by fallen trees get flooded. They provide drinking water for the land animals and a home for species that live in water for some or all of their life cycles. Including any form of standing water in your garden will greatly increase its attractiveness to wildlife, with a fully established, vegetated pond best of all.

Making a pond If there's no room for a pond, supply a source of drinking water for birds in a wide, shallow container – an old dustbin lid is fine. It is important that the container is shallow, as small mammals may fall in and be unable to escape if it's too deep. Replenish the water as required.

To make a 'proper' pond you'll need to dig a suitable hollow with sloping sides and a range of depths, line it with sand and a sheet of waterproof material and weigh the edges down with stones. Then you can add clean water (water from an existing pond may contain bacteria). You'll need to add some plants like water milfoils to keep the water oxygenated, and planting wet-loving plants around the margins will provide help for insects like dragonflies, which mature under water then crawl out to assume their adult forms. Low flat stones half-submerged in the water provide perches for birds to use when they drink. Small native fish like Sticklebacks can live in a good-sized pond, but if you want to attract newts you should not introduce any fish.

WOODPILES AND STONE STACKS

Damp, decaying wood might not be top of your list for garden beauty, but a woodpile offers food and shelter for many small creatures. Beetle grubs and some wasp larvae munch through the wood, while earwigs and woodlice hide in its depths. This makes the woodpile a happy hunting ground for predatory beetles

A LOAD OF RUBBISH

If you have a garden, you need a compost heap. Not only does it save you throwing away your food waste and gives you (eventually) a high-quality fertiliser when it has rotted down, but it also attracts wildlife. Many other invertebrates will join the worms and microbes to help break down the contents of the heap, and Slow-worms may come and dwell in its warmth.

Grass cuttings can go on the compost heap, or you can leave them where they are or pile them up in shady spots. Besides other wildlife, they may entice a passing Grass Snake to lay her eggs there, especially if your garden has a pond with a supply of tadpoles for the baby snakes to hunt.

← Among the rotting apple cores and garden trimmings of your compost heap you may spot the gleaming scales of a half-hidden Slow-worm.

and bugs, spiders and small insectivorous birds like Wrens. Fungi will colonise the wood and produce their fruiting bodies in autumn.

A pile of stones is a drier version of the woodpile, providing shelter for just as many small animals. You can build this up into a proper drystone wall (though you may need some help from an expert to ensure your wall is stable, and sourcing the stones may be tricky). The holes between the stones provide hiding places for insects and, if big enough, cavities which may attract nesting birds and small mammals. Openings at the bottom of the pile will provide shelter for amphibians over winter.

↓ Any kind of fresh water could attract Grey Herons, though you're most likely to see them if you have a very large pond on your property.

BEYOND THE GARDEN

Most of us do our wildlife-watching either in our garden or at various nature reserves, or both. There's plenty of other countryside out there, though, but because most of it belongs to other people, we keep to the footpaths and don't hang around too long. However, many landowners are more than sympathetic to wildlife and wildlife-watchers, and if you're willing to ask, you may get permission to do some more active wildlife-watching in the wider countryside.

WILD FEEDING STATIONS

If your garden bird table attracts a good number and variety of birds, just think how many more could be enticed to visit a feeding station in the middle of a woodland. Or how about on the boundary between woodland and farmland, where species like Yellowhammers and partridges may be encouraged into view? If you've noticed a promising-looking spot in your local area, why not find out who owns the land and see if you can get their permission to set up a bird feeding station there?

The beauty of this kind of set-up is that if you are allowed to go just a little way onto private land, you can be sure that your feeding station will be almost completely undisturbed. By screening off your approach to it and using a hide, you will ensure that you don't disturb the feeding birds either.

↓ Many farmland birds, such as Red-legged Partridge, will be attracted to feeding stations – a substitute for the split grain they used to feed on in days of simpler farming methods.

PUTTING OUT THE BAIT

If you've found an animal living locally which you're keen to study more closely, you may be able to entice it to spend more time in a particular area. This can be accomplished by putting out a suitable form of bait (again, you'll need the landowner's permission for this).

A cache of nuts and seeds on the ground or slightly elevated should attract small rodents as well as birds. Dog or cat food (soaked if the dry variety) may entice larger mammals such as Hedgehogs, Foxes and Badgers.

OTHER WAYS TO ATTRACT WILDLIFE IN THE WILD

If you have found yourself a sympathetic landowner, why not see whether you can get permission to do a little habitat enhancement work

↑ Red Kites are scavengers, searching the ground below for roadkill and other casualties, and may be attracted to strategically placed fresh meat.

on the land? You could put up nestboxes for a variety of bird species, ask for dead trees to be allowed to rot in place to feed invertebrates, help with hedge planting or pond landscaping – the options are endless. Always be willing to offer to show the landowner 'their' wildlife, and help instil in them the same sense of wonder you're feeling at the wildlife encounters you are enjoying. At the same time, always be respectful that you're on someone else's land; if you meet resistance to an idea don't argue or push, and don't assume that because you have permission to stray off the path, that will apply to all your friends too.

↑ A woodpile on this scale is out of question for most gardens, but in a privately owned wood it is quite feasible and offers great shelter for wildlife.

↓ Flowery meadows are now rare in the UK – if you can persuade a landowner to leave a patch of grassland to grow wild it will attract many insects.

SPORADIC OR CONSISTENT?

Supplying food for wildlife should be done either just once in a while or a regular basis, and nothing in between. If you start supplying food regularly, and then stop, the animals may suffer without a resource that they have come to depend on. Establishments like Gigrin Farm in Wales, which attracts hundreds of Red Kites along with many Buzzards, Ravens and other birds to the daily feed, illustrate just how quickly wild animals can come to depend on handouts. Unless you can be sure that you will be able to keep up the supplies long term, it's best for the wildlife to stick to ad hoc food provisioning.

MOTH TRAPS

We have already touched on what moth traps are for and what they're made of in Chapter 3. Now we take a more detailed look at the process of using your trap, whether in your garden or in the wider countryside. With more than 2,000 British species, moths form an endlessly fascinating animal group, ranging from the spectacular to the fiendishly difficult to identify, and with a moth trap you can open the door to studying them in all their diversity.

TRAPPING IN YOUR GARDEN

Most beginner moth trappers will set up their gear in the back garden. You might think that because you haven't observed many moths in your garden the results will be disappointing, but give it a try, you may well be very pleasantly surprised by the results. Even quite small gardens could attract more than 200 different species of moths through the years.

It is wise to warn your neighbours if you are going to be running your trap, especially if it uses a mercury vapour bulb, as these are extremely bright. Place the trap somewhere where the light won't shine straight into anyone's windows (including your own). You should not use the trap on consecutive nights as you'll end up retrapping some of the same moths that you caught the night before (unless you have a very big garden and are able to site the trap somewhere different each time you use it).

↓ Interesting captures like this Poplar Hawkmoth can be kept safe in collecting pots for a short while if you want to show them to the rest of the family.

← If you want to take a clear photograph for identification, try gently encouraging your moth onto a clean white background. This is a Willow Beauty.

CHECKING THE CATCH

You could stay with your trap into the night, then switch off when you go to bed, or you could leave it unattended and check it in the morning. If you do the latter, make it early in the morning for the moths' sake, as there will be some that didn't get inside the trap but are resting nearby, and these will be snaffled up by birds if you don't rescue them.

If you have a small, uncluttered but windowed room, this can be ideal for emptying your trap as any moths that make a break for it will settle on the window glass where you can examine them or easily catch them in a pot for closer study. Otherwise, go through the trap contents outside and accept that some of your moths may fly away before you have had a good look at them (though many become very docile in the daytime and can easily be coaxed onto your hand or into a pot). Whatever you do with your moths after capture, whether it's a close look under a hand lens or a few photographs, don't detain them too long, and if they refuse to fly to safety, place them in cover where they'll have a good chance of being overlooked by predators.

BRANCHING OUT

When trapping at home, you can run your bulb from your home's mains electricity. If you are keen to trap somewhere out in the countryside (and have permission to do so) you may have to purchase or hire a generator to power the bulb. If your trap uses a less powerful actinic bulb rather than a mercury vapour bulb, it can be powered from a car or a motorcycle battery. If trapping away from home, it's very sensible to team up with another trapper or two, so you can share your resources, and from a safety point of view you'll be able to look out for each other.

That's not a moth!

Light doesn't just attract moths. Alongside your Black Arches, Feathered Gothics and Hebrew Characters, you may find lacewings, ichneumons, beetles and sometimes even wasps or hornets. Many of these are harmless and are just as interesting to the amateur entomologist as any moth. Others could be bad news for both you and your moths. Wasps can be removed without too much trouble if you do it first thing in the morning. If you don't, they will become increasingly active as they warm up and will be more likely to sting you and to kill your moths.

↑ The Skinner moth trap is the 'industry standard', ideal for garden use, and can be purchased from suppliers like NHBS (www.nhbs.com).

STUDYING SMALL ANIMALS

Catching small insects and other invertebrates can be done without injuring or stressing them, and with some species it's easy to replicate their natural environment and give them an artificial home for a short time, while you observe their behaviour. This is something you can do easily and cheaply at home, and it's a great way to get the whole family involved in 'nature study'.

↗ A suitable habitat for a group of captive Woodlice should include soil, stones and decaying wood and vegetation, kept somewhat damp.

↓ A pitfall trap is a simple way to capture walking insects and other invertebrates. You can prop up the jar's lid with a stone if it is a rainy day.

SETTING UP A VIVARIUM FOR INVERTEBRATES

You're going to need a fish tank, but it doesn't have to be completely watertight so you might be able to pick up a bargain. It will need a lid, though, which supplies ventilation. What goes into the vivarium next depends on what you'd like to keep in it and for how long, but if you're not sure, just put in some earth and a few stones from your garden to start with. Later on you could add some small plants, dead vegetation and perhaps some dead twigs which you can poke into the ground.

CATCH

Now it's time to catch your subject or subjects. For this, you could use a pooter (see Chapter 3 for how to make one) or, for a more relaxed approach, try a pitfall trap. These are easy to make – you just dig a hole in the ground, sink a jam jar or similar receptacle into the hole so the top of the jar is level with the earth around,

and retreat and wait. Sooner or later, an inattentive woodlouse, centipede, beetle or other small animal will fall into the trap. Inspect your pitfall traps every hour, as there is a slight chance you could catch a shrew, which will not survive long if it can't climb back out again.

Other ways of catching ground invertebrates include putting out bait such as soft, overripe fruit, painting a sweet mix of honey and beer onto tree trunks or laying a white sheet under a bush and shaking the foliage so insects fall out onto the sheet. Or you could just pick up stones which have lain on the ground undisturbed for some time, and put them straight in the tank along with the creatures that will inevitably be clinging to their underside. Once you have the animals you want inside the tank, you can remove any unwanted hangers-on and add any extra resources that your chosen creatures will appreciate.

WATCH

Now you can take a look at what your creatures do with themselves. Some animals won't do very much, but others will exhibit some fascinating behaviour. If you catch a spider, you may be lucky enough to witness it constructing its web. If you put a few snails in your vivarium, you may get to observe their extraordinary and protracted courtship and mating ritual. Whatever you catch, you should release it after a day or be prepared to find out more about its diet and habits in order to make sure you're meeting all of its needs for a longer stay.

↑ Garden Spiders are not great travellers, so you can keep one reasonably happy in a tank or muslin 'bug cage' as long as you provide flies for it to eat.

Water life

It's possible to establish a tank of miniature life similar to what exists in your garden pond (obviously for this the tank will have to be watertight!). Your community could include pond snails, aquatic insect nymphs and tiny swimming organisms, such as rotifers and water fleas, which you'll only be able to watch properly with a strong lens. Setting up and managing a tank like this is quite demanding, if you want to run it for more than a day. You'll need a good layer of mud on the tank bottom, some oxygenating plants and perhaps also a pump. The water should be taken from an actual pond. If you are keeping insect nymphs which you wish to rear to adulthood, you may need to give them some supplementary food. However, if you just want to observe small aquatic life for a short while, you can simply transfer some water from pond to tank and watch, but make sure you put the tank in a shady place or it could rapidly overheat.

RAISING CATERPILLARS

Rearing caterpillars to maturity has long been a popular activity among amateur naturalists. You get to see the caterpillar grow and feed, witness the whole extraordinary magic of metamorphosis, and at the end of the process (all being well) release a perfect new adult moth or butterfly into the wild. It is a wonderful activity for children to get involved in and, in a small way, can even help improve the local fortunes of the species you're rearing. Don't rear from caterpillar kits as releasing non-local species into the wild can upset the ecology of your area.

↑ Mature caterpillars like this Oak Eggar may be found wandering far from their food plants, looking for a place to pupate – which you can provide.

→ A bug cage consists of muslin pulled tight around a simple frame, and makes an ideal container in which to raise caterpillars.

KNOW YOUR CATERPILLAR

It really helps if you can identify the caterpillar or caterpillars you've found before attempting to rear them. This will help inform you about what the species' exact dietary and habitat requirements are, and will also help you avoid disappointment when your 'caterpillar' transforms into a sawfly or beetle rather than the expected butterfly or moth.

If you can't make a positive identification, get to know your caterpillar as best you can by observing its natural behaviour in the wild before you bring it home. What is the plant species it is eating and will you be able to get fresh supplies of that plant? Does it favour small new leaves or more mature ones? Does it keep to the shade or bask in the sun? Does it feed alone or cheek-to-jowl with its brothers and sisters? Armed with as much information as possible, you are well placed to offer the caterpillar a safe and appropriate home.

THE SET-UP

Put several stems of the foodplant in a container filled with water, then seal off the top of the container with cotton wool so the caterpillars can't fall in. Now place this inside another container such as a fishtank. Transfer your caterpillars onto the leaves from the plant on which you brought them home, using a soft paintbrush. Now place the assembly into another, larger container, such as a fish tank, with muslin stretched and taped across the frame of the lid to allow air in and out. Keep the set-up somewhere where there is at least partial shade, lots of circulating air and no artificial heating.

WHAT NEXT?

The caterpillar or caterpillars will munch up the leaves and poo a lot. Provide fresh leaves whenever the caterpillars have nearly finished the ones they have or if the leaves start to look droopy. The caterpillars should grow rapidly and shed their skins at regular intervals.

Some caterpillars overwinter before pupation. Others will overwinter in their pupal form while some complete the whole cycle before winter. Once your caterpillar is ready to pupate, it will usually leave its foodplant and begin wandering about, so be ready and provide some suitable sites. Some moth caterpillars pupate among leaf-litter or in soil, while many butterflies pupate suspended from twigs. Cover all eventualities by providing a layer of soil, topped with dead leaves, in the tank and poking some upright sticks into the soil. The books should tell you how long the species you're rearing spends in the pupal state.

↑ You must release the adult moth or butterfly as soon as it is mobile, as it will want to seek a mate or (like this Brimstone) feed up to prepare itself for hibernation.

EMERGENCE

It's easy to miss the big moment, so check your pupae frequently when the 'due date' is approaching and look out for any changes of colour or signs of movement. The pupa will usually split along the back, and the adult insect climbs out through this hole. At first its wings are small and crumpled and its abdomen bloated, but the wings gradually expand, stiffen and straighten. When this process is complete, it's time to take a quick photo then let the adult insect go.

POTENTIAL PROBLEMS

If your caterpillars don't seem to be thriving, you should return them to where they came from and accept that you might not find out this time what was going wrong. One problem that may not be obvious until it's too late is attack by parasites. Ichneumon flies lay their eggs in caterpillars' bodies, and the first sign of this is often when the caterpillar stops moving and the fly larvae emerge and pupate. Gruesome though this is, it is still a natural and interesting process to observe.

← To find eggs and caterpillars, keep a lookout for female butterflies (this is a Common Blue) or moths discreetly laying their eggs.

TALK TO THE ANIMALS

Great apes can be taught to use sign language, but most other species seem to lack the ability or inclination to learn how to communicate with human words. However, we can sometimes find ways to speak their languages, and we can use these to get a glimpse into their worlds. Animal communication is extraordinarily complex and much of it will always be beyond our grasp, but trying to communicate with them is fun and wonderful, when it works.

→ 'Pishing' or making squeaky noises by kissing the back of your your hand may attract shy birds like this Chiffchaff.

↓ Tapping rapidly on wood may attract the attention of a Great Spotted Woodpecker.

BIRD-SPEAK

Most bird sounds are variants of a whistle, so if you can whistle you have the means to try a few conversations with wild birds. Many songs are too complex and rapid to follow, but you could try certain phrases. The drawn-out, thin '*seee seee seee*' section of a Nightingale's song is easy to imitate, and your rendition may be enough to tempt the songster itself out of the undergrowth to have a quick look at you. Try imitating the long, low, quavering whistle of a Tawny Owl's hoot after dark, and see if you can elicit an answer. Don't keep it up for more than a minute, though, as the birds have other things to do

SECRET SIGNALS

It is possible to attract the attention of a Great Spotted Woodpecker by knocking a piece of wood against a resonant tree trunk. You can imitate the rapid 'drumming' they perform in spring by rattling a short stick against a branch fork.

Nightjar males proclaim their territory by flashing white patches on their wings – a clear visual signal to other males. You can sometimes persuade a Nightjar to come closer to you by flicking a white handkerchief in the air or, for extra height, throw a white table-tennis ball in the air.

↓ A skilled human whistler can produce a fair imitation of a Blackbird's warbling song, enough to pique the bird's curiosity at least.

CATCHING A BUTTERFLY'S EYE

Butterflies are mainly attuned to home in on certain colours (as well as smells) as they fly along, and you can take advantage of the fact that their vision delivers poor detail by placing something of about the right size and colour in their path. Male butterflies are always looking for mating opportunities and will drop down to investigate anything that's about the same size and colour as a female of their species. A piece of white paper will attract a white butterfly, while a Meadow Brown may be drawn to a strategically positioned dead leaf. Flower colours are also important. Swallowtail butterflies, which roam over Broadland reedbeds to find the few concentrations of flowers, are attracted to anything pink or purple – even a cerise sock draped over the reeds may tempt them down.

↑ This is what male Green-veined White butterflies are looking for – a female. But anything white of about the right size will draw them down for a closer look.

Tape-luring and why you shouldn't

Playing actual birdsong while you're out, via an MP3 player with a speaker, is a technique widely used by researchers to attract territorial male birds. The practice is called 'tape-luring' and can be very effective. However, it should not be used by amateurs, and no one should use it to excess.

The male bird responds to the song because it convinces him that a new rival male has arrived in his territory, and he comes over to find and drive away the challenger. This kind of occurrence does happen naturally, so male birds are equipped to deal with it, but serious territorial challenges are usually rare and are highly stressful for the birds concerned. Therefore, tape-luring should be kept to an absolute minimum to ensure the male does not suffer too much stress or neglect his duties towards his mate and nest.

AMATEUR POWER

In these days of grant-chasing research scientists, it's easy to forget that our nation has a long tradition of amateur science, represented in the field of natural history perhaps more than any other. Actually, things haven't changed as much as you might think, as today there are still thousands of amateur naturalists contributing huge amounts of data to scientific study. You don't need a laboratory or expensive equipment to make scientifically valuable observations of nature – just a front door.

A MYSTERIOUS WORLD

Whatever plant or animal species you care to name, it's a pretty safe bet that there are some large gaps in our knowledge about it. The same goes for general phenomena, such as how birds navigate, how plants respond to changes in day length through the year or whether climate change is having a real impact on our wildlife. At the end of the 20th century the House Sparrow, surely one of our most familiar animal species, began a steep and catastrophic decline, and we still don't know exactly why.

Natural history is generally defined as the study of living things through observation rather than experimentation, and so there's a huge amount that the more casual observer can contribute. You can sign up to a large number of surveys to add your data in a formal way, but you may also sometimes make an interesting 'ad hoc' observation, which, if passed on to the right people, could add a new piece to the huge jigsaw puzzle that is our growing understanding of nature.

→ In order to save rare species like Dartford Warbler, you need to study exactly how they live, to protect the ecosystem on which they depend.

SAVING LIVES

Scientific research isn't just about furthering knowledge for its own sake. Many species of plants and animals are in trouble, both here and abroad, and we need to learn as much as we can about their ways of life in order to work out how best we can help them avoid further decline and extinction. Then it's a matter of putting into practice what we have learned, and that can mean physical labour as we modify and manage habitats to best suit their needs.

There are many ways in which you can help support the work of the scientists and conservationists striving to understand and safeguard our wildlife. By getting involved in research or conservation projects, you'll be doing your bit to ensure that the wildlife you enjoy watching today will still be around in your later years, and for future generations.

↑ You will soon become attuned to unusual observations, such as this juvenile Moorhen helping its parents by feeding one of its young siblings.

↓ The Small Skipper and Essex Skipper were only recognised as different species in 1889 – now scientists are studying their ecology.

NATURAL HISTORY OR BIOLOGY?

Natural history used to have a very broad meaning back in the days of the Victorian naturalists, including such diverse areas as astronomy and geology. Many of the wealthy naturalists of those days had wide-ranging interests, especially those who had the time and money to completely devote their lives to their interests. Now that we have formalised our definitions of the different scientific disciplines, natural history has been somewhat subsumed by biology – the study of living things and life systems, and the term 'natural history' is now generally only used to cover the study of plants, fungi and animals. A further distinction is that biology's research methods include plenty of experimental work that is undertaken in a lab.

JOINED-UP THINKING

The most straightforward way to help conservation bodies is to join them. Depending on the organisation, your membership fees go into the pot to be spent on buying and managing land for nature reserves, carrying out surveys and other research, campaigning against potentially destructive developments, and liaising with landowners to help them encourage and look after the wildlife on their land. In return, you'll get various benefits, often including free access to some wonderful wildlife-watching places.

THE RSPB

↓ Many RSPB reserves are in remote wilderness but some, like Lodmoor in Dorset, are close to towns.

With a million members, the Royal Society for the Protection of Birds is the UK's most significant conservation charity. It was founded in 1889 by a group of women concerned that the lavish use of bird feathers in hats and other garments was causing severe declines in species such as Great Crested Grebes. From these simple beginnings the society has grown fast in terms of both its remit and its membership and influence. Today, it manages more than 200 nature reserves, covering almost 143,000 hectares of superb wildlife habitat, and is a powerful and significant voice in support of all wildlife, not just birds. It is also the UK partner of the global organisation BirdLife International.

GO GLOBAL

There are many wildlife charities active abroad. The Worldwide Fund for Nature (WWF) is heavily involved in saving some of our planet's most spectacular and threatened wildlife, while BirdLife International offers you the chance to join the World Bird Club and support conservation work on some of the world's rarest birds.

Membership benefits

As an RSPB member, you get free access to the majority of these reserves, plus the stunning quarterly magazine *Birds*. For young members there is *Wild Times* magazine (for under eights), *Bird Life* magazine (for 8 to 12 year olds) and *Wingbeat* magazine for teens. All of the publications are packed with a wide variety of articles about wildlife of all kinds, illustrated with spectacular colour photos and artwork. On joining you'll also receive a free gift, which may be a bird book or a feeder for your garden.

THE WILDLIFE TRUSTS

All 47 of the Wildlife Trusts are concerned with protecting local wildlife in both town and country. The Wildlife Trusts buy and manage land as nature reserves, and members will get free access to those reserves for which a fee is normally payable. Overall, the Trusts have 800,000 members and manage 2,300 reserves, from very small pockets of land within our cities to grand-scale wild spaces. All members receive the Natural World magazine, and some Trust branches publish their own magazines too.

THE WILDFOWL & WETLANDS TRUST

This charity, founded by Sir Peter Scott, protects outstanding wetland areas and their wildlife. There are nine WWT centres across the UK, all with lavish visitor facilities and the opportunity to see some impressive wildfowl gatherings as well as (at some centres) a collection of exotic waterfowl from around the world, where globally endangered species are bred with a view to reintroduction in their native habitat. Members get free entry to the centres as well as a joining gift and the quarterly *Waterlife* magazine.

↑ Most Wildfowl and Wetlands Centres have a collection of exotic wildfowl – great for learning different species before you head for the 'wild' part of the centre.

OTHER ORGANISATIONS

The British Trust for Ornithology is concerned with bird research, studying everything from migration to breeding success in all species. Members receive an exciting free gift on joining and *BTO News* magazine six times a year. Butterfly Conservation is a charity promoting the conservation of butterflies, moths and their habitats, and manages more than 30 reserves in England, Wales and Scotland. Members receive *Butterfly* magazine three times a year. Buglife works to study and protect all invertebrate groups – one of the benefits for members is a free day out with a bug expert. The equivalent organisation for plants is Plantlife, which includes fungi in its remit and manages 23 reserves. Members receive *Plantlife* magazine three times a year and are invited to various exclusive events. The Mammal Society offers similar benefits for all those interested in mammal conservation.

→ The organisation Butterfly Conservation has several reserves managed to encourage butterflies – this is Park Corner Heath in East Sussex.

COUNTING BIRDS

When you see your first Swallow of the spring or hear your first Cuckoo, who are you going to tell? Who's going to be interested to know that you have Treecreepers nesting in your garden for the first time? Friends and family, perhaps, but researchers also want to know. The general public is a potentially huge source of data on all kinds of bird observations, and you can easily make real and meaningful contributions to many large-scale projects.

↑ The UK is internationally important for many wetland birds, including Pink-footed Geese. Take part in the BTO's Wetland Bird Survey to help keep track of them.

RSPB SURVEYS

■ **The Big Garden Birdwatch** takes place over the last weekend of January each year and is the world's biggest bird survey. It's ideal for all the family to get involved, as all you need to do is watch your garden (or someone else's) for one hour at some point over the weekend and record all the birds you see. After 30 years of results, the survey has highlighted interesting changes in garden bird numbers, including dramatic declines in House Sparrows and Starlings.

■ **Big Schools Birdwatch** Related to the RSPB's Big Garden Birdwatch, the Big Schools Birdwatch count is performed on school premises, for one hour during a school day. Schools who register get lots of help, including identification charts, instructions on how to make simple bird feeders and tips for attracting birds.

■ **Other public surveys** Other RSPB surveys to which you can contribute include the RSPB National Swift Inventory, recording breeding territories for this enigmatic bird, and the Bird Conservation Targeting Project, a collaboration with the BTO and others to identify important sites for uncommon birds outside of nature reserves.

BTO SURVEYS

The BTO has numerous research projects, some short term and others continuing year on year indefinitely. As an amateur, you can contribute to many of them.

▥ **Birdtrack** is perhaps the most accessible and significant one of all – it collates sightings of all species week on week, producing a complete picture of their movements through the seasons. Unusual sightings of migratory species are of particular interest, as are records of large flocks, and unseasonal sightings. However, 'everyday' observations are the backbone of the project. Registering and submitting sightings is easy, and you can view the results in various forms including animated maps.

▥ **Breeding Birds Survey** To participate in the Breeding Birds Survey, you'll need to visit a designated 2km square area three times between April and June and record all birds seen. The Garden Birdwatch and Garden Nesting Survey are simple counting surveys. You can also submit details of any nesting birds in your garden, or nests you observe in the wider countryside to the Nest Record Scheme. This project has yielded some extremely valuable data for conservation research. For example, the Kestrel is currently in a period of decline. The Nest Record Scheme records that chick survival from Kestrel nests has actually increased, which indicates that the decline is caused by increased mortality of adults and/or juveniles, rather than any problem at the egg or chick stage.

▥ **Wetland Bird Survey** If you live close to a wetland area, you can take part in the Wetland Bird Survey (WeBS) and count all waterfowl at your site on designated dates. This long-running survey of non-breeding wetland birds has helped identify key sites for concentrations of waterfowl of all species, and to reveal trends in their abundance and the timings of their migrations year on year.

↑ The Big Garden Bird-watch is an annual event for everyone who has access to a garden – just count the birds you see over an hour and submit your results online.

Rings and tags

Once in a while you'll see a bird (or find a dead bird) wearing a ring or rings on its legs, or some other kind of marking such as a wing tag or neck collar. Researchers use these to track the movements of individual birds, and resightings or recoveries of ringed birds can teach us a great deal about their behaviour and migrations. If you find a marked bird and can see or note the details of its rings or tags (colour plus any numbers or letters), send the details to EUring (European Union for Bird Ringing), which coordinates all ringing and tagging projects in Europe – www.euring.org. You should hear back about where your bird was originally marked, its age and any other known details about its life.

← Ringing studies tell us about birds' migrations and longevity. If the full code or number on a ring or tag can be seen, send the details to EUring.

SPOTTING A RARITY

For some of us, the ever-present chance of finding a rarity is really enticing and can persuade us to go out with binoculars and camera in all weathers. When you do find yourself looking at a bird or other creature which you know is really rare, the excitement can be overwhelming. What you do about your sighting is up to you. Others may want to see it, too, but it's not always wise to 'spread the news' willy-nilly. However, one number you should definitely call is that of your local recorder, who collates all records of unusual species for your area.

→ Some rare birds are extremely distinctive. A Spoonbill, with its unique bill shape, is unmistakable as long as you get a reasonably good look.

SURE OF WHAT YOU SEE

Everyone who goes out to look at wildlife will, sooner or later, see something which they think is a rarity or scarcity ('rare' being less common than 'scarce'). If you think you've found something special but aren't sure, you should try to get photos or make sketches, and write a written description – but it's also worth getting hold of someone a bit more expert than you to take a look at what you've seen. If you're lucky, there will be other wildlife-watchers nearby who you can ask for help. If not, try calling a fellow naturalist and, even if they can't meet you to verify your sighting, you can at least give them a description while you're looking at your potential rarity, and they can ask for more pertinent information.

SUBMITTING A RECORD

For most groups of animals and for plants and fungi there will be a local recorder whose job it is to collate sightings. Since the most likely rarities you'll be reporting are birds, we'll look at the procedure for reporting a scarce or rare bird as an example.

■ **County bird recorders** are listed on the BirdTrack website at: **www.bto.org/birdtrack/bird_recording/**

↑ Most 'little brown jobs' or 'LBJs' will prove to be something common, but once in a while you'll find something unusual, like this Bluethroat.

county_bird_recorder.htm. In the first instance, send in a brief description of what you've seen and where. Some species are classed as 'description required', which means you have to supply a more detailed description which will then be assessed to judge whether you have indeed made the correct identification – the recorder will let you know if this is the case with your sighting. If the description includes good photos then there is unlikely to be any dispute, but if it is words only, the recorder must be satisfied that you have ruled out any possible 'confusion species'. If the sighting concerns a particularly rare bird, the local recorder will send it to the British Birds Recording Committee for further scrutiny.

PUTTING THE NEWS OUT

When a rare bird turns up, often many people will want to see it. So as well as informing your county recorder, you may want to inform a publication such as Rare Bird Alert or Birdguides, who quickly make news of rarities available to their subscribers. This way, other local people can enjoy 'your' bird, but there are other times when it would be ill-advised to pass on the news.

■ **Private land** If you find your bird on private land which you have permission to access, you should speak to the landowner first, and only with their permission should you pass on any news.

■ **Scarce breeding birds** If you have found scarce birds which look like they may be breeding, you should not spread the news to avoid disturbance. The RSPB may in due course be able to arrange safe access for visitors, as happened with the Purple Herons that nested at the Dungeness RSPB reserve in 2010.

■ **Sensitive habitat** If you find your rarity where other wildlife (especially breeding birds) would be vulnerable to disturbance from a large arrival of people, this is another time to keep quiet.

WELFARE COMES FIRST

Discoveries of rare birds, flying insects and other mobile animals can teach us a lot about their migratory behaviour. However, in all circumstances the well-being of the rare animal itself, plus that of all the other wildlife in the area, must take priority. That means that some rarities will inevitably 'get away' from many of those who want to see them, because of difficulties of safely accessing the site or because the rarity simply departs before access can be arranged. While this can be disappointing, it's absolutely necessary for the future of our hobby that respect for all wildlife is always upheld.

↓ Rare birds like these Glossy Ibises can attract lots of birdwatchers. You must give the birds lots of space to feed and rest, and watch from a distance.

↑ Rare ducks like this female Hooded Merganser from North America are often more likely to be escapees from captivity than wandering wild birds.

SURVEYING THE SCENE

While birds are probably our most easily observed wildlife, there are other surveys out there for you to participate in, involving pretty much every animal and plant grouping you can think of. Some require a reasonable time commitment, or a certain skill or experience level, but others are simple and would make ideal family or school projects. All of them give you the opportunity to turn your wildlife-watching into a valuable contribution towards conservation research.

↑ the RSPB's Wildsquare scheme charts all wildlife in a given area. The plants you find will help predict which insects are likely to be there – this Birdsfoot Trefoil attracts various butterflies.

→ Butterfly Conservation's surveys, which involve counting butterflies in a set area, are helping to track population changes in species like the Marbled White.

RSPB WILDSQUARE

The premise of the WildSquare project is very simple. You pick a 1km square somewhere convenient for you to visit, and register on the RSPB's WildSquare page: **www.rspb. org.uk/wildsquare/index.asp**. Then you can take part in a wide variety of surveys, finding and counting your local fungi, butterflies, mammals or flowers, as well as various bird species. The WildSquare project is designed for children, and the surveys are perfect for families.

BUTTERFLY SURVEYS

Butterflies are excellent subjects for beginners to survey because they are highly visible, relatively easy to identify and (best of all) most active on pleasant, sunny days. They are also valuable 'indicator species' of habitat quality – if butterfly numbers start to fall, you can be fairly certain that other, less obvious wildlife is suffering too. Butterfly Conservation needs volunteers to take part in various surveys, including the Wider Countryside Butterfly Survey which requires you to note all butterfly species seen in a 1km square of 'general countryside' (as opposed to on a nature reserve). The charity is also introducing a National Moth Recording Scheme.

OTHER SURVEYS

■ **Mammal surveys** The Mammal Society's current surveys include examination of small mammal remains by dissecting owl pellets and a monitoring project assessing the spread of the Muntjac Deer in Britain, while previous surveys have included examining the distribution of Foxes and Polecats. The society has also launched the National Small Mammal Monitoring Scheme, which looks for populations of mice, voles and shrews using a variety of methods from searching suitable areas for Harvest Mouse nests, to using approved live-trapping methods to catch small mammals, so they can be identified before release. Anyone can take part – the society will send you all the information you need.

■ **National Moth Night** Butterfly Conservation has joined forces with the butterfly, moth and dragonfly journal *Atropos* to promote National Moth Night, when everyone interested in moths is encouraged to go in search of them on a designated night, whether by just checking what comes to the kitchen window, running a trap in the garden or attending a local event. The survey now also seeks sightings of bats. The surveys are not necessarily annual so keep an eye out if you want to be involved. The charity Buglife organises several surveys investigating insects and other invertebrates in Britain, while Plantlife does the same for our flora and fungi.

↑ Most sightings submitted to the Harlequin Ladybird Survey involve adults, but observations of Harlequin larvae are also very welcome.

SPECIALIST SURVEYS

Some surveys are organised by much smaller organisations with a very specialised remit. You can often find links to them via the pages of the more main-stream conservation bodies. They include the Harlequin Ladybird Survey, a project looking at the spread of this invasive species, and the UK Glow-worm Survey, researching the distribution of this fascinating insect.

The OPAL Water Survey is one of several projects organised by the Natural History Museum. To participate, all you need is a pond and a few simple tools, many of which can be made at home. The survey needs you to analyse the animals and plants living in your pond, and to supply details of the pond's location, size and depth, and the pH of the water.

→ The OPAL water survey records aquatic wildlife. The presence of certain species, like stoneflies, can be a strong indicator of good water quality.

GOING IT ALONE

Organised surveys are a fantastic way to make good use of your wildlife observations. However, for those pioneering and independent wildlife-watchers, there's no reason you can't design and conduct your own surveys – and they could yield results that are just as useful and valuable. This is the perfect way to recapture the spirit of the Victorian naturalist and possibly make your own unique contribution to scientific knowledge.

↑ Some animals leave very prominent signs behind. Counting the empty yellow pupal cases of Six-spot Burnet moths will give you an idea of the local population.

WHERE TO GO

As most survey types with one data recorder (you!) will only yield meaningful results if you carry out several observations, somewhere local is the obvious choice to begin. You could start in your garden or go to your local patch. Wherever you choose to carry out your study, it should be somewhere that you can visit often, ideally at the same time once a day or once a week.

WHAT TO STUDY

Counting is the simplest form of surveying and it's a good place to start. You could count the number of birds visiting your garden feeders over a designated period, similar to the RSPB's Big Garden Birdwatch but not restricted to just one day. This will eventually give you a picture of the annual population fluctuations for various species in your garden and, by extension, your local area.

Breeding birds
On your local patch, you can get a good idea of how many breeding pairs there are of one or more bird species by visiting regularly through

← Various simple 'nature studies' are easy to devise and everyone in the family can join in – getting fresh air and exercise into the bargain.

→ Noting where male birds like this Whitethroat are singing on your local patch makes it possible to map out the territories of the different individuals.

spring and noting where you hear singing birds. Over the weeks you should build up a clear idea of which individual bird is which, and where the limits of its territory fall. You could even begin to map out the territories by plotting the points where you hear the singing birds on a simple map, which will tell you how large they are, and in which parts of the territory the bird spends most of its time. Cross-reference this with a survey of the general vegetation on the patch, and you'll see what habitat features are most important for the different species.

Investigating insects
One easy way to study study ground invertebrates is to put down hiding places for them, such as pieces of slate or squares of old carpet, and then check what's living underneath, but not too often – once a week should be sufficient to give you a good idea. If you spot anything unusual among the miniature community, you can use a pooter to catch the individual for further examination.

WHAT TO DO WITH THE DATA
Local recorders (for whichever group of animals or plants you're studying) may be interested in your findings and have suggestions for future studies. If you gather a lot of data and want to analyse it, there are various statistical tests you can do to see if you can identify any trends. Practice like this will stand you in good stead if you want to do more formal wildlife survey work in your future career.

→ If you decide to study garden birds like Coal Tits, comparing photos of them may enable to you to consistently identify particular individuals.

TAKE A RIGOROUS APPROACH
If you're going to make a proper study of wildlife, you need to be a bit disciplined in going about it. Experiments are all about controlling irrelevant variables so they don't skew your results, but with observations, you should try to be as consistent as you can in the way you record information and the time that you do it. Taking the garden bird-feeder study as an example, if on week one you only count birds that you see perched on your feeder but in week two you decide to also count birds you see flying overhead, you're obviously recording two different things. The answer is to decide right at the beginning what you're going to look at and what your methods will be. If you begin your study and then decide that your methodology isn't right, you should start again and not include the data from the 'failed' part of the study in your results.

SQUARE DANCING

Many studies, whoever they're organised by, work by making a 'transect count' over a particular area – usually a predefined 1km or 2km square. Another method for counting plants involves using a quadrat – a 1m-square frame which you place on the ground and then count what's inside it. Both techniques take a little practice to master but doing them correctly will help ensure you get good and useful data.

FINDING A SQUARE

For surveys organised by the BTO, Butterfly Conservation and so on, the transect squares are predefined, and finding one is usually a matter of contacting the survey organizer or a local coordinator to find out which squares local to you are in need of coverage. If you want to do an independent transect survey, you can define your own square, using a large-scale Ordnance Survey map to work out the boundaries.

↑ You can order bespoke maps from the Ordnance Survey, centred around any point you choose – ideal for locating places to do transect counts.

WALKING THE TRANSECT

Some surveys require you to cover your designated square thoroughly, perhaps in a set time. For others you just walk a straight path through your square, and some don't designate a measured square at all but just a patch of habitat. If you're doing your own research you can make the rules, but one universal rule should be that you work consistently. Move at a steady pace, and don't stop at a particular point. It can be tempting to do so if you know the site well and know that a certain species favours a particular spot, but the other species you see while you're waiting could skew your results. If you're counting butterflies or birds, have a camera handy to grab photos of fast-moving individuals so you can identify them later.

Note your sightings as you make them, rather than relying on memory. It may

Transects for everyone

Transect counts and quadrat use might sound quite complex, but after a bit of practice they become very simple to conduct, and provide a great way to give a new and interesting twist to a family country walk. If you have a 'wild patch' in your garden you can do quadrat counts there, to encourage your children to find out more about the kinds of wild plants that grow there and the small creatures that depend on them. For older children with an interest in biology and natural history, this kind of study can be tied into schoolwork and can help establish skills that will be very helpful to them in their future academic career.

be helpful to write a list of likely species before you set off, and then you can record each observation with a simple stroke mark against the name.

THE QUADRAT

The typical quadrat has a narrow wooden frame, is a metre square and may have wires across the midpoints to further divide it into four 50cm squares or into smaller subdivisions. It is a very useful piece of kit for the surveyer, as it enables you to do random sampling of plant or small invertebrate numbers. Using the walk-through method for these groups could produce skewed results, as you are much more likely to notice some species than others. Using a quadrat enables you to take a complete, detailed sampling from a random selection of 1m squares.

Sampling   Once you have worked out (using a map) a selection of random places from which to sample, place your quadrat on the ground at the first designated spot (or close by it if it happens to be occupied by a large tree!) and then get low down to do a detailed check of its contents, working in a consistent direction. If you are counting slow-moving invertebrates such as snails, remove them from within the quadrat once counted so you don't count them twice.

↑ A quadrat (this one is available from NHBS) is a convenient way to mark off a measured area, to study plant and small invertebrate communities.

↓ Insect activity, like damselfly courtship and mating, happens more on sunny days, so take this into account when planning your counting days.

YOUR LOCAL RESERVE

Your local nature reserve, whether it's managed by the RSPB, Wildlife Trusts or another organisation, needs you. Offer your time as a volunteer worker at any reserve and there's very little chance you'll be turned down. Whether you can make a regular commitment or a one-off, there will be something that you can do to help, and it's a great way to give something back to the organisations that help safeguard our wildlife. It's also a great way to meet like-minded people, and to find out more about how conservation works at grass roots.

HABITAT MANAGEMENT

↓ Common Terns nest on the ground – your local reserve may need volunteers to build artificial islands to give the terns a safe nesting place out of reach of ground predators.

A lot of the important work on nature reserves is to do with making sure the habitat remains suitable for wildlife or to make it more suitable than it currently is. This includes work like clearing scrub away from grassland, digging ditches to manage drainage in wet pasture, coppicing, felling or planting trees, cutting back reeds and so on. Some of this is quite hard physical work, but very necessary (as well as great for improving fitness!). Many species rely on transient habitats, for example, wetlands which would, left to their own devices, dry out and become overgrown. As wildlife-rich wetlands are now rare in the UK, wetland reserves are managed to maintain them in this state rather than allowing nature to take its course.

Jobs for all Other physical work involves improving access for visitors, and this might include building boardwalks, putting up fences or erecting signage. If you have a driving licence you could help with moving materials around the site. Other lighter practical work could include filling bird feeders, keeping the visitor centre shelves stocked with supplies, updating the wildlife sightings board and so on.

MONITORING AND PROTECTION

Most reserves carry out their own surveys of the wildlife present to build a detailed and accurate picture of the biodiversity. This will help the reserve wardens to check whether habitat management is working to support certain target species and alert them to any significant new arrivals. You may need

some identification skills to help with surveys.

Another important role for volunteers concerns the safeguarding of particular rare species. On reserves where species occur which are particularly vulnerable to deliberate disturbance or destruction – such as certain birds of prey – volunteers are often needed for day and night vigils to ensure that nothing like this happens.

↑ One of the tasks that volunteers working on nature reserves may be asked to do is to carry out regular counts of birds and other species.

↓ Lowland heath is a scarce habitat, and left to its own devices it can be encroached upon by Bracken and other scrub – volunteers can help by removing the scrub.

PEOPLE SKILLS

Working on a nature reserve isn't just about working with nature – volunteers are also needed to assist visitors on the reserve. This may be manning the reception desk to take admission fees (if required), preparing and serving food and drink, or helping to ensure visitors get the most out of their day by explaining what wildlife is about on the reserve and perhaps pointing out some of the more interesting sightings.

Naturally, you'll want to share your enthusiasm for your reserve and its wildlife, and many visitors will be eager to learn from you. However, be careful not to overwhelm visitors with information. Try to get a feel for what the different visitors are looking for, and know when to step back and let the wildlife speak for itself.

VOLUNTEERING FURTHER AFIELD

As your interest in wildlife grows, you'll probably start wanting to plan all your holidays around wildlife-watching. One way to do this and also gain the satisfaction of giving something back is to plan a working holiday, where you'll be spending your time helping with conservation projects. This kind of work can take you anywhere in the world, although if money is tight be wary of the more exotic projects. On the other hand, spending a week as a live-in volunteer on a UK nature reserve is a fantastic way to have an inexpensive, profoundly rewarding and wildlife-rich holiday.

↓ There are numerous projects based at bird migration hotspots around the Mediterranean area, with placements of a week or longer.

RSPB RESIDENTIAL VOLUNTEERS

The RSPB has a long tradition of providing accommodation for volunteers in exchange for their help with all aspects of running a reserve. Many reserves offer long-term placements of several months, although for newcomers to this kind of work it's often best to begin with just a week-long stay. The long-term placements are a fantastic way to gain solid practical experience

REAL WORK

Because working with wildlife is so popular, conservation organisations can attract a lot of volunteers. Although the work you'll be doing is unpaid, it's important that you still check that the organisation can offer you the support you'll need while you work for them, particularly if it's not one you've heard of before. Make sure you'll be fully insured and that if there is any particular situation you need to avoid (for example, heights or full days of walking) that you'll be able to do so. Having satisfied yourself that everything is above board and will suit you, go out with a positive attitude, prepared to put in some hard work, and you should thoroughly enjoy your time.

of habitat management, ideal for anyone working towards a career in conservation.

How it works

You'll be given all the training you need and a comfortable place to stay. You'll only need to fund your travel to the reserve and back, and your food while you're there. You'll normally work about eight hours a day for five days a week, though if you are on a reserve with rare nesting birds you may need to work late shifts to cover a round-the-clock watch on the nest or nests. The work will be varied – at more remote reserves it will be largely habitat management and survey work, while at busier reserves there will be opportunities to work face to face with visitors. While for some work you'll need to be able-bodied, there may also be placements suitable for disabled people. A driving licence is often useful but not essential, and anyone who's 16 or over can apply for a placement.

↑ Want to get away from it all? The RSPB needs long-term residential volunteers on many of its most remote nature reserves.

↓ Overseas voluntary work will give you the opportunity to see wildlife that you're unlikely to find close to home, like the spectacular Black-winged Stilt.

BTCV

The British Trust for Conservation Volunteers is an organisation for anyone looking for voluntary conservation work, both in the UK and, through its international partners, abroad. There are a huge range of projects on offer, from the simple to the challenging. You could clear litter from beaches, lead nature walks for adults and children, establish and manage wildlife gardens, or any of numerous other projects. The longer-term conservation holidays could take you to Estonia, Cameroon or the USA among many other places.

OTHER PROJECTS

There are also numerous opportunities to volunteer for conservation work over a weekend, a week or longer. You could join BirdLife Malta as they monitor bird migration and deter illegal hunting activity on the island every spring and autumn, or join the Mgahinga Community Development Organisation to study gorillas in Uganda. The website Environment Job (**www.environmentjob.co.uk**) lists volunteering opportunities around the world, as well as at home in the UK.

CONSERVATION CAREERS

It's the dream of many a wildlife-lover to find a job that puts you at the heart of an exciting wild area, spending your time surrounded by nature and working to encourage and safeguard this special place and its wildlife. Nature-reserve wardening jobs are few and far between, but this and related work is certainly a valid career choice. You can do much to increase your chances of successfully getting into this line of work – working as a volunteer warden will certainly help, and doing appropriate study will boost your chances even more.

↑ Doing short courses in woodland management techniques will help you find paid work as a nature reserve warden.

ACADEMIC OPTIONS

You can study various aspects of conservation at degree level. BSc courses currently listed with various UK universities include Wildlife Conservation with Zoo Biology (Salford University), Conservation Biology and Management (University of Stirling), Animal Conservation Biology and Biodiversity (Hadlow College in Kent) and Zoology with Conservation (Bangor University). Courses like this will include practical modules as well as theoretical study. You'll generally need Biology A level and other science subjects to gain a place, but mature students with other relevant qualifications or experience are often encouraged to apply too.

OTHER LONG-TERM COURSES

■ **Foundation courses** Foundation degrees (FdSc) are career-focused, degree-level study

← The UCAS website will help you to search for a suitable course, and guide you through the application process.

courses which you can take over two years (full time) or three to four years (part time). Many conservation-related foundation courses are offered by specialist establishments such as agricultural colleges as well as by universities. Because they are aimed at people looking to get quickly into the workforce rather than those who may want to pursue a career in academia, entry requirements are usually less strict, but be prepared to work just as hard. However, the part-time option is a good compromise if you cannot afford to stop 'normal' work.

■ **Vocational qualifications** BTECs, City & Guilds and OCR Nationals are all types of vocational qualifications which you can often study full or part time for a year or sometimes more. In terms of level of difficulty they may be equivalent to GCSE level or A level (City & Guilds levels 2 and 3 respectively) or above (for example, a BTEC HND – Higher National Diploma – qualification). As with academic study, there are lots of options; for example, you could take an HND in Countryside Conservation at Aberystwyth University, or a City & Guilds Level 2 or 3 Diploma in Work-based Environmental Conservation at Bromley College in Kent.

Choosing a course can be difficult. Do your research and talk to anyone you know who's already working in the field that interests you for more advice about which kind of course would be best for you.

← The Barn Owl Trust works to conserve this beautiful bird, and offers short courses to teach monitoring techniques to anyone who's interested.

↓ Some wildlife-related jobs are very specific – for example, the RSPB employs a House Sparrow Officer whose task is to help curtail the decline in this species.

SHORT COURSES

In addition to the long-term courses above, there are any number of short courses (from a half day to a few weeks) covering all aspects of conservation work. Some are extremely specialist, for example, the Barn Owl Trust runs courses in surveying and monitoring Barn Owls, and the Bat Conservation Trust offers a day course to help tree surgeons and other tree workers do their jobs without endangering roosting bats. Short courses with more general applications cover things like hedge-laying, building drystone walls, using chainsaws and introductions to habitat-surveying techniques. Many will be helpful for those looking to find paid work in conservation. Many will also be valuable if you're just interested in improving your wildlife-watching or managing your garden to make it a better place for wildlife.

OTHER WILDLIFE WORK

Going into practical conservation work is one way to make a living out of your wildlife-watching, but it isn't the only way. There are plenty of other options to turn your hobby into a career. In general, this kind of work doesn't attract large salaries compared to other sectors, but the rewards are rich nonetheless, as you'll be doing something you love and you'll also know that what you're doing is helping wildlife.

A CAREER IN RESEARCH

If academic study is your thing, you can build a career in research biology by going into post-graduate study. A PhD or doctorate qualification (which usually includes an MSc) in your chosen field of interest will normally take four years or more of serious study, at the end of which you'll need to write up your findings in a thesis and then survive a question-and-answer session about your work with professional academics (a viva). Many PhD students have returned to study after some years in other employment. You will normally be based at a university, though distance study on a part-time basis is also possible. With a PhD you are well placed to secure work as a research scientist, perhaps with the RSPB or some other conservation body.

↓ At the time of writing, applications are being invited for a PhD studentship at Nottingham Trent University, to study Yellowhammers and their conservation.

WILDLIFE RESCUE AND REHABILITATION

Throughout the UK there are wildlife 'hospitals', set up to treat, rehabilitate and eventually release rescued wild animals found by the public. These establishments often rely on volunteer workers, but the larger centres also employ staff. You can learn the relevant skills 'on the job' (perhaps after a stint as a volunteer) or transfer veterinary or animal-care skills gained while working with domestic animals. Learning how to take care of wild animals in captivity can also give you useful experience if you are interested in working on reintroduction projects, such as the ongoing scheme to return Red Kites to parts of Britain where they had become extinct.

RECRUITING, FUND-RAISING AND ENGAGEMENT

If you have a persuasive personality, you could find rewarding work raising money for conservation groups and projects. This kind of work ranges from directly

recruiting members for conservation bodies to seeking sponsorship from companies. You could also be a 'public face' for your organisation, talking to visitors and the media or working as a field teacher, educating visitors of all ages about wildlife.

OTHER OPTIONS

With a bit of imagination, you could find work in a variety of fields with a link to wildlife. You could work for a publisher producing nature books or magazines or at a wildlife photographic library. You could be a ranger in a country park or a horticulturalist working on propagating rare plants from Britain or abroad. Conservation bodies need a wide range of staff besides those working directly with nature reserves, from administrative staff and IT support personnel to cooks and cleaners. Whatever kind of work you're looking for and whichever hours you want to work each week, you should be able to track down something suitable that also links you into the world of wildlife conservation.

WORKING FOR YOURSELF

Self-employment is an exciting but challenging path, which demands real passion if you're going to make it work. Channelling your passion for wildlife into your own business idea may be a daunting prospect but is also potentially hugely rewarding. You could try selling your photos or artwork, set yourself up as a tour guide or become a wildlife consultant, advising individuals and businesses on wildlife-related issues. If you are lucky enough to own some land you could try organic, wildlife-friendly farming. The options are only constrained by your imagination.

↖ Voluntary work in wildlife rehabilitation, helping injured birds like this Buzzard to return to the wild, is hard but immensely rewarding.

↑ The British Birdwatching Fair, held in Rutland every August, is a great place to make wildlife-related contacts.

↓ Becoming a professional wildlife photographer is many a wildlife-watchers' dream – but competition is fierce.

YOUR CONDUCT AND THE LAW

When you're out in the countryside, the last thing you'll want to do is cause any disruption or harm to wildlife, or to the people who make their living from farming and other outdoor activities. Avoiding problems is largely a matter of common sense, but you should also observe appropriate formal codes of conduct.

↓ Most of us enjoy the great outdoors, and with a little consideration we can make sure that our activities do no harm to wildlife, wild places, and country people's livelihoods.

THE COUNTRYSIDE CODE

This code of conduct, compiled by the Countryside Commission (a statutory body which has now evolved into Natural England) began life as the Country Code and was updated in 2004, in collaboration with the Countryside Council for Wales.

The sections that apply to the general public are as follows:

1 Be safe, plan ahead and follow any signs
2 Leave gates and property as you find them
3 Protect plants and animals and take your litter home
4 Keep dogs under close control
5 Consider other people

The Natural England webpage on the Countryside code (**www.naturalengland. org.uk/ourwork/enjoying/countrysidecode/default.aspx**) goes into more detail on these individual points.

→ The Birdwatchers' Code exists to protect the well-being of all wild birds in Britain, from the commonest, like the Blue Tit, to our rarest and most vulnerable species.

In Scotland

Scotland Natural Heritage has produced its own code of conduct for exploring the outdoors, called the Scottish Outdoor Access Code. You can see the details at a dedicated website: **www.outdooraccess-scotland.com**. Its main points are summarised as follows.

1. Take responsibility for your own actions
2. Respect the interests of other people
3. Care for the environment

THE BIRDWATCHERS' CODE

The Birdwatchers' Code has been put together by a team of 13 different bodies with an interest in bird welfare, including the RSPB, BTO and Wildfowl and Wetlands Trust. It is a detailed code of conduct for all birdwatchers, and can be viewed in full here: **www.bto.org/notices/birdwatchers_code/bwc.pdf**. The key points are as follows.

1. Avoid disturbing birds and their habitats – the birds' interests should always come first
2. Be an ambassador for birdwatching
3. Know the law and the rules for visiting the countryside, and follow them
4. Send your sightings to the County Bird Recorder and the Birdtrack website
5. Think about the interests of wildlife and local people before passing on news of a rare bird, especially during the breeding season

SPECIAL PROTECTION

Some species enjoy particularly strict protection from any form of disturbance in the wild, and you should be aware of which they are. If, for example, you put up a portable hide to photograph a Kingfisher or Barn Owl at its nest, you could be breaking the law, as these are listed on Schedule 1 of protected species and must not be disturbed at the nest. The Wildlife and Countryside Act of 1981, which you can view here: **http://www.jncc.gov.uk/page-3614**, lists all species for which special protection is given.

OTHER CODES OF CONDUCT

These include the Code of Conduct for the Conservation and Enjoyment of Wild Plants, published on the Natural History Museum's website: **www.nhm.ac.uk/hosted-sites/bps/Code of Conduct**. This code covers the importance of protecting wild plants and their habitats and being aware of the laws that cover them. Many local conservation bodies publish their own codes of conduct.

FURTHER READING

There is a huge wealth of books out there on all aspects of natural history. For your 'core library' you will need field guides covering the species groups that you're most interested in, but if funds allow it's easy to build a wonderful wildlife library covering everything from photographic techniques, individual monographs on single species and compilations of poetry, to swashbuckling Victorian travelogues, wildlife site guides and glorious coffee-table books of stunning artwork or photography.

FIELD GUIDES

Collins Bird Guide (Lars Svensson, Killian Mullarney, Dan Zetterström and Peter J. Grant), Collins, 2010. The definitive field guide for British and European birds, in an updated second edition.

Birds of Europe (Lars Jonsson), Christopher Helm, 1992. A superb field guide by one of Europe's most gifted bird artists and ornithologists.

RSPB Handbook of British Birds (Peter Holden and Tim Cleeves), Christopher Helm, 2006. A field guide to British birds, with extra detail on habits, migration and distribution.

Black's Nature Guides series, A&C Black 2008 onward. A series of guides for Britain and Europe, illustrated with many colour photos. Titles include trees, wild flowers, fungi and birds.

RSPB Pocket Guide to British Birds (Simon Harrap), Christopher Helm 2007. A good-value beginners guide covering 174 popular species.

RSPB Handbook of Garden Wildlife (Peter Holden and Geoffrey Abbott) published by Christopher Helm, 2008. A field guide to garden wildlife, covering more than 200 species.

Butterflies of Britain and Ireland (Michael Easterbrook), A&C Black, 2010. A combined field and site guide for all of Britain and Ireland's butterflies, illustrated with colour photographs.

Field Guide to the Moths of Great Britain and Ireland (Paul Waring, Martin Townsend, Richard Lewington), British Wildlife Publishing, 2009. Comprehensive and beautifully illustrated guide to British moths.

Colour Identification Guide to Moths of the British Isles: Macrolepidoptera (Bernard Skinner and David Wilson), Harley Books, 2009. The definitive identification guide to British moths, in a new updated edition.

Collins Complete Guide to British Wildlife (Paul Sterry), Collins, 2008. A single volume covering all of the commoner animals, plants and fungi.

FOR CHILDREN

RSPB Children's Guide to Birdwatching (Mike Unwin and David Chandler), published by Christopher Helm, 2007. A 'how to' guide for young birdwatchers, with a field guide section covering the most commonly seen species.

RSPB My First Book of Garden Birds (Sarah Whittley, Rachel Lockwood and Mike Unwin), published by A&C Black, 2006. An ideal first bird book for young children, with charming pictures and descriptions of common garden birds.

RSPB My First Book of Garden Bugs (Mike Unwin and Tony Sanchez), published by A&C Black, 2009. Introduces young children to common garden insects and other creepy-crawlies.

RSPB My First Book of Garden Wildlife (Mike Unwin and Tony Sanchez), published by A&C Black, 2008. For young children, this book describes 20 common birds, insects and other garden creatures.

SITE GUIDES

RSPB Where to Discover Nature (Marianne Taylor), published by Christopher Helm, 2009. A visitor's guide to all visitable RSPB reserves, this book describes what wildlife you're likely to see at each reserve and gives full access information.

Where to Watch Birds in Britain (Simon Harrap and Nigel Redman), published by Christopher Helm, 2010. A new edition of this classic compendium of great birdwatching sites. Helm also publishes more detailed county and regional *Where to Watch* guides.

GARDEN WILDLIFE

RSPB Gardening for Wildlife: A Complete Guide to Nature-friendly Gardening (Adrian Thomas), published by A&C Black, 2010. An inspiring guide to creating the perfect wildlife garden.

RSPB Birdfeeder Guide (Robert Burton and Peter Holden) published by Dorling Kindersley, 2003. The ultimate guide to feeding your garden birdlife, from which feeders to buy or make to which foods are best for the various species in your garden.

COLLECTIBLE

Poyser monographs, published by T & A D Poyser. These distinctive white-jacketed hardbacks mostly cover individual bird species, though some deal with multiple species or with other bird-related phenomena. Written by acknowledged experts and packed with detailed research, each one is a treasure trove of fascinating information. Out-of-print titles are now available to be printed on demand.

Collins New Naturalists, published by Collins. Another set of hardbacked books in distinctive livery, the New Naturalists books cover a wide range of subjects in authoritative detail. This publisher is also reprinting older titles on demand.

USEFUL ADDRESSES

Here you'll find a list of contact details – addresses, phone numbers and/or websites – for some of the many organisations which are involved with wildlife-watching.

CONSERVATION BODIES

Royal Society for the Protection of Birds (RSPB)
The Lodge
Potton Road
Sandy
Bedfordshire
SG19 2DL
Tel: 01767 680551
Email: enquiries@rspb.org.uk
Website: **www.rspb.org.uk**

Wildlife Trusts
The Kiln
Waterside
Mather Road
Newark
Nottinghamshire
NG24 1WT
Tel: 01636 677711
Email: enquiry@wildlifetrusts.org
Website: **www.wildlifetrusts.org**

British Trust for Ornithology (BTO)
The Nunnery
Thetford
Norfolk
IP24 2PU
Tel: 01842 750050
Email: info@bto.org
Website: **www.bto.org**

Wildfowl and Wetlands Trust (WWT)
Slimbridge
Gloucestershire
GL2 7BT
Tel: 01453 891900
Email: enquiries@wwt.org.uk
Website: **www.wwt.org.uk**

Butterfly Conservation
Manor Yard
East Lulworth
Wareham
Dorset, BH20 5QP
Tel: 01929 400 209
Email: info@butterfly-conservation.org
Website: **www.butterfly-conservation.org**

Plantlife
14 Rollestone Street
Salisbury
Wiltshire
SP1 1DX
Tel: 01722 342730
Email: enquiries@plantlife.org.uk
Website: **www.plantlife.org.uk**

Buglife
First Floor
90 Bridge Street
Peterborough
PE1 1DY
Tel: 01733 201 210
Email: info@buglife.org.uk
Website: **www.buglife.org.uk**

RETAILERS

RSPB Shop (for bird feeders, nestboxes and other garden wildlife supplies, also optics and gifts)
Website: **shopping.rspb.org.uk**

Wildlife Watching Supplies (for hides, camouflage material and clothing)
Website: **www.wildlifewatchingsupplies.co.uk**

NHBS (for books and wildlife studying equipment)
Website: **www.nhbs.com**

PUBLICATIONS

Birdwatch magazine
www.birdwatch.co.uk

Bird Watching magazine
www.greatmagazines.co.uk/store/displaystore.asp?sid=329

British Birds magazine
www.britishbirds.co.uk

Birding World magazine
www.birdingworld.co.uk

Atropos magazine
www.atropos.info

British Wildlife magazine
www.britishwildlife.com

INFORMATION

Natural England
Website: **www.naturalengland.org.uk**

Countryside Commission for Wales
Website: **www.ccw.gov.uk**

Scottish Natural Heritage
Website: **www.snh.gov.uk**

Rare Bird Alert
Website: **www.rarebirdalert.co.uk**

DISCUSSION FORUMS

RSPB Community
www.rspb.org.uk/community/forums

Birdforum
www.birdforum.net

Wild About Britain
www.wildaboutbritain.co.uk/forums/index.php

→ The skippers form a potentially confusing butterfly group. A good field guide will help you pick out the features that identify this as a male Large Skipper.

INDEX

ACKNOWLEDGEMENTS

Firstly, I'd like to thank the team at A & C Black for taking on this project, especially Julie Bailey who got the ball rolling, and Lisa Thomas who was an unflappable and always helpful and efficient guiding hand through the later stages. The text was ably copyedited by Wendy Smith. Austin Taylor created the delightful page designs, and was a joy to work with throughout the project, showing exemplary patience with a sometimes painfully indecisive author. I'd also like to thank Laurie Taylor for putting the index together. Mark Boyd of the RSPB checked the text for this book and provided much helpful criticism.

My partner Rob Cardell provided about half of the photos for this book, and unfailingly came up with the goods when I asked for specific images. Some patient friends agreed to be models for us – thanks are due to Dianne Cardell, Michéle Trott and Jonathan Newman. Many thanks to Carol Trott and Susan Paine for allowing me to use their back gardens as photo studios. I must also thank those people we met while out and about who agreed to be photographed, but whose names I didn't get at the time.

As ever, friends and family offered invaluable support, advice and, when needed, distraction. Special thanks to my father, Alison, Mike, Sue, Claire, Michéle, the three Steves, the Gents of Science, the aikido gang and the Ladies who Run.

Rob was his usual wonderfully supportive self throughout the writing and putting-together of this book. He read through the proofs and nailed a few mistakes, as well as making helpful suggestions about photo choices. He also brought me plenty of tea, and was always willing to listen and help with any worries I had.

It's my hope that this book will help encourage its readers to discover the wonderful hobby of wildlife-watching, and I'm delighted to have the RSPB's backing. From the time my parents bought me a membership to the YOC (Young Ornithologists' Club – then the junior division of the RSPB) when I was very young but already obsessed with wildlife, the RSPB has been central to my experiences of getting to know wildlife in Britain. The network of RSPB reserves place our most fabulous wildlife within reach, and protect precious habitats which would otherwise be lost forever. I hope all readers will get out there and see some of these wonders – and consider joining the RSPB to help fund their vital work.

Finally, I want to thank my father and my late mother for fostering my passionate interest in nature, and making sure I was given so many opportunities to read about, write about, draw and above all watch wildlife as I was growing up. This book is for them.

PHOTO CREDITS